It Happened In Brazil - Chronicle of a North American Researcher in Brazil II

Mark J. Curran

Order this book online at www.trafford.com
or email orders@trafford.com

Most Trafford titles are also available at major online book retailers.

Print information available on the last page.

ISBN: 978-1-4907-5933-3 (sc)
ISBN: 978-1-4907-5932-6 (e)

Trafford rev. 05/06/2015

www.trafford.com
North America & international
toll-free: 1 888 232 4444 (USA & Canada)
fax: 812 355 4082

Another in the Series "Stories I Told My Students"

TABLE OF CONTENTS

LIST OF IMAGES

PREFACE

This book is the continuation of the narration of life lived in diverse moments in Brazil. It follows the spirit of a volume of some years past, "Adventures of a 'Gringo' Researcher in Brazil in the 1960s" and will really be Volume II of "Adventures" but with another title. It will be similar yet not similar. The format will continue that of the various trip diaries, but moments will be described in the form of vignettes or short "chronicles," in some cases, very short. I would like it to be understood that the inspiration for this format comes from one of my very favorite Brazilian writers, Luís Fernando Veríssimo. For more than twenty years, traveling for sundry reasons to Brazil, one of my first stops would be the bookstore, always enthusiastic to see what was "new" from Luís Fernando. And I note, an aside, that his father also contributed inspiration with his large chronicle "Black Cat in a Field of Snow, or "Gato Preto em Campo de Neve," the story of the elder Veríssimo's time in the "white" United States as a diplomat in the late 1940s. This latter book was one of the first I ever read about Brazil in those early days as a graduate student in Spanish-Portuguese and Latin American Studies at Saint Louis University in St. Louis, Missouri. I thought of this once when traveling late at night on a city bus in Salvador, the only "branco" on the bus.

The mention of these Brazilian writers and the debt owed to them ends on this note. Far from having the talent of a writer like Luís Fernando or his wonderful, unique sense of humor, and mainly not being Brazilian, I could not possibly dream of arriving at the literary heights of this author writing about Brazil. But in spite of this, I always tried to keep my eyes open to any eventuality on the many research trips to Brazil, including tourism and professional moments through the years. I think yes that we have in common the observation of people, of seemingly unimportant events and moments of daily life, but there the analogy ends. And some of my headings were inspired by readings of the great Brazilian novelist, Joaquim Maria Machado de Assis.

So it is that the reader will enter into contact with professors, folklorists, writers of Brazilian literature, poets from the "literatura de cordel," scenes from Brazilian folklore, and small moments of life in Brazil that caught the attention of the "gringo," but also the mention of the political times and the changes that I saw in Brazil, for better or worse. Between the lines the reader will see the evolution of a small portion of the Brazilian reality. And there is lots of tourism.

This chronicle will portray happy moments, but also times of loneliness, sadness and disappointment, most of these a result of the long odyssey of attempting to publish my writings in Brazil. Now in 2015 one only has to see www.currancordelconnection.com to see how it all turned out for the best. I thought about not including the account of the trials of research and publication in Brazil, but reconsidering, I don't think it is just my story, but that of friends and colleagues who have their own similar stories to tell. We all were living in the familiar terrain of "publish or perish" in the battle to achieve university tenure and then advancement in the academy. Hopefully any one of my colleagues who may read this narration will nod his or her head in agreement, remembering such moments, but I humbly borrow a conceit from a great hero of readings past, Machado de Assis when he addresses "Dear Reader" and gives him permission to skip a few pages (not really applicable in Machado's ironic style, but maybe the case in "It Happened"). I for one will not be offended if such is the case. Skip these parts and move on to something less "chato" and a bit happier. Good times are to come. I assure you that after the final chapter of this book, the last particularly happy in itself, better times are to come in regard to the academy and publications in Brazil.

What I wish most is that this second volume in a series may continue to express my original love for Brazil, the love affair that continued for forty years. And that it may express my love for the Brazilians, something I was not always able to verbalize, but was always felt in my heart during all those years of teaching, researching, traveling and getting to know Brazil and its people.

THE RETURN IN 1969

THE ARRIVAL IN BELÉM WITH SOME "CURIOSITIES"

So it was that the odyssey in Brazil would continue in June of 1969 returning to do research on Brazil and the "literatura de cordel." The big difference however was that now I was an Assistant Professor of Spanish and Portuguese at Arizona State University and the object of the trip would not only be research but the search for the means of publication of my Ph.D. dissertation and related research articles in Brazil. So there was definitely a certain change in status from that first year of 1966-1967 when I was ABD and with no job title. But my attitude toward Brazil was the same. Brazil represented for me an exotic world and a place I loved, and I wanted to learn more about it; the "love affair" was still serious. So I will not speak just of research, but of those small moments that impressed the North American researcher in the land of Brazil.

This time I flew on the famous Varig Airlines, the route from Miami to Belém do Pará and on to Recife which would be my "base camp" for this year's research. The service on Varig was the well-known of the times: gum drops or Chiclets before taking off, the steaming hot towel to "refresh oneself" before the first meal, slippers to ease the swollen feet during the long flight, beautiful maps of Brazil and Varig's routes throughout the world, the day's newspapers and magazines and then the meal itself: pre-dinner cocktails and appetizers ("tira-gostos"), the first course of salad and salmon, the main course of filet mignon with potatoes and vegetables, and then the pastry for dessert and the excellent and fine aroma of Brazilian demitasse coffee ("cafezinho"). All was accompanied (I like the Brazilian word from Jorge Amado: "regado") with pre-dinner drinks, wine during the meal and liqueurs later. Wonderful! What a way to toast our imminent arrival in Brazil. And this all was in economy-tourist class. As we all would see, there would be a sad change to all this in coming years, but not yet!

We arrived at the International Airport of Belém do Pará at 2:30 a.m. There was the usual bureaucracy – too many passengers, too few airline employees to handle them all and the resulting slow and inefficient scene at the airline counter. There was one agent to attend to all the passengers traveling on to various cities in Brazil: he was to check passports and visas, see the original tickets and issue new tickets and boarding passes to the Brazilian destinations, and on top of that make sure the luggage stickers were properly done. The poor fellow was sweating profusely, visibly nervous, checking each airline ticket (in those days you had a cardboard coupon for each destination, international and national; it could amount to a good sized stack), rechecking the same, forgetting what he had already seen, trying to deal with luggage, cleaning and recleaning his glasses and swearing at all the "peon" employees there to assist him. Finally the new ticket was issued along with the boarding pass and I was ready to continue the flight to my final destination of Recife.

Then the unexpected, or perhaps the expected, occurred. I could only assume that Varig had been doing this route for months if not years, that everyone knew "the drill," and not to what would just happen. The huge Boeing 707 continuing its route to I do not know where, perhaps the return flight to Miami, started the four engines, revved them up, and backed out of its spot in front of the passenger terminal. But then it turned, still in reverse, with all four thrusters facing the front of the terminal. The four engines at full blast hit the large glass windows of the terminal directly in front of the airline counter where I was standing and suddenly shattered them all. Huge pieces of glass were flying through the air and without time to think, I sat down on my haunches (like a good northeasterner from the interior of Pernambuco), thus avoiding the glass flying overhead. I was luckily unscathed from the flying sheet of glass and somehow saw no others injured. In fact all seemed to be quite normal; the plane taxied away from the terminal, no one said anything more.

I had arrived in Brazil.

RECIFE, 1969

The city in 1969, two years after my initial research of 1966-1967 told in the book "Adventures of a 'Gringo' Researcher in Brazil in the 1960s," was in a growth rhythm, lots of new construction including tall buildings on the side of the Capibaribe River in downtown, but one could still see much poverty along the rivers and streets of the city. There was more traffic on the large arteries of the City Center; people were still walking across the many bridges and ragged beggars were to be seen, some with evidence of Schistomiasis with bandaged wounds on their swollen legs. I was overwhelmed by the increase in traffic and the resulting barrage of noise in the streets, some of them yet the old colonial cobblestone ("paralelepípedo"). Rush hour was now part of old Recife, in the morning movement to work, at mid-day for those still driving home for the big mid - day meal, and in the afternoon or early evening when the sound of engines, blowing horns and exhaust smoke filled the air.

My old hangout to rest and recreate with friends, Boa Viagem Beach, was different with new skyscrapers, among them, hotels and tall apartment buildings. The young girls now wore biquinis instead of the old one-piece "maillot" of just two years past, the sign of both small and great changes to come in future years. The ubiquitous soccer games were still scattered all along the beach of Boa Viagem and to the north toward Pina; I wondered if this was due to the unemployment that still was the norm for the poor boys and young men of Pina.

I lived in a "Republic" of college age students in the Brazilian substitute for college dorms: several fellows in a "boarding apartment" often run by a widow needing the income. This was thanks to good friend Jaime Coelho of the old days in Recife. It was on a high floor of a tall apartment building near the old Law School of Pernambuco whose library was much frequented by me in the 1966-1967 research times. I might add that the colorful boarding house, "The Rose House" or "Chácara das Rosas" of the earlier time, sitting on prime real estate, had been demolished and a tall, shiny apartment building was going up in its place. If not a step in financial gain for the perhaps greedy or or more likely, opportunistic owners, (Good Lord, I have a Luis de Góngora "barroquismo" here!) it certainly represented a loss of "character" for the neighborhood. The "Chácara" was well-known in those parts.

Living conditions were a lot better than in 1966 both in regard to comfort, hygiene of the bathrooms and in the food. The "Dona" prepared a mid-day meal of rice, beans, a portion of beef, tomatoes, onion, and with a "cafezinho" and a slice of guava jam for dessert. The evening meal might be fried eggs, tomatoes, onion, French bread, bean soup, banana, and "café com leite."

Shortly after arriving in Recife, I went to my old spot ("ponto") for research, the São José Market in old Recife, in search of "literatura de cordel" at the old poetry stand of Edson Pinto. I noted that I spied only one "cordel" vendor in the entire market, a big change from 1966.

Years later I would be shocked at the change in customs in the Northeast, one example being the festivities of St. John's Day on June 24th. I had seen a documentary on Brazilian television criticizing the excesses in the festival in years around 2000, people burned and even maimed by the fireworks, the drunkenness and the violence. But that June of 1968 I and friends enjoyed the festivities in Camarigipe, a beautiful celebration and not dangerous at all. There were two bands, one of northeastern country ("caipira") music and one of Brazilian rock and roll of the times ("a música iê-iê-iê"), fireworks and beautiful northeastern "square dancing" ("quadrilhas"). It all reminded me of Jorge Amado's descriptions of the same festival in his novels on the cacao zone in Bahia.

There were articles in the newspapers each day complaining of the not too appealing Brazilian economic situation. The year of 1969 was particularly one of crisis: high inflation, fear of "Yankee Imperialism" controlling Brazil, cries for a higher minimum wage, and the lack of money in peoples' pockets and even in the coffers of the government with one result bringing to a halt the local efforts in public and social works trying to ameliorate the situation of the chronic droughts in the Northeast.

A Cultural Note for Those Interested in Folklore

I saw the film "Maria Bonita Queen of the Bandits" ("Maria Bonita, Rainha do Cangaço"), a totally romanticized version of the story, only slightly based on the life of Lampião and his consort. It was new and in color, but with the same romanticism of the classic "Bandit" ("O Cangaçeiro") made years earlier by Lima Barreto. The former films, like "Stream of Blood" ("Riacho de Sangue") were in stark contrast to the films with northeastern themes so important to the Brazilian New Cinema ("Cinema Novo") of directors like Glauber Rocha of those times. "God and the Devil in the Land of the Sun" ("Deus e o Diabo na Terra do Sol") is an excellent example of the latter. Only coincidences, but maybe not much, were the Italian "Spaghetti Westerns" of similar days like Clint Eastwood in "The Good, the Bad and the Ugly."

Another sign of the times: the paranoia from the Right, the fear of communism, communists and "subversives" had grown exponentially in those two years. With the fear came the government repression, now a constant in life in Brazil. The much beloved music of the MPB ("Música Popular Brasileira") linked to the annual festivals televised nationally with the nation's love affair with Chico Buarque de Holanda, Nara Leão, the young Caetano Veloso, Milton Nascimento and others had taken another direction. Samba still reigned but Chico was in "voluntary" exile in Italy, Nara Leão sang little, Caetano Veloso was in England, and the star of Jair Rodrigues was ebbing. Most important was the absence of Gerardo Vandré and the Festival of 1967 with his "anthem" "Disparada," the singer-composer either disappeared or dead. So what was left? Roberto Carlos the King of Brazilian Rock and the "iê-iê-iê" and the so called "western" singers imitating United States' country music ("os sereseiros"). And "forró" was coming just now coming into its own. Music now was to entertain and not comment on society. The one good thing of all this is that in future years the censorship and repression would lead to arguably the most creative Brazilian popular music of all time with the satire, double-entendre and witticisms of those heroes of MPB who returned to live in Brazil, oppose the dictatorship in their limited ways, mainly "driblando a censura" but leading to a great moment of the return of Brazilian democracy in the "Direction Elections Now" campaign of 1984-1985. Chico Buarqu de Holanda, Milton Nacimento and others in mind.

The political climate of the times was also visible across the nation, always present in the movie previews ("trailers") dealing with the activities of the military in the rhythm of "economic development" and the "March to the West" and what would become the "Pharaohonic" projects so criticized in the coming years. Economic Minister Roberto Campos and more importantly the Minister of the Interior Delfim Neto would come under fire, the latter seemingly growing fatter as the years of the dictatorship went on, all this time with the promised "slice of the big cake" of economic development never delivered to the masses. But back to the movie previews: when yet another ribbon was cut by a general or admiral revealing yet another statue of military heroes, when there had been whistling, catcalls, jokes and even booing and jeering two year ago, now there was utter silence in the movie theater. A deafening silence.

Mark J. Curran

The Cultural Moment – The "Auto da Compadecida" and Federal Censorship

Ariano Suassuna at Home

In those days in the headlines of the "Diário de Pernambuco" I read of my mentor and guide to Northeastern culture, Ariano Suassuna (his "The Rogues' Trial" – "Auto da Compadecida" – had been one of the chapters of my Ph.D. dissertation, this because it was the Brazilian work that most used the "literatura de cordel"). It turns out that the "Auto" had been made into a commercial film and in these days was awaiting its "première" in the Brazilian cinema. There was only one problem: the government censors in Brasília were not ready to "liberate" the film. The author would have to travel to Brasília and defend his text and the film! I would talk about this with Ariano himself a few days later, but all was eventually resolved. The doubts of the government had to do with the author's comments in his text as to bureaucracy and corruption in the Brazilian government (one should recall that Suassuna wrote and produced the play in 1955 years before the "Redeemer" Revolution of 1964!) Also it was being bandied about that the cause of the censorship was the fact that the author chose to place a black (!!) Jesus Christ in the cast, a fact that he attributed to "American Racism." Well, this was just one of the many signs of political change and the political climate that this author would see in 1969. The paranoid government of the generals saw "leftist subversion" everywhere, even in the text of this so innocent and so northeastern folk drama! The irony of the moment came later: the film broke all attendance records up to that time for Brazilian Cinema.

I would learn a lot more about all this in a visit to Ariano's home a few days later. The house was in the colonial style, surrounded by walls and a large steel entry gate. It was surrounded by gardens with all kinds of tropical plants and flowers. The outside front of the house was ablaze with the blue tiles inherited from the Portuguese and Arabic Traditions in Portugal. Inside there were high ceilings, all the rooms open to the open air. (Hey, we are in tropical Brazil!) The furniture was all in the colonial style, mostly of Brazilian rosewood or "Jacarandá" in the form of no less than four rocking chairs and two benches, all " caned" in the style of the tropical Northeast and its colonial heritage. The living room was a true museum of northeastern art, painted portraits of the Baptism of Jesus, others done by Ariano himself, and yet others by Fransico Brennand and Samico (friends of Suassuana, the former now attracting hundreds of thousands of dollars for his works and Samico not far behind). They were all colleagues in that great effervescence of northeastern cultural life in the late 1940s and 1950s, a real Renaissance of art in the region. There was a statue of St. George (São Jorge) in the corner, impossible to leave out! And the floor was of northeastern tiles without any carpeting. I would make repeated visits to Pernambuco and the house in future years and the paintings might change, evidence of the future "Romance da Pedra do Reino" ("Romance of the Rock of the Kingdom") and the important intellectual-artistic movement initiated by Ariano, the "Movimento Armorial" ("Armorial Movement"). A minor note, but interesting for the North American, was the use of mosquito netting in all the bedrooms, recalling the "muriçocas" or mosquitoes of the "Rose House" in Recife in 1966 and 1967.

Perhaps a reflection on Ariano and 1969 and the decades to come would be interesting. Ariano declared in the 1960s that he would do anything to avoid travel to Rio, São Paulo or even Brasília preferring the image of the "intellectual of the provinces" (he was in good company – Brazil's most important folklorist Luís da Câmara Casudo, adopted the same stance). But time passed, the times changed, and Ariano had to make an exception to the rule for no less than the occasion of being accepted into the august company of the "acadêmicos" in the Brazilian Academy of Letters in Rio de Janeiro. A subsequent moment, of much greater national exposure, was when one of the Samba Schools of Rio chose as their theme "Ariano Suassuna" and Ariano, our humble servant, somehow acquiesced to ride on the float in the huge carnival parade in Rio. This means, in the Brazilian parlance, "You have arrived!" To put it all in perspective, singer-song writer, novelist, social protestor "par excellence" Chico Buarque received the same honor in those times.

The Day to Day "Normal" in Recife 1969

Many other things had not changed, moments that caught the "gringo's" attention in the Northeast. One evening I was seated at the counter of a café near Guararapes Avenue just eating a sandwich. I felt or perhaps just sensed some movement behind me, turned around, and about three inches from my rear end was the headlight and bumper of a Volkswagen "Bug." Keep in mind this is between the lunch counter and the wall just a few feet away. It turns out that was the best place for the owner to park his car each night. I knew street parking space was at a premium but didn't figure it would interrupt a snack!

There are many bridges linking the mainland of Recife to the peninsula, the peninsula to the island all in greater downtown Recife with the three rivers that run through it, and many of the bridges yet in 1969 were "spots" for beggars, some with their swollen legs wrapped in bandages. And there was talk of Schistomiasis, a disease still present in the Northeast in those times, a fact verified by several of my United States Peace Corps Volunteer friends. The disease came from a parasite in the form of a worm, in its early form a type of snail, which grew in the intestines of its victims, the worm being found in the stagnant waters of ponds and small lakes and even the rivers of the interior. The worm grows in the intestines and can be up to one meter in length! The symptoms are stomach pains, blood and horrible damage to the liver. Just a thought – is this why so many northeasterners in the 1960s were all taking prescribed medicines ("remédios") for their liver? ("Mal de fígado!") Even the young college guys seemed to be on the medicine. And of course, totally unrelated, but a "must" reference to Brazilian literature is the great Monteiro Lobato's short story "O Fígado Indiscreto," the story of a young man betrothed to a fine young lady and his "engagement" dinner at the family home when he was served, yes, a huge slab of liver. He of course had an aversion to the same, in fact detested it, and the rest of this hilarious story is how he attempted to avoid eating it and at the same time not offending his perhaps future mother-in-law. I can say no more; please look up the story and read it.

The Second Hand Bookstore in Recife

The store is famous; I met its owner Mr. Brandão in 1966 when I was searching out and buying so many "classics" of northeastern folklore which were only available through him (and the Livrara São José in Rio de Janeiro). Anyway, we met again in 1969 in Recife. In those years of the late 1960s Brandão was in his heyday – a "Golden Age" of "blank check" sales to major

United States Universities greedy to get the best of Brazilian books for their libraries in a sort of "book race" (read "space race") for predominance in the field. The University of Texas comes to mind. Brandão informed me that there was a new national law in place in Brazil: at the death of a writer, artist, or intellectual, the individual's library (and these people were true Bibliophiles!), had to remain intact in Brazil. The collections could not be sold and taken out of the country. The activities of booksellers like Brandão were considered by a large portion of Brazilians to be another type of capitalist exploitation by the United States of poor, third world countries. Brandão told me he had already been accused of selling "rarities" to the United States. This is but a small "vignette" of the anti-United States views from the Left in Brazil at the time; it existed side by side with the right wing paranoia already described

The Quest for Publication

There were several days and encounters with the folks at the Instituto Joaquim Nabuco de Pesquisas Sociais in the "Casa Forte" district of western Recife. I had done serious research there in 1966, perusing classic works on Brazilian folklore and checking out the "cordel" collection. It was there I fell asleep in a Gilberto Freyre lecture after the big mid-day meal, and where I waxed enthusiastic hearing the wonderful lectures of Brazil's most famous folklorist Luís da Câmara Cascudo (I would travel to Natal to have private sessions with him, all narrated in "Adventures of a 'Gringo' Researcher of Brazil in the 1960s"). So in 1969 I arrived with manuscript in hand, offering a text based on my Ph.D. thesis of 1968 for publication. There were courteous chats with the "masters" of the Institute – Sylvio Rabelo, Mauro Mota, and Renato Carneiro Campos. The latter took some interest in the text and drove me out to the "Casa Grande" to see the famous founder of the IJNPS Gilberto Freyre. The entire endeavor of the research institute was founded in part on the fact Freyre was a descendant of the sugar cane aristocracy of the Northeast, had a large hunk of property on one of the old sugar cane mill "fazendas" which he would convert into the modern Institute, incidentally named after a major Northeastern intellectual of the 19th century, Joaquim Nabuco, but also, parlaying Freyre's prestige as a federal congressman, this in turn reflecting his intellectual fame – author of "Casa Grande e Senzala" ("The Masters and the Slaves") a classic of Brazilian history and sociology, incidentally the off-shoot of his M.A. Thesis at Columbia University in New York. He was as we said in the old days in the Northeast the "manda-chuva" or even the "bamba do bairro" - the "big cheese" making it all go! A "yes" by the master and my manuscript would magically appear in print. He indeed agreed that it would, at least in part, be a nice article in the review of the Institute.

However, the <u>entire</u> study was seen by Ariano Suassuna as a small monograph or book to be published by the University Press of the "Universidade Federal de Pernambuco." It took years and a thick file of letters back and forth from Tempe, Arizona, to Brazil to make this happen, but it did! The manuscript eventually came out in 1973 as "A Literatura de Cordel" with a wonderful woodcut by the now world master J. Borges on the cover! Sometimes you live right. Ariano himself insisted on doing the proof reading (which I think he did a little too rapidly). At any rate, he accompanied me in a chauffeured car of "The Department of Extension and Culture" one fine day that June to the University Press, introduced me to the director, and it was a "done deal." Ariano was my "guide" in the whole matter. After a brief chat with the director of the press (who knew who he was talking to) Ariano said, "All set. You are the boss and your wish is my command." Or something to that effect. He said he himself would take care of the revision of the text and the book should come out in August of 1969, just two months later. It indeed did come out in 1973 and I'm thankful for that. Only four years wait! Years later the final book of publishing academically in Brazil would come out in São Paulo after a mere seven years' wait! I wrote somewhere else and repeat here: one of the realities of daily life as a professor at Arizona State University during a career of 43 years was the waiting for the mail to come in with, a letter, a package or even a book, from Brazil. And e-mail did nothing to change the wait; Marshall McLuhan said about that time, "The Medium is the Message." Anyway, on one happy day in 1973 there was a small package waiting for me – my first published book and great happiness and cause for celebration.

The Times - Military Repression

Students and Friends at the "Student Republic" and Military Repression

In 1969 I and some student friends in the "Republic" boarding apartment in Recife were celebrating the birthday of friend Jaime Coelho, all with great enthusiasim. Someone, as a joke, shouted "Viva Cuba!" Just a few short minutes later there was a loud knocking on the door; it was the police wanting to know what was going on and threatening to haul us all down to the city jail. Only after much conversation did we convince the sincere police officer that it was all a joke, but the year 1969 was not much of a joke for Brazilians. Years later after the political "opening" in 1980 many stories would come to light about the oppression of that era.

As proof of the atmosphere of those days there were newspaper articles each day about the threats to the "Red Bishop," Dom Hêlder Câmara of the Arch Diocese of Recife as well as news of the assassination of a Catholic priest in the city. Once more, the paranoia of the Right, the fear of communism, of the Left and of the "subversives" was augmented in the city. It was precisely in 1969 that a serious note came out in the newspapers of Recife. The house of the "Red Bishop" was machine gunned, the bullets scarring the front of the episcopal house, and the bishop threatened with death. In those same days a certain Father Mello was assassinated in the Jesuit University, a message to the "Progressive Church" and to the clergy leaning toward Liberation Theology to not speak or take any action unfavorable to the military regime.

An Aside. A few years later in 1978 my wife Keah and I attended the International Eucharistic Congress in Philadelplia and learned that the main honorees were Mother Teresa of India and the same Dom Hêlder Câmara. These two were present and Keah and I, far away in the lofty heights of the auditorium, saw the tiny figures on stage and heard their words. It was a very important moment in our religious life.

And yet in another year I was in Recife, waiting for a flight in the "Aeroporto dos Guararapes" in Recife when I saw from a distance this short little fellow in clerical garb with a leather briefcase in one hand, and I said to myself: "It's him! Dom Hêlder Câmara!" I stammered a stupid question, "Sir, are you Dom Hêlder Câmara?" The short northeasterner smiled and said, "No, I'm his brother." Then, after the joke, we had an altogether too short conversation but one unforgettable for me. I shall never forget the "Red Bishop's" mantra: "The greatest violence on the planet is hunger."

The Street Vendors and the City Government in 1969

In those years it was common to see on the streets of downtown Recife all manner of "semi-legal" commerce. It was legal to sell anything on the city streets as long as you had a license. Just the same the streets were filled with the "illegal" vendors especially near the Post Office. In a feeble attempt to stop the street selling, the city employed a large open bed truck circulating on the streets with the ostensible purpose of catching the vendors "red handed," confiscating their goods and who knows what fate if they actually caught the vendors. I, probably on my way to the post office one morning, saw the following hilarious scene.

Avenida Guararapes was jammed with traffic, cars and buses belching smoke, and the normal mass of humanity in the streets. Suddenly outside the steps of the Post Office all the vendors were yelling at each other and waving madly, giving the sign that the "fuzz" ("o rapa") was coming down the street, that is, that big lumbering truck of the city. One poor little vendor tried to pick up his wooden stand filled with limes, trying to hide it behind a concrete post at the Post Office, and it all went splattering wildly in the street, limes in all directions and the vendor in another, and he shouting the whole time warning his buddies of the "rapa." Suddenly there was a wild scene with all the street vendors running in all directions, all shouting to each other, and hiding behind columns and posts of buildings and the post office itself. The crowd in the streets, witnessing the scene, all yelled and rooted for the vendors. One of the latter ran in front of the city truck, crossed the bridge on the river, and a few minutes later returned to his hiding place behind a column of the post office, a broad "shit eating" grin on his face the whole time.

It was all a bit ironic since the "contraband" they sold consisted in some limes, oranges bananas, and let's face it, some BIC ink pens (used by the folks entering the Post Office to write last minute letters to be mailed that day). Some of us fans of Luís Fernando Veríssimo can only recall the stories of "Ed Morte," that street wise comic detective created by Veríssimo and his humbling scene when he is desperate to buy the morning paper and has to pawn his "collection of BICs" to get the daily paper. I was thinking that there ought to have been more important matters to concern the Military Police and the City than to harass street vendors, but evidently the "legitimate" businesses along Guararapes felt threatened by the hordes of street vendors in front of their shops and complained to the "fuzz." However it was the horde of street vendors hawking all manner of wares, even shouting their wares with the age-old Pernambuco tradition of the "pregões" that made for a colorful life in Recife yet in those days. If one kept his eyes open, there was no end of surprises and I'm happy to report the same.

Small Time Hoodlums

There is an article in the newspaper today about the small time, young thugs at the open air food market in Olinda. There are young boys who work at the market offering to carry home the groceries or other purchases, most often in small wagons or carts. Evidently the thugs offer "protection" and want "protection money" to leave the young boys alone. No money and you get a whipping! Despicable! The tiny article caught my attention because of my research in Salvador da Bahia in later years. The famous "cordel" poet Rodolfo Coelho Cavalcante who would go on to be the most prolific poet of all times with perhaps 1,700 booklets of narrative poetry did the same job as a child – carrying goods from the market - "fretando na feira" in his home town in Alagoas State.

The "Gringo Artist" in the Campina Grande Night Club

On one of those nights in June, 1969, I went with friends Jaime and Flávio to the nightclubs in the town of Campina Grande in the interior of Paraíba State. We checked out the "Venézia" and the "Esquisito," the latter with a big crowd and a live band. I was encouraged by my buddies, perhaps after several "Brahma" or "Antártica" beers, to take part. So I was introduced, climbed up on the stage, picked up an electric guitar and proceeded to sing some "Rock" songs from the 1950s, stuff from Elvis Presley, Bill Haley and the Comets, Little Richard, Ricky Nelson, and Buddy Holly, the guy who sang "Peggy Sue." It really was no big deal, small potatoes, but the novelty in the northeastern interior was that the songs were in English, and gossip soon spread the next day about the "gringo" who "put on a show" ("Deu um show") on the preceding night. It just goes to show the times and the atmosphere in the towns in the northeastern interior in the late 1960s. I might add that the next night, in another foray to yet another night club a guy pulled a gun on all of us.

Justice in the Interior

The informed reader on things Brazilian will know of the history of injustice and the role that it played in the making of the northeastern bandits Lampião and Antônio Silvino ("cangaceiros") – the two supposedly entered into banditry when members of their family were murdered in political disputes in the northeastern interior and the official of justice turned a deaf ear to their pleas. The family of a good friend in Campina Grande, Paraíba, told this story: one of his sisters became engaged; the finance was shot to death; the suspected killer had political "pull" ("pistolão") with the police and politicians in the city and region and was never arrested not to mention being brought to trial.

Nationally known Glória Pérez of fame as the creator of some of the most successful of television soap operas ("telenovelas") in Brazil in recent years told me a similar story to that of the murder in Paraíba, this while visiting in her office – studio in Rio de Janeiro. Her story of course involves the real life murder of her daughter Daniella in the1990s in Rio de Janeiro. Daniella was the heroine Jasmine of the TV "telenovela." She was murdered by her real-life costar when art became life and life became reality. The story is complicated and macabre, but it really happened. My unexpected connection to Gloria and this event was unusual: the story became national news on all the media, and even the humble poets of the "literatura de cordel" wrote several best-sellers on the hot topic. Thus I wanted to talk to Gloria because I was in the process of doing my book "História do Brasil em Cordel" to come out in 1998 and the Daniella episode was an excellent example of modern cordel journalism. With utmost courtesy and cooperation Gloria filled me in on the details: the creation of the "Telenovela", the cast of characters, her daugher's participation, the role of the villain who eventually killed her in a suburb of Rio, and the murky connection to Brazilian spiritism "Umbanda" in the whole thing. I will deal in detail with the entire episode in a future volume but it is apropos here in relation to the question of "Justice in the Interior" of Paraíba in 1969.

Kardec Spiritism in Campina Grande 1969

The Coelho Family, Campina Grande and Kardec Spiritism

The following lines reflect an interview with the father of my friend Jaime Coelho in Campina Grande in 1969. Mr. Coelho was a "Medium" of Kardec Spiritism. Allan Kardec was the founder of the spiritist movement in France in the years around 1850, all reported in his book "The Book of the Spirits" ("O Livro dos Espíritos"). Kardec Spiritism is based on, among other things, the communication with the spirits of the dead, the talent of the spiritist medium to cure the sick, tell the future, and to write down the sayings, conversations, thoughts of deceased authors (known as "escritura mediunística") and a belief in the evolution of life after death, a type of Reincarnation. Mr. Coelho treats some forty "patients" or "clients" per day. He believes he has the gift ("o dom") of healing, of course less than that of Jesus Christ, but derived from Christ and his disciples. Therefore, Mr. Coelho believes that his gift is a gift from God, and he of course cannot and does not charge for his "services." His reputation is such that "clients" need to request an interview with him one month in advance. Of note is that the persons I saw waiting in line did not at all have the appearance of the downtrodden, poverty stricken people common at that time in the Northeast. They were as the locals liked to say, "decent people" ("gente decente").

The consultations take place in the "annex" to the main house, in the exterior patio. There are various rooms to wait in with benches to sit down, with images on the walls of Jesus Christ, St. George and Father Cícero Romão. For our readers, it is noted that in northeastern folklore in those days and yet today St. George ("São Jorge") is mostly known as a saint upon horseback with sword extended in the act of killing a dragon and is the stock northeastern image of "the man in the moon." Father Cícero Romão Batista is the local parish priest in the tiny town of Juazeiro do Norte Ceará who became known for his "miracles" and later for great works of charity amongst the poorest of Brazil's poor, the victims of the droughts in the interior of Brazil's Northeast in the 19th century. One miracle began it all: while distributing Holy Communion to a "Holy Woman" Maria de Araújo at a daily mass in Juazeiro, the host purportedly was turned into blood in her mouth. News of the event spread like wildfire resulting in a study by the local bishop, Father Cícero's faculties to say mass or distribute the sacraments suspended. His fame grew throughout the backlands and a cult grew with national repercussion in Brazil.

There is a "meeting room" or "session room" to the side with a long table and on the walls are images or photos of famous "médiuns," some seven in all. The "sessions" take place two times each week. Also, on the first floor below the "curing room" there is an entire room filled with prescription medicines donated by the traveling salesmen of pharmaceuticals in the entire region, the greater part being samples.

Mr. Coelho is known in the entire region, but has links to other well known "médiuns," especially to one lady in Salvador da Bahia. He goes there two times a year for conferences. He possesses the gift of healing, but she is a "vidente" or "seer" of things (something I think related to the case of the famous Chico Xavier, a "medium" in Minas Gerais known for "Mediunistic Writing"). In the sessions the "médiuns" are capable of entering into contact with the spirits of deceased persons, family or friends, resulting in conversation with the living. Mr. Coelho believes in and cites Biblical Verse as the source of his "gift." He believes his son Jaime, my friend, guide and informant to folklore in Paraíba, has a gift even greater than his own. However, Jaime is studying traditional medicine in the university, like his two sisters. (He will eventually become a medical doctor and practice in far off São Paulo).

I observed Mr. Coelho "working." In the cases that involve spirits, he prays, places his hand on the heads of the patients; in "physical cases" he makes an immediate diagnosis and recommends a prescription medicine from his "pharmacy." He says that of ten cases of "mental disturbance" he sees eight improve after his consultation. (He adds, "An average significantly better than that of the state mental hospital." He accepts no one from the Afro-Brazilian religious rites or from "low spiritism" ("baixo espiritismo"). Mr. Coelho's consultations have been going on for fifteen years.

The family does not wholeheartedly approve of all this business, but obviously allows it to continue. It is this type of spiritist healing in Brazil that is associated with Master Arigó, a famous healer from Minas Gerais known for his eye surgeries without the use of anesthesia. In the late 1960s it was bandied about that the University of Princeton Medical School sent a team with cameras to record Arigó's surgeries and witness his successes.

If I learned anything in Brazil over all these years, it was to not close my eyes to possibilities, in effect, to other religious beliefs beyond those we are used to in the United States. This is a good example of the same. Another will be described later, a visit to a Spiritist Center in Rio de Janeiro with research colleague, friend and guide to the folklore scene in Rio, Sebastião Nunes Batista, this years later in the 1980s.

I might mention, in retrospect, there were other events that occurred earlier in 1966 and 1967 with visits to Xangô religious rites in Olinda, Pernambuco, "Candomblé" in Salvador, and the "Umbanda" rites on the beaches of Rio on New Years' Eve of 1966.

Tourism – Blum Fort in Recife

Blum's Fort in Recife was begun in 1626 by the Portuguese and completed by the Dutch in their occupation of Pernambuco in 1630. This was during the time Spain controlled Portugal, hence a consequence was the latter country had fewer resources to control its colony. The Dutch and the French took advantage of the moment to make serious incursions in Brazil and created lots of problems. We saw heavy cannons, thick walls of three to four meters, and portals for the cannons. The Dutch remained in Pernambuco until 1654 and the Battle of Guararapes; the main avenue of the city is named after the Brazilian patriots who opposed and defeated the Dutch. With the defeat there was the expulsion of many of the Jews who had thrived under the Dutch and were instrumental in the development of the sugar cane industry in Pernambuco and the Northeast. Peter Eisenberg, a research colleague of the 1960s in Recife would complete his study and write and publish a fine book on the subject some years later. I understand that the sugar cane industry fell into complete decadence in the following years and many of the Jewish owners, financiers and industrialists migrated to sites in the Caribbean to continue the endeavor.

A Return to "Jubiabá"

I dedicate this moment to the student of Brazilian Literature with knowledge of the works of the master Jorge Amado. We went to the main docks in the old port of Recife one morning and this scene awaited us: there was a huge cargo ship docked, the holds opened in wide spaces, and there were stacks and stacks of boxes and sacks in view. On the dock there were dozens of men, mostly black, all dressed in ragged t-shirts and shorts and sandals or flip-flops, all sweating profusely in that tropical sun of Recife, moving the sacks and boxes from the cranes to the beds of long bedded trucks and/or semi - trucks. They used a sort of gunny sack over the head and shoulder for their only "tool." The sacks were all labeled: "Donated by the People of the United States of America." It was dried food from the Alliance for Progress of the times in Brazil. This of course was a carryover from the regime of John F. Kennedy and the swell of a new alliance with Latin America and a period of increased friendly relations, notwithstanding Cuba and the Bay of Pigs. But now the enthusiasm was ebbing, and even though Brazil's military government was receiving aid from the U.S., the masses, particularly the masses of the northeast, distrusted the U.S. and thought of it all as another part of "Yankee imperialism." They considered the food donations a disaster, believing that most ended up sold by thieves, and that it would be far better for the U.S. to send machines, like road building machines. (I wrote of that phase of the Alliance in "Adventures" in 1966; see the story of the rusting bulldozers, tractors and heavy road building equipment at the docks of Natal, donations from the United States "buried" in Brazilian bureaucracy and corruption of the times.)

In another part of the dock it was a true scene from "Jubiabá" and its stevedore hero turned boxer Balduíno: large ships carrying raw sugar from Brazil and many black stevedores loading the heavy sacks weighing 80 kilos each onto the ships. The sugar was brought by many large trucks to the docks from the sugar cane mills and refineries of the northeast interior, all waiting in lines to be unloaded. I noted that it was not the white refined sugar we see in supermarkets and dinner tables at home, but the brown "raw" sugar in use in Brazil. The many stevedores were dressed in rags, mostly black men but some mixed, both mulatto and "caboclo" (Indian-White) mixtures from the Northeast.

Man on the Moon, July 20, 1969

"Man on the Moon"

It was a historic moment: the United States' astronauts landing on the moon. It was all televised, but on the black and white screens in the Northeast. I saw the entire scene on a TV in the window of an ice cream shop on a street corner in Recife near the Law School. Friends from my boarding apartment and many others whom I did not know rushed up to me, offering big embraces ("abraços") or shaking hands, congratulating me on the event as though I had something to do with it! The next day there would be story-poems from "cordel" selling like hot cakes in the city markets and on downtown street corners, notably in the coming days three different editions by the poet-singer José Soares known as the "Poet Reporter of 'Cordel'" in Recife. He was known for "scooping" the major dailies upon occasion with his quick journalistic style booklets of verse.

Of the several story-poems on the Recife scene I noted the different approaches taken by the poets: one with perhaps the very detailed operations of the landing itself, but also curiously others with major emphasis given to the food the astronauts ate and how they ate it. Perhaps significant or not in a "hungry" northeast interior, these details in some stories had more pages dedicated to them than the feat itself. And one should note that yet in the late 1960s everyone in the Northeast was aware of the "Space Race" between the United States and the Soviet Union, of "Sputnik" and the Russian success a year or two before, and the failure just days before the U.S. moon landing of the Russian attempt on the moon. Many skeptical, humble northeasterners in the interior still believed the whole thing was a "set up," a cinematic "creation" by the U.S. and not the real thing. The Cold War, fear once again of U.S. imperialism, and the case of Cuba, Fidel, and Ché Guevara all figured in this atmosphere. But for me that day in Pernambuco, it was good to be an American!

An Aside. Many years later in 2011 there was a symposium on the "Literatura de Cordel" at no less than the Library of Congress in Washington, D.C., sponsored by the American Folk Life Center. The unlikely event matched the equally unlikely reality that the largest collection of "cordel" in Brazil were to be located in no less than in the archives of the Ruy Barbosa Foundation in Rio de Janeiro. This is another story that needs to be mentioned here: because the great Ruy was a famous polyglot and the scholars had no better place to study the Portuguese language then at his foundation, why not study as well the "language of the people!" So it was that the Research Center with the famous "relics" of Master Ruy also would contain the collection of "popular literature in verse" or the "cordel."

At the aforementioned symposium the person who would represent all the "literatura de cordel" and its poets happened to be Gonçalo Ferreira da Silva of the folkloric museum "Casa de São Saruê" in the Santa Teresa District of Rio de Janeiro. I knew Gonçalo from years back so I ended up as his "guide" ("cicerone") in free time in Washington. I found something close to Brazilian rice and beans in an eatery not far from the Capitol, but also took the poet to the Smithsonian Mall to see the sights. We ended up at the Air and Space Museum and at one point right in front of the Lunar Landing Vehicle from that first landing on the moon and Gonçalo could almost not contain himself with the surprise and joy of being right there! Why? It turns out he had done a story-poem in "cordel" in 1969 about the landing on the moon, basing his poem on the reports from the Rio de Janeiro dailies and television, and he was now "reliving" the story! It was an incredibly moving moment for him, and I was happy to share it.

The Fame of Ariano Suassuna in 1969

Ariano Suassuna at Home Again

In those days Ariano was the head of the DEC, "Department of Extension and Culture" of the Federal University of Pernambuco. One day in his office we were discussing my upcoming book. A young professor from Lima, Peru, was ushered into the office and spoke to us of the great success of putting on the "Auto da Compadecida" in Peru. It was presented first in the church atriums and in the public plazas of the municipalities – free to the public and in the spirit of the originals performances by the author in the Northeast in the 1950s. At that point the Peruvian clergy complained labeling the play as "anti- Catholic." It was the first theatrical presentation in Peru given this label, not all a bad thing because the subsequent publicity attracted the public to come see it. The play was later put on in municipal theaters and finally in the famous "Teatro de la Comedia Española" in Lima. According to the Peruvian professor Suassuna is now the Brazilian author most read in Peru. Interestingly enough, the play as presented in Spanish was based on an English language translation – this because there was no

Portuguese version to be found in Lima! It's a good example of the lack of cultural exchange between Spanish and Portuguese in Latin America in the 1960s.

An Aside. The phenomenon also explains the risk taken by "Editora Orígenes" in Madrid of publishing my book "Antología Bilingüe de la Literatura de Cordel Brasileña – Portugués – Español" in 1989.

Suassuna spoke of the prizes won by the play in Colombia, presentations in France and Germany, and a horrible translation to Spanish that he learned of. He said that when he wrote the play in 1955 he never dreamed of national or even international success due to the strong regional tone of the play. I got the impression that Ariano really had little idea of his success "out there." For certain, he said, he had received few royalties. He said he does not pay much attention to any of that; "Only those folks over in the State Department" (Itamaraty) deal with that stuff." He added that "If I spent time on all this stuff I would not have any time to write." The more I got to know Ariano, the better I liked him. The friendship would continue sporadically over the years, meeting again in 1981, 1988 and especially in 2000.

The "Gringo" in the Post Office, Guararapes Avenue, Recife 1969

On the research trips in 1966, 1967, 1969 and 1970 while in Recife I depended on the post office for correspondence with my family at home in the U.S. I received my mail in the building of USIS (United States Information Service) and it involved a long walk from the boarding house near Boa Vista Avenue and Guararapes Avenue in City Center to the Island where USIA was located. On the return, always with letters from home in Abilene, Kansas, I would stop in an open air café on Avenida Guararapes, buy a "Time" Magazine in English to "cure my homesickness" ("matar saudades" as they say in Portuguese), and drink an icy "Guaraná" or perhaps a "Brahma Choppe" beer while I read the letters from home or from my girlfriend at that time, Keah Runshang.

Sending letters home was another story. A citizen of the United States was not prepared to deal with the "battle" that would take place in the post office. Allow me to explain. First of all one encountered all the commerce going on outside the building on the post office steps; it all seemed like a bazaar in Istanbul! Vendors were selling oranges, bananas, "cafezinhos" from thermos bottles, cigarettes and boxes of wooden matches and of course writing paper, envelopes and BIC pens. The local custom for many was to buy the writing materials, write the letter on the spot, and then go into the Post Office to mail it.

An Aside. Yet today I cannot help but smile thinking of the BIC pens. Any student of Brazilian Literature has to remember Luís Fernando Veríssimo and his "chronicles" of those years and in particular the stories of that very Brazilian creation – the detective "Ed Morte." An unsuccessful Brazilian version of "Guy Noir" of Lake Wobegon Fame, or even a take - off on Mickey Spillane, Ed worked out of a tiny cubicle in Rio, his office populated by cockroaches and mice scurrying about. On at least one occasion Ed had to pawn his "BIC collection" to get the local paper.

It turns out the envelopes and even the stamps you bought after waiting in long lines did not have glue on them. The "deal" ("jeito") was to buy said envelope and stamp and then go to a tiny, round table in the middle of the big room where there were small glue pots with tiny brushes in them. For a person who can play classical guitar other tasks needing dexterity were a challenge to me (like wrapping Christmas presents – my dream of the "job from hell" would be as Christmas package wrapper in Macy's). So I ended up with a mess: glue all over the outside of the envelope, wet stamps with too much glue, and worse, glue all over my fingers, hands and the shirt I wore that day.

Then the next "adventure" began. With envelope sealed and stamped one gets in line to send the letter "regular" mail, or "registered mail", or perhaps to send as "registered air mail," each requiring a separate line. The Brazilians did not seem to mind the long wait, all loudly conversing with much laughter. Not so the "gringo" accustomed to just an air mail stamp and dropping the letter in the proper post office box. I knew no Brazilian that even minutely believed that a letter sent by "regular mail" would ever arrive at its destination. But I noticed something funny: behind each steel "guichê" or cage where the employees sat there was a huge pile of letters, all casually tossed there from the respective cage. Did the Brazilian Post Office ever separate the different letters from that huge pile? Did each have the same fate?

The post office employees were notoriously badly paid and it was no surprise to observe their usual bad humor ("casmurros" or ill-humored, a term taken from the famous novel by the great 19th century Brazilian novelist Machado de Assis: "Dom Casmurro") and then have to deal with it. I would customarily greet said employee with great courtesy: "How are you today? I hope all goes well for you and your family" and hope for the best.

A final note: in all those many years of going to the Guararapes Post Office to mail letters and also large packages of books to be sent home to Abilene, Kansas (the books are another story: the wrapping paper was fragile, easily torn; the packages wrapped with twine and with the mandatory slit which had to be reinforced with clear "Scotch Tape" so one could see that indeed there were books inside), never but never was a package lost. They all arrived safely, often torn beyond recognition, the destination address in shreds. I sent so many the U.S. Post Office "knew" what to do with them.

And it is also fair to say that at least living in a large city and dealing with the U.S. Post Office in recent years may not always be much of an improvement. For sure the Brazilians took it all in a better spirit.

A CHANGE OF SCENE –
"FLYING DOWN TO RIO"

The Times – "Embratel" (The Brazilian Communications Company)

On the flight from Recife to Rio there was an interesting conversation. In those years there was a rapid expansion of the communications network in Brazil, largely via satellite, all accomplished by the government firm/monopoly EMBRATEL ("Brazilian Company of Telecommuications"). Seated beside me on the airplane was a man who had been working for months in Recife doing the installation of the network. He complained of the inefficiency, the laziness, and the outright thievery of the northeasterners involved in the operation. And he believed it was a very bad use of federal funds in the Northeast. He has no sympathy for the plight of the Northeast and believes that if northeasterners would learn to work harder they would be more efficient. (I do not recall where he was from; the reader can only surmise.) This attitude has not disappeared in Brazil. The prejudice continues.

Changes on the Buses in Rio de Janeiro

The system has changed drastically since 1967. Before, on the sign in the center at the top of the windshield of each bus one would see the destination of the bus: i.e. Downtown, Botafogo, Maracanã, etc. And below, in the right hand corner, a placard would actually show the route to the destination: "Downtown via Jardim Botânico" for example. Now the placard above has only a number, i.e. 420, 325 or the like, and no one knows the relation of the number to the actual destination. There is mass confusion. With the passage of time eventually it did all get sorted out and the public learned the relationship between the number and the destination. Supposedly there was a guidebook with all this pertinent information available at the time, but I met no one that had such a book. After several rides, including getting lost more than once in Rio, I gradually was able to learn how to get around. The good news is I got to know a lot of Rio I had not counted on knowing!

Changes on Copacabana Beach 1969

Changes on Copacabana Beach

The city planners have a plan for a significant widening of Avenida Atlântica (the avenue next to the beach in Copacabana). If memory serves me there were only two lanes in 1967, one lane each direction. The plan is for two or three lanes in each direction. So where does this space come from? That's where it got complicated and Rio planners devised an amazing project: they dug tunnels and brought hundreds of thousands of tons of sand through them with the effect of broadening or widening the beach itself. And space would be created for the new "multi-laned highway." It was a huge success and what you see today is a result of the original plan, a large, wide avenue with many lanes of traffic. There is only one problem: together with this engineering feat come others: the massive increase in the production of steel, the subsequent mass production of automobiles, the creation of easy-credit plans for folks to buy cars, and the huge increase in traffic on the roads of Brazil's large cities, particularly São Paulo, but with Rio de Janeiro, Belo Horizonte, Salvador and Recife not far behind. So, there are still massive traffic jams in Copacabana. In 1969 there were only two ways to get from the south zone (Leblon, Ipanema, Copacabana) to downtown: one through the center of Copacabana via Avenida Nossa Senhora da Copacabana or Avenida Atlântica to the east,through the tunnel to Botafogo, and over the viaducts to the "Aterro" in Botafogo, or "the back way" through Ipanema and Leblon, around the Rodrigo de Freitas Lake, through the tunnel to the back of Botafogo, down jammed main streets of Botafogo, back to the main street on the beach at Botafogo Bay and on to the "Aterro" of Botafogo to downtown. Normal life and traffic were charactersized by terrible traffic jams no matter which route one chose.

In the back part of Botafogo there is a huge "favela" on top of the hills. They say there is a government plan to bulldoze the "favela" and move all the people out to a "proletarian housing district" in the "Baixada Fluminense." There were some "mysterious" fires in the "favelas," thus partially accomplishing the task. Another case was the "Praia do Pinto" Favela behind Leblon. It was announced that it soon would be leveled in the name of "progress." When the inhabitants refused, there was a "mysterious" fire and it was destroyed. Similar events took place in the "invasões" in Salvador or the "mangues" or "mucambos" of Recife. It made sense that the "povão" did not want to move from the "favelas" in the center of Rio to the "Proletarian" districts in the Baixada, a region known for its terrible pollution, climate, disease and crime. These people worked in Rio as doormen, maids, washing ladies, construction workers and the like, and the increased cost of train or bus fare into Rio was just one of the good reasons to not want to move. But "progress" leveled the "Praia do Pinto" and the next step is due to be Rio's largest "favela" on the other side of the "Lagoa."

An Aside. How the times have changed. Attitudes have changed tremendously over the years; the "favelas" are now known as "comunidades" or "communities." And especially with the arrival of the World Cup in 2014 and the Olympics to come in 2016, great efforts are being made to better the conditions in the "favelas," just one example being the shiny new cable car up to Providênca near the Port of Rio.

The Northeastern Fair at São Cristóvão 1969

Early in the morning on a Sunday I caught the bus in the South Zone; it was loaded with maids, doormen, construction workers, many from the Northeast, taking advantage of their day off to "kill homesickness" ("matar saudades") at the Fair. It was a cloudy morning and upon arriving to the downtown and to the north zone there was considerable pollution caused by the traffic, the buses and the factories in the north zone of Rio. Before that however one saw the beautiful Botafogo Bay (polluted itself) in the distance, the clouds up above, the beaches now replete with people playing soccer in the league and make-up games, but few daring to go in to the water at Botafogo due to that nasty polluted water.

The bus was from the line "Jacaré-Jardim de Aláh" ("Alligator- Allah's Garden") and I think there may be something symbolic in all that. Jardim de Alah is a beautiful small park in the south beach district of Leblon and Jacaré is a poor suburb in Rio's North Zone. The bus was jam packed by the time we got out of Ipanema, the majority of the passengers dark complected and short, the stereotypical Northeasterners.

Now in downtown Rio, the center of town, after leaving Avenue Getúlio Vargas on the way to the North Zone and the many tall buildings of Avenida Rio Branco, there was a complete deterioration at the side of the streets. One could see the old 19th century two-story buildings, poorly cared for, beat up, and old and torn down warehouses, some in the process of being bulldozed. To the right there was a hill with a "favela" almost invisible through the fog and the smog, and on the back side of the hills separating the north and south zones; the north side was full of poor construction.

After heading west a bit on Presidente Vargas the bus curved and entered "Avenida Brasil," (in 1969 the "freeways" of four lanes or more that today connect the South Zone to the Galeão Airport on the Island of the Governor did not exist.) Avenida Brasil passed by factories, a canal pitch black with evil, badly smelling "water" which was the color of coal from the factories. Later after passing through the district of Meier, we arrived at São Cristóvão, its plaza being the connecting point of bus, train and cargo trucks from the northeast and north and west of Rio. To the side of the plaza was São Cristóvão Pavillion, the fair or market surrounding it on three sides. The fair is the "home away from home" for the northeasterners ("pau de arara, caipira") who frequent the scene each Sunday morning. This particular Sunday the fair shares its space with the "National Beer Festival" inside the pavilion, a less than healthy circumstance.

Folklorist Raul Lody has written the best and most detailed description of the fair that I know of, all in a long article for the "Revista da Campanha de Folclore Nacional" of Rio de Janeiro. The stands in the fair sell almost everything one could find in Caruaru or Campina Grande or Feira de Santana: all types of food, tools, household needs, clothing, and hammocks. Folk culture of the Northeast is readily evident: blind folk singers, "forró" trios – sound box, triangle and drums – the kind of music Luís Gonzaga will make famous throughout Brazil in coming years. (One needs to recall his song, the "Anthem of the Northeast," "Asa Branca" ("White Wing"). This author comes close to tears each time he hears it! The trios play "baião, xote" and other northeastern rhythms. There are vendors of popular medicines and remedies, preachers of the Bible with the Good Book in hand, snake charmers, "sword swallowers' and "fire swallowers" as well.

The "Cordel" Poet "Azulão" 1967

My special interest was the presence of the "Literatura de Cordel" and its poets singing or declaiming their verse. The poets of "cordel" as well as the "singer-poets" ("cantadores") are more present than in my last visit of 1967. Principal among them is José João dos Santos (Azulão) living now in the State of Rio de Janeiro, but originally from Paraíba. He sells using a small sound system with a microphone (the strident roar of the "forró" music in the fair creates a tremendous obstacle to the poets). He was well turned out, clean, close shaved, and perhaps gaining a kilo or two from the last time we saw him in 1967. He had a female assistant who worked as "money collector" while he would "sing" or recite the cordel story. Azulão sings and declaims in the best of the "cordel" tradition, this by virtue of the fact he is both accomplished "cantador" and "poeta de cordel." The audience was impressive, both in the number of persons surrounding the poet and their enthusiasm. While I was there he sang "The Man on the Moon" and sold many copies of the same. He was kept quite busy with his audience so I tried to stay out of the way and not draw any attention (any "gringo" was quite evident in the market). Azulão had story poems in the two styles of the times: the traditional covers of the northeastern story-poems and those by Editorial Prelúdio of São Paulo with the colored covers with a sort of "comic book" cover design. I noted the customers seemed to prefer the São Paulo design.

The "Cordel" poet Antônio Oliveira was also present (I had met him in 1967) with a good stock of poems, among them the "classics" of Ceará and Pernambuco States. He was an old veteran of São Cristóvão. And I spotted three or four other vendors as well.

Poet-Singers in the Fair of São Cristóvão 1969

There was a "dupla" or pair of poet-singers, that is, improvisers of verse, nearby, the two in dark suits, with white shirts and tie. They were seated on wooden boxes under the shade of a tree. When I arrived and indicated I wanted to take a photo, they immediately launched into improvised verse, singing poetically about the "foreign guy" who had just arrived. I offered a tip and the improvisation went on.

All in all, the totality of "cordel" poets and singer-poets was the best that I had seen in this trip to Brazil. It seemed like the Fair was indeed prospering.

The "Water Yell" ("O Berro d'Água")

My friend Daniel Santo Pietro (Fulbright Scholarship to Brazil in 1966 -1967, Harvard, Economics, and now in the management of "Caritas" in Rio) introduced me to this great place and I returned several times over the next few years. The scene was impressive; originally a high rise hotel or apartment building was to be built on the spot to the side of the Lagoa Rodrigo de Freitas behind Ipanema and Leblon beaches. According to the story financing fell through but the company decided to at least do something with the property. What remained was the superstructure itself of concrete and steel with several floors, but no walls or finished floors. So they put in an elevator shaft to the top and finished that floor only with a night club – restaurant. It is a very strange sensation to enter the building, dodging construction materials on the ground floor, sometimes climbing over them, getting to the ultra-modern elevator and being whisked up to the top floor, some ten stories up. Even then you have to walk carefully on a partially finished floor to the entrance to the nightclub. The restaurant itself is elegant and the dance floor outside in the open air is spectacular! You dance under the stars, on one of those good nights in Rio, and through clouds or fog you see the Christ Figure on Corcovado far to the right and directly ahead the Rodrigo de Freitas Lake with the beach district of Leblon and Ipanema beyond that. The name of the place comes from a "novella" by Jorge Amado: "A Morte e a Morte de Quincas Berro D'Água" ("The Death of Quincas Wateryell" by one translation). The main character Quincas is a real expert on the diverse types of "cachaça" in Salvador, knowing them well by color, "perfume," and taste. On one occasion he is the victim of a joke by his drinking buddies: they serve him a small glass of the "branquinha" which is really water. Quincas slugs it down, chokes, coughs, and spits out the drink, yelling "ÁAAAAGUA." On a night in Rio with a soft breeze, Bossa-Nova music playing quietly in the background, the moon and stars and the scene already described, it may have been the most romantic spot in Rio in those times. I won't say who all I managed to take up there, but my wife Keah was thrilled by the scene in 1970. I ask myself now in 2015 at this writing, could it still be there? Naaaah.

An Aside. Speaking of Those Days, I don't recall if I wrote in "Adventures," but on the return flight to the U.S. in 1967 the Varig Flight turned into Carnival time. The plane departed from Rio, stopped in São Paulo where we picked up Miss Brazil (she sat directly across the aisle from me) and then stopped in Lima, Peru, where we picked up no less than Miss Peru, Miss Bolivia, Miss Paraguay and Miss Argentina. You have to know Brazil and the Brazilians to not be surprised at what happened next: an open, full bar, music and "samba" in the aisles until Miami! Never have I been surrounded by such beauty since, including the pretty Peace Corps girl who traveled on the other side of me during that flight. Ah youth! Ah to bachelor days in Brazil!

BRAZIL 1970 WITH KEAH

INTRODUCTION

I was off to Brazil one more time with a small summer research grant from Arizona State University and plans for a project, but with a big difference – tourism! This time I am taking my brand new wife Keah (married in December, 1969) to get to know "My Brazil." It would be followed by a very quick trip to my other "favorite" country of Guatemala. The two would represent a true Latin American "honeymoon" (the original honeymoon was a short three day affair in Hot Springs, Arkansas (we were married in Little Rock). Needless to say Brazil and Guatemala would hold sway.

It was the first time Keah really knew and understood the necessities of my career: research in Latin America. She was not a student of languages and knew just the bare basics of Spanish and Portuguese, a result of auditing my Introductory Portuguese course at ASU and a "quicky" conversational night course in Spanish in Tempe, Arizona. But she had a great "ear" for language and there were moments when she understood the native speakers when I did not, a lesson in humility for the professor but a happy circumstance.

CHANGES

With the atmosphere of terrorism against the military regime now in Brazil in 1970, the sequesters of businessmen and even diplomats, and bombs thrown at banks and the like, there was a huge change in the security at airports including passenger and luggage checks. The introduction for us was at the airport of Belém do Paraá where we entered Brazil on our way to Recife, Pernambuco, and our first destination (the reader may recall I did the same route in 1969). After spending the night at a very modest hotel on Avenida Getúlio Vargas in Belém, we got up at 4:00 a.m., arrived at the Belém airport at 5:00 a.m., and our flight left for Recife at 8:30 a.m. due to all the security restrictions of the DOPS. At least they used uniformed female security personal to check the ladies, even then a "personal" body search, I mean a personal search of the entire body!

EMERSON FITTIPALDI "SYNDROME" AND BRAZILIAN AIRLINE PILOTS

Keah's introduction to the "machismo" and the "esprit 'de corps" of Brazilian airline pilots began on the Belém – Recife flight. At the end of the flight from Belém we were arriving at our destination of the Guararapes International Airport in Recife but with unstable weather and heavy thunderstorms. Upon entering into the flight pattern for landing, the airplane descending rapidly and precipitously, at the moment the wheels should make contact with the tarmac the plane suddenly lurched upward, gaining in velocity. Looking out the small window, I noticed that the landing strip was well to the left of our flight path. Then the pilot pulled the "Emerson Fittipaldi" Indianapolis 500 maneuver: he "goosed" the engines, climbed at a g-level speed and veered the airplane sharply to the left. We suddenly were flying over the Atlantic Ocean! Then the airplane circled and we landed on the proper runway, this on our second try. Keah was with "wet palm syndrome," a result of her introduction to Brazilian aviation. I thought at that time: "No North American pilot would dare to undertake the abrupt maneuvers we had just witnessed on the Varig." (I'm not so sure about that today vis a vis the emergency landing by the captain of the plane on the Hudson River in New York a few years ago.) Looking back, it was all a lot of fun.

Keah had arrived in Brazil.

FLOODS AND "BUGS"

Floods and "Bugs" Recife 1970

We were staying in the home of old friend Flávio Cavalcanti Veloso who at the moment was in São Paulo doing graduate work in engineering. His brother Sérgio with his recent diploma in medicine was a guide. As always in the month of June (like in 1966, 1967 and 1969) it was "winter" in Pernambuco and heavy tropical rains brought serious flooding to the city. The flooded streets were the result of the "blowout" of all three rivers running into this "Venice of Brazil" as a result of the rains in the interior of the Northeast. Sérgio, driving us around the city, came to a street with high water, didn't hesitate for a moment and floorboarded it directly into the water. His explanation: "VW Bugs float!" In his defense I think we did float just a bit. In the U.S. there would have been a barrier barring entrance to the street. The Brazilians knew better.

THE MOMENT - PEOPLE AND TOURISM DURING THE TRIP: WHAT WE DID AND WHAT WE SAW

The Golden Chapel in Recife dating from 1699. It is one of the best baroque churches to be seen in all Brazil and is characterized by its gold leaf and stained glass windows.

"Capoeira" in Salvador da Bahia by Master Bimba ("Mestre Bimba"), one of the most famous masters of all time in Bahia. The show was in the Pelourinho Plaza.

Keah's Introduction to Rio was a quick visit to the lavish apartment of the James family (he was the representative of the Library of Congress in Brazil, formerly in several African countries) in Parque Guinle with its distant view to the Bay of Guanabara. Jorguinho Guinle in those days was perhaps the playboy about town in Rio. The family not only owned the Copacabana Palace Hotel but the prime real estate in all Rio in what would become Parque Guinle. Jorginho touted himself as an "intellectual Marxist!" Interesting! A professional aside: Jerry James in his capacity as Library of Congress Director in Brazil happened to see my book on a list of future publications for the University Press of Pernambuco, a good sign for the future. The book would actually be in print three years later.

News from the Casa de Ruy Barbosa. Professor Theirs Martins Moreira director of the Research Center during my formative years in research and sometime mentor has passed away. His project of the book of studies on popular literature in verse ("cordel") is continuing as planned. Professor Adriano da Gama Kury is the new Director of Philology and will become a good friend in the future. It was he who edited and corrected my Portuguese in the future study for the book: "Satire and the Poetry of Leandro Gomes de Barros."

I met for the first time the renowned Théo Brandão, folklorist from Alagoas and in my view the second best in all Brazil following only Luís da Câmara Cascudo in Natal. He had seen my article in the "Revista Brasileira de Folclore" and was now deep in research on the classic poem of "Cordel," "The Gambling Soldier" ("O Soldado Jogador"). It was rather unbelievable to learn that he had 500 manuscript pages written so far and is not finished!

I met the "Cordel" poet and publisher Joaquim Batista de Sena from Fortaleza, Ceará, a relative of Sebastião Nunes Batista. The encounter took place in the library of the Casa de Ruy Barbosa and was a pleasure; Joaquim was a major figure in northeastern "cordel" in the 1950s and 1960s. Upon his death his works and stock of "cordel" would be obtained by Manoel Caboclo e Silva in Juazeiro do Norte.

I met for the first time the ubiquitous and perhaps infamous professor from the Sorbonne, Raymond Cantel; he would really put "Cordel" on the map in Brazil with his interviews with major dailies and weekly news magazines. I do not know where else I mentioned it, but there is almost a "folklore" grown up around this man, both pro and con. He would arrive on the direct flight from Paris to Rio or São Paulo, immediately contact the press and garner interviews. A bit of an intellectual dandy, he also became known for his amazing collection of "cordel" which he guarded zealously in Portiers, France. He never published in quantity, but certainly in quality and certainly did cause intellectuals dragging their feet in Brazil to take notice of the "cordel." (This folk-popular poetry was truly looked down upon and/or ignored by most of the Brazilian intelligentsia in the 1960s.) When I heard the professor speak on a couple of occasions his papers were incredibly clear, free of jargon and fine work.

Tourism in Rio with Keah: we went to Corcovado, to Sugar Loaf and to the aforementioned Panorama Palace Hotel with the "Berro D'Água" nightclub.

Henrique Kerti and Wife Cristina, Rio de Janeiro

There was a fine reunion with my first Brazilian friend dating from undergraduate days at Rockhurst College in Kansas City, Missouri. Henrique and Cristina were married at the Igreja do Carmo in the center of Rio with the wedding reception at the Copacabana Palace Hotel and honeymoon in Amsterdam. I stayed with the family in my very first days in Brazil in June of 1966, getting to know Henrique's mother and brother Cristiano.

Those were sentimental days prior to his marriage, in effect, his bachelor days. Henrique introduced me to Copacabana nightlife and took me to my first Brazilian soccer game, a doozy at the Maracanã. My first Brazilian "Love," that rosewood Di Giorgio classic guitar (the same model as Baden Powell played), was kept in their house while I did fieldwork for six months in the Northeast. There would be many encounters over the years and I may recount them upon occasion in these notes.

The "Colombo Confectionary" ("A Confeitaria Colombo"), Rio de Janeiro

I introduced Keah to the famous "Confeitaria Colombo" in downtown Rio. We enjoyed terrific "cafezinho" and the serious pastries it is known for. The Confeitaria was founded in 1894, thus is now over one hundred years old and cannot be separated from the cultural and culinary history of Rio de Janeiro. It is now an official part of the historical patrimony of the city. Carioca high society were among the clients to enjoy the "high tea" of the afternoon, the many chocolate treats (like "Brigadeiro" but many more and fancier ones) and all the rest in the "Fim do Século" atmosphere in Rio. The place, in time, became a famous restaurant with its clientele of the "gente fina" – economically, socially and politically.

I saw the seminal documentary film by Tânia Quaresma on "cordel" and the folklore of the Northeast. It was a "classic" from the 1960s with the scenes of poet-singers ("cantadores"), the northeastern cowboys in their outfits of leather from head to toe, scenes from the Cariri region of Ceará (the land of Father Cícero and the"holy women" of Juazeiro), and Father Cícero's successor Friar Damian. What I would not give to see it again now. It was one of the first efforts to capture that amazing folkloric scene of the Northeast on film, albeit in the black and white of the times.

A Brazilian Institution: the "Despachante"

This is a Brazilian institution. The "dispatcher" or ""despachante" is a person or agent who is hired to "cut through" the terrible red tape and bureaucracy of Brazilian life. My friend Daniel Santo Pietro in Brazil on a temporary visa in order to work for CARITAS (Catholic Relief Services) came home to the apartment and showed us what seemed to have been a two-inch thick billfold full of the documents needed for him to simply leave Brazil, go to New York City, marry his fiancée and bring her back to Brazil to live with him, as husband and wife. Daniel, a veteran of Brazil's ways if there ever was one, was finally forced by inaction and exasperation to hire a "despachante" who was ever so slowly getting through the process.

Of all sources to know about the "despachante," one of the best accounts on the subject is by novelist John Grisham in his novel taking place in Brazil called "The Testament." Grisham writes (fiction of course, but not far from reality), "No official document is obtained in Brazil without waiting in long lines. The "despachante" knows the city clerks, the courthouse crowd, the politicians, and the customs agents. He knows the system and how to grease it to get things done. The job requires a quick tongue, patience and a lot of brass." (Quoted by Robert de Paolo in "Doing Business in Brazil").

This is a professionalized example of the "jeito," the source of such things. It means finding a way to get around something, a law, a custom, a rule, and all done in good faith with all parties satisfied. My own best example was using political "pull" ("pistolão") in getting an exit permit from the Pernambuco Police (customs in that state) to leave Brazil after a very innocent year of studying on a Fulbright Hays Grant n 1966-1967. It took the word of a retired Brazilian Admiral to get my slip of paper saying I had not committed a crime or owed any taxes.

For Daniel, the good news is it turned out all right. And for us too; while he journeyed to New York for the wedding, Keah and I rented his modest apartment in Ipanema. It really turned out to be second honeymoon ("lua de mel") for the two of us. Thank you Daniel.

The Hairdresser

While living that short month in Ipanema Keah found that she needed a haircut or something of the sort. So we marched down the main street of prosperous Ipanema until passing a very decent salon. I entered with Keah, speaking Portuguese to the main person in charge, said hairdresser. I asked if he knew English; "Of course, of course" was the answer. So, confident that one could not do better than Ipanema I left poor Keah in his "good hands." I returned one hour later and scarcely recognized my newlywed spouse. She now had an entirely new hair style of tightly knit curls ("caracóis" the Brazilians call them) looking much like a brunette and older Little Orphan Annie. Keah reported that the hairdresser knew one word in English:

"Yes." Like Daniel and the "despachante" Keah and the "cabeleileiro" turned out well; the curls gradually diminishing lasted Keah trhe rest of the trip. We actually had a good laugh about it and she was actually pretty cute looking with those curls. There's got to be a moral to this story somewhere.

End of the Trip

These notes were brief because it was a short trip, a beautiful trip consisting mainly in tourism. Today, decades later, I recognize that my own happiness in Brazil, at least in regard to socializing, for the most part would be attributed to those happy moments with Keah in 1970 and again in 1985. There were, as I shall tell, other moments of solitude and even loneliness, not all bad, to be reported.

BRAZIL 1973

INTRODUCTION

Such things happen rarely in the life of a North American professor (unless you are a "super star," not applicable here), but one of them happened to me in 1973. I was living the calm and normal life of a young assistant professor at Arizona State University, that is, teaching Spanish and Brazilian Portuguese and the respective cultures from the Peninsula and Latin America and doing research on Brazil's folk-popular poetry ("a literatura de cordel"). I received in the morning mail an unusual letter marked "Air Mail Special Delivery" on Varig Airline stationery from Los Angles. It said: "Please get in touch with us at Varig regarding your pre-paid transportation." "What in the hell is this?" I thought to myself. I telephoned Varig in Los Angeles and they repeated "We have a paid airline ticket for you to Rio de Janeiro." They did not know why or from whom, but just had the paid passage with travel dates. I asked them to see if they could find out a bit more about it. Anyway, that's how the ticket fell out of thin air!

A good professor always has something ready in the desk drawer and that was my case. I had prepared a few months earlier a study treating the relationship between the theme of the heroic in the "cordel" and the masterpiece of João Gumarães Rosa, "Grande Sertão: Veredas" ("The Devil to Pay in the Backlands"). Young, ambitious, still at the beginning of my career, and yet not knowing the reason behind the air line ticket, I agreed, packed my bag and caught a flight from Phoenix to Los Angeles. Happily, in Los Angeles Varig had received an answer and explanation for the mysterious ticket. The ticket had to do with an invitation to attend and participate in the "First International Congress of Portuguese Philology" in Rio de Janeiro and Niterói. Not being a Philologist and probably having only a vague idea of what it was, I learned only after arriving in Rio that a small part of the big congress would be dedicated to "Popular Literature in Verse" as the "Cordel" was correctly known at that time. Due to my assiduous research on the "cordel" at the Casa de Ruy Barbosa in 1966, 1967, 1969 and 1970, they had decided I deserved an invitation. Not being a gambler, certainly not in Brazil's famous numbers' racket ("O Jogo do Bicho") I had "hit" the number and won the prize. So that's how I ended up writing these notes, memories and meditations on the trip that would turn into a new adventure for the "naïve 'gringo'" ("o gringo sem jeito") in Brazil.

At the Varig airline counter in Los Angeles, upon printing out the boarding pass the employees laughed at the situation, not making a big deal out of any of it. "Hey, go on and go, and have a good time" was their advice. There was a time of waiting, really, two; the first when no one was able to open the door on the big Boeing 747 to allow passengers in, and later, the heavy night fog in Los Angeles. We were called back to the tarmac from the take off strip due to the dense fog. So all of us passengers enjoyed the incredible "on board service" of Varig seated in our comfortable seats waiting for word from the tower announcing permission to taxi and take off. At mid night there were before dinner drinks, salmon, tomatoes and eggs, French bread and cheese, chicken breast, lemon dessert, and that delicious Brazilian "cafezinho." At two in the morning we took off and after five hours arrived at the international airport of Lima in Peru. Everyone left the airplane to stretch their legs and experience a bit of Lima, and after one or two Pisco Sours probably donated by the local tourist agency with the hopes of us loosening our pocketbooks for the tourist shops, once again all climbed aboard and we took off with a direct flight to Rio.

THE ARRIVAL IN RIO DE JANEIRO

Much to my surprise there were people to meet me at the Galeão Airport, my old friend from the Casa de Ruy Barbosa, Ana Maria Barroso. At that point everything came together and I finally got the "big picture" of the purpose of the trip.

Ana Maria explained the name of the Congress or "Conference" as we say in the U.S., was the euphemistic name reflecting Portuguese and Brazilian rhetoric - "The First International Congress on Portuguese Philology and Luís de Camões." How did I fit in, certainly not a Philologist or the like? It turns out there would be a session on "Popular Literature in Verse" (the academic name for "cordel" in those days, a correct and very accurate name indeed), the "cordel" being housed in the Philology Sector of the Research Center of the Casa de Ruy Barbosa. That is all a very complicated story, but I think was really only a "jeito" for an entity dedicated to the life and works of the "polyglot" and statesman Ruy Barbosa to have a collection of the "literatura de cordel," a literature extremely looked down upon in those years. The second "jeito" was perhaps that the "cordel" in fact did represent the "popular language of Brazil" of the Northeast. Get it? Language of the masses in the sector on the study of Language and Philology. Be that as it may, Ana Maria took me to the conference hotel, the old and famous "Hotel da Glória" in the district of the same name in the old part of downtown Rio.

The "Hotel Glória" and Sugar Loaf Mountain 1973

The Salon of the Emperor Dom Pedro II, "Hotel Glória"

An Aside. The Hotel had a large salon dedicated totally to Imperor Dom Pedro II with beautiful paintings of him, colonial furniture of the times, gorgeous Portuguese tile scenes of the era, a real sight to admire (it made me think of Dom Pedro's museum in Petrópolis outside of Rio). On the other hand, there was, for the times, a bit of a "doubtful" side to the hotel: it was known as the site of the famous "Transvestite Ball" of Rio's carnival; at least that was its fame in 1973.

And of note in 1973 Avenida Rio Branco the main business, banking and cultural avenue of the city was totally torn up for the construction of Rio's new subway. Brazil was in a frenzy of modernization at the time and Rio could not fall farther behind the "Locomotive of Brazil," the huge metropolis of São Paulo which already sported a large subway system.

Anyway, the hotel would house and host the "elite" of the Portuguese and Brazilian academic world – the "crème de la crème" of intellectuals in Philology, Literature, and most important, experts on the Portuguese Epic Poem, "Os Lusíadas" ("The Lusiads" of Luís de Camões, by far the most famous work of literature of that nation). I was introduced to Américo Ramalho, Celso Cunha, Massaud Moisés, Artur Torres, Joel Pontes, Hernani Cidade of old Portugal and the important Raymund Cantel of the Sorbonne. The latter, as perhaps mentioned earlier, was the intellectual who "put the 'literatura de cordel' on the map in Brazil!" I, young, just a beginner, would have my baptism into the intellectual world of international congresses.

It is worthwhile to tell my impressions of the Congress portraying thusly certain interesting customs from that world, a world so different from that of the United States. It was Old World – New World with a European Flavor and me as a tiny footnote.

THE LITERATURE CONGRESS

The "Solemn Session" – the Opening

It all took place in the auditorium of the Rectory of the School of Letters of the Federal University of Rio de Janeiro in Niteroi. The first thing was of course the singing of the Brazilian National Anthem. For the reader who does not know it, the anthem is extremely lengthy, complicated for the English or North American ear, and yes, a bit funny. All the fine intellectuals in all their finery, dark suits, white shirt, tie, cufflinks, polished shoes, in short, immaculate, seemed to bounce up and down with the rhythm.

Then came the first orator. It was "The Cadillac" (a local joke because he showed up everywhere, perorating, uttering grand seemingly "Baroque" speeches) Pedro Calmon, a famous Brazilian historian from the crown prince of Brazilian locution, Salvador da Bahia, deserving of the attention of all. Humor aside, I have to confess that I owe a great personal debt to him for it was he who planted the intellectual seed for my most successful book in Brazil, this because of his own very modest book of years ago, "History of Brazil in the Poetry of Its People" ("História do Brasil na Poesia do Povo"). The volume treated popular poetry and history just before the advent of "cordel.

The Lunch or Mid-Day Meal to Follow

This is an entire lesson for the foreigner on Brazilian culture and life. The mid-day meal in Brazil in those days and to an extent yet today was the "almoço," in fact the main meal of the day. It was not one of those "cardboard" fairly tasteless poor lunches at academic meetings in the United States. It took place in a Brazilian "steakhouse" or "churrascaria" in the neighborhood (think of "Fogo de Chão" or the like today, or maybe Rio's "Porcão"). There was all manner of salad, French fries, manioc flour, and the main attraction – all possible cuts of beef, pork, and chicken. It was followed by ice cream and an excellent "cafezinho." (I will not go into a long description of the "churrascaria" but you get the idea.) The problem was, as also is the Brazilian custom, and I love the Brazilian saying, "Tudo foi regado" ("All was irrigated") with an opening "caipirinha," a choice of Brazilian wines and of course icy cold Brazilian draft beer. A beer drinker and not thinking of the consequences, I participated a fair amount in the draft beer. The result was the afternoon session rewarded me with terrible drowsiness and perhaps a short nap or two during the proceedings. I assure you I was not alone.

During the "almoço" I met more of the intellectual "crème": Gladstone de Mello, a famous Brazilian philologist, and two wonderful colleagues of future "cordel" research in Brazil Théo Brandão, a nationally known folklorist (in my mind second only to the great Luís da Câmara Cascudo of Natal) and Sebastião Nunes Batista, research colleague and friend at the Casa de Ruy.

Impressive for the young North American in the session that afternoon was that the large auditorium was jam packed, not an empty seat to be had. I calculated some 500 hundred persons in the audience. This would never but never occur at an academic congress in the United States, and beyond that, I discover that the audience PAID TO ATTEND!

Speaking of that, during the long afternoon, a pretty young lady came to my chair in the audience and handed me an envelope. It was full of bank notes, national money, I think in the neighborhood of 500 cruzeiros (the Brazilian "dollar" of the times). Even considering rampant inflation, it was a fairly significant amount of change which would end up paying for small purchases, beer or soft drinks, taxis, or extra meals. The young lady explained that it was "walking around money." Jeez! ("Nossa!" in the parlance of the times in Brazil!) The tradition of the honorarium for the principal speakers in U.S. congresses, notwithstanding, would never be paid in a white envelope full of cash in the middle of the congress! Over the years as a faculty member of a major university in the U.S., in regard to an annual conference, my university would pay airfare and one night's lodging and meals; the lodging and meals went by the board later on. So compare this with Brazil in 1973 in that country of the "Third World" in the midst of economic development. I can't explain it and why should I complain? It is indeed "small potatoes" in the larger world picture of business, government and such things most of us never see or experience. So we the academic specialists those few days were the "privileged." "Congressistas" at that!

Returning that afternoon to the hotel the mode of transportation was the old ferry boat Niteroi-Rio, with a slow and calm passage with the view of Rio; I found it incredibly beautiful and even, may I say, romantic.

An Aside. News of "Cordel." Zé Bernardo da Silva poet and owner of the São Francisco Typografia in Juazeiro do Norte with ownership of the works of Leandro Gomes de Barros and João Martins de Atayde, has died. Also deceased is Sylvio Rabelo of the Joaquim Nabuco

Institute of Social Sciences in Recife. Among the best of the private collections of "cordel" in Brazil, that of Evandro Rabelo, has been sold, I believe to an entity in Pernambuco. All the above mentioned played roles in my original research in the Northeast in 1966-1967.

Friend, research colleague and cultural guide to the folklore of Rio de Janeiro, Sebastião Nunes Batista, at that time was full-time as a student at the Federal University of Rio de Janeiro, trying valiantly to obtain a university degree. This is another story to tell. Sebastião was of humble roots, one of the sons of Francisco das Chagas Batista from Paraíba, one of the pioneering poets of "cordel" and colleague of Leandro Gomes de Barros, the greatest name in all "cordel". Sebastião was a modest civil servant in the Ministry of Agriculture in Rio de Janeiro. It was through the "pull" ("pistolão") of Professor Theirs Martins Moreira of the Casa de Rui that Sebastião was guided in gaining entrance to the university, not an easy task. Sebastião told me that the area of specialization did not matter, only having the degree. Years later he would win in life, gaining both the degree and the subsequent respect of co-workers in the Casa de Rui.

Second Day. The Session in the "Portuguese Royal Reading Room," "O Real Gabinete de Leitura Portuguesa" in Rio de Janeiro

If memory serves me, the session treated Luís de Camões, Portugal's main claim to international literary fame with his renowned epic poem "The Lusiads" which told of the epic voyage of Vasco da Gama and the Portuguese to India in 1497. The session began with a flowery speech by "The Cadillac" Pedro Calmon. Incidentally famous professor Hernani Cidade of Portugal, elderly and deaf, was deep into a nap. And once again all began with the hilarious (to me) national anthem with everyone present bouncing up and down to the rhythm. There were baroque speeches by the Bahian Calmon and one of his fellow "conterrâneos" Hélio Simões, these contrasting with the pragmatic discourse, replete with facts and statistics, of Segismundo Spina of the University of São Paulo. Should I have been surprised? It was the old Bahia-São Paulo stereotype.

There were other things that I would see various times in congresses in Brazil. There were problems with the microphone: the Brazilians were accustomed to speaking with the mouth too close to the microphone thus causing distortion and always at too high a volume. So, repeatedly, the orator would be interrupted by a "peon" trying to adjust that devil of a microphone creating even more confusion and great difficulty in both giving and understanding the speech. It was such small detail that possibly kept me from falling asleep during the talks.

Another Inconvenience. The bathroom in the "Real Gabinete de Leitura Portuguesa" was located directly behind the large horseshoe shaped wooden carved speakers' podium, just a short distance from the orators' microphone. Inevitably after one of those huge mid-day mels including wine and beer, there were many "necessitados" or those in need, thus there was the constant opening and closing of the single bathroom door (it squeaked) and worse the sound of the loud flushing of the commode.

Many of the esteemed "consecrated" ("consagrados") professors fell asleep during the afternoon talks. And on the upper floors of the library, surrounding the speakers' table and podium, two or three stories high, there was constant foot traffic of those purportedly using the stacks or just hanging out, looking at the "band passing by" below. An appropriate aside: it was in these years that the young and talented Chico Buarque de Holanda composed and sang many of his hit songs of the MPB in the Festivals, and one of the best known was "A Banda", a great song epitomizing the essence of carnival in Rio, and those watching "the carnival bands pass by."

Suddenly there was a flurry of noise and activity, confusion and loud talking in the reading room. It was the arrival of the ambassador of Portugal to "bless and address" the ceremony. He arrived with sirens and a police escort, all this in the middle of a high falutin' speech by the esteemed Camoes' scholar from Germany. You can only imagine the fact that Germany and the German were not to be interrupted! But what can you do? It's the tropics! As I would learn later, it really was nothing new, and certainly nothing to be surprised about, not a big deal, just academic procedure and life going on in the tropics. In a speech replete with high rhetoric, the ambassador himself inaugurated a bust of a statue outside the building, of whom I cannot say. He was accompanied by the "Cadillac" in the middle of it all. Thus I survived the afternoon.

The Portuguese and Brazilian Academicians in the Bar of the "Hotel Gloria"

That night there were drinks in the "Chalaça" Bar of the Hotel Gloria with Hernani Cidade, Segismundo Spina, and Massaud de Moisés comparing academic life and practice in Portugal, Brazil and the United States. I think they were just "putting up" or a bit curious about the presence of the young "gringo." Amongst other things we all compared salaries and sabbatical leave policies, etc. One topic in the conversation was the writer Jorge Amado (I should have known better than to bring him up, but he was my favorite Brazilian writer). Hélio Simões of Salvador discoursed on Amado, the artist Carybé, the "afoxés" or black carnival blocks of Salvador, and Jorge de Sena, the Portuguese poet at Brown University in the U.S.

The only other North American attending the congress was historian Thomas Skidmore, at that time still at Dartmouth (he would move on and up to Wisconsin and finally to Brown in the Little Ivy League). He was probably the best known North American scholar of Brazilian Politics and History of the moment, together with E. Bradford Burns of U.C.L.A. The books of both of them would be invaluable to me in preparation for my future book "História do Brasil em Cordel" at the University of São Paulo in 1998.

On Another Day. Camões in the Morning at the Portuguese Royal Reading Room in Rio de Janeiro

It was during these moments of the congress that I really arrived at understanding and appreciating the role of the author of the "Lusiads" in the intellectual tradition of Portugal. I can say that not only have I read the work in graduate school but have taught the same on one occasion in a reading and conference course to a graduate student, years later in Arizona. And in 1987 I would kneel in homage before his tomb in the Jerônimos Monastery in Belém (Lisbon).

The Session on "Popular Literature in Verse" ("Literatura Popular em Verso," ou seja, "A Literatura de Cordel"), the Conference in Rio de Janeiro and Niterói

The Most Important – The Session on Popular Literature in Verse in the Auditorium of the Rectory Building in Niterói

The auditorium was full to capacity, an unbelievable moment for me. The first speaker was the young Arnaldo Saraiva from the University of O Porto, a casual acquaintance whom I would only get to know better in the coming years. Our most recent contact was at a conference in João Pessoa, Paraíba, in 2005. It was also the most memorable: Arnaldo had matured in age and wisdom but it was an informal moment I shall always remember: on the return bus ride from Campina Grande to João Pessoa, the bus microphone was passed around and much improvisation and singing took place (I did a couple of country songs from the U.S.). Arnaldo stood in his very Portuguese, continental attire, full formal suit, tie, vest, cufflinks and the like, and improvised a ribald poem for us all.

Next was a short but incredibly complimentary introduction to my talk by the then director of the Research Center at the Casa de Ruy, the successor to Professor Thiers, Maximiano Campos.The talk went over well, albeit one of the more "academic" talks over the years: "Influência da Literatura de Cordel em 'Grande Sertão: Veredas'" ("Influence of the 'Literatura de Cordel' on 'The Devil to Pay in the Backlands'") by João Guimarães Rosa. Later the talk was expanded into a short monograph, eventually winning a prize in Brazil in 1985 and finally, after no end of on and off letters came out in a fine journal, "Brasil/Brazil" from Brown University.

Then came the pragmatic, non-baroque presentation of Raymund Cantel of the Sorbonne, the "Star of the Speechifiers." And after all the talks there was a performance of singer-poets ("cantadores") who improvised verse to a delirious audience! The star was Azulão of "cordel" fame in Rio de Janeiro from the late 1950s up until know.

An Aside. Volume I of the series of studies on "Literatura Popular em Verso" was published coinciding with the congress, and there was a wonderful "noite de autógrafos" held in the formal salon of the Casa de Ruy Barbosa with a festive atmosphere of food and drink, music, joking and laughter, some impromptu dancing and a truly momentous meeting of the "crème de la crème" of the intellectuals from the congress. I at the young academic age of thirty-two would now always be in the company of Manuel Diégues Júnior, Ariano Suassuna, Raquel de Queiróz, Arnaldo de Saraiva, Théo Brandão, Bráulio de Nascimento and Sebastião Nunes Batista by virtue of the volume of studies. A second edition would come out years later by Itatiaia Press in Belo Horizonte. The book is seminal in its early extensive studies on "cordel" and is now a "classic" in the genre. My participation was due to all that hard work in the past years, research in that old tiny room of the library for research at the Casa de Ruy, painstakingly taking hand written notes from the booklets of "cordel," notes incidentally I used throughout my academic years. The work was appreciated by then Research Center Director Thiers Martins Moreira who on an occasion or two gave me impromptu lectures on the role of "cordel" during the Rubber Boom in the Amazon ("SEMTA" during World War II). What most surprised me that evening were the many students who spent their hard earned "cruzeiros" on the book. I noted: "They really read these things!"

A small note: on the return that p.m. from Niteroi on the Rio-Niteroi ferry I had a chance to talk to Professor Cantel and to Professora Luciana from the University of Rome while we stood under umbrellas in one of the tropical rains.

Another Day: I "Split the Scene"

I truly needed a break from academia and congresses so I took the next day to get around Rio and see some of the old hangouts from past research trips, one of them the old "pé sujo" café in Copacabana with the still reasonable prices while sitting on a bar stool at the counter. I and others could enjoy filé mignon, vegetable salad, "vinagrete" topping, French fries, icy cold beer and delicious "cafezinho" for the price of $2.90 U.S. Yet I noted in 1973 that prices were considerably up from the last research in 1970. On the other hand the beach scenery was better: now the young ladies were in "tangas" and "fio dental" (eventually "the thong" in English, but translated "dental floss bikini"). I wrote, "Makes a young man weak!"

One result of the day off was missing the outing to the residence and gardens of Roberto Burle Marx, the most famous landscape architect in all Brazil, truly a "mortal sin" due either to the ignorance of the "gringo" or the simple fact I could not take another intellectual day and more "academia." Burle Marx was of the first ecologists in Brazil and early in his career implored Brazil and Brazilians to save the Amazon rain forest (I would meet North America's great advocate, Tom Lovejoy, only decades later on the National Geographic Explorer and the 125 year anniversary trip to Brazil. Lovejoy told the entire story of the battle to save the rain forest. I played a much lesser role talking of Brazilian culture, religion and folklore.) Burle Marx was a partner with Lúcio Costa and Oscar Niemeyer in Brasília. One of Burle Marx's last projects was the gardens of the "Igreja de Pampulha" in Belo Horizonte. But perhaps he is most famous for the design of the plantings on Copacabana, Ipanema and Leblon beaches in Rio and the famous "mosaic" sidewalks and later the central garden of Brasília. My loss!

Yet Another Lecture, The Dinner Party and Then "Samba"

I attended the lecture by the professor that impressed me as the one to "stand out" for his manner, his eloquence and especially his personal appearance: Leodevigário de Azevedo Filho was certainly the best dressed of the congress and all its intellectual "crème." He sported a fine dark suit, an impeccable white shirt with cuffed sleeves, fine cuff links, and a handsome tie. His talent for peroration was no less impressive marking his presence in the congress. I would see him "in action" again in later years.

A short but important moment was a chat during lunch with Professor José Aderaldo Castelo a luminary in the culture and literature of Brazil's Northeast, thus our common interests. I believe he was a professor in São Paulo at the USP at the time; we would meet years later at an autograph party in that city.

I truly have never been a "name dropper" in my entire academic career (although the preceding paragraphs may seem to contradict that), but the "cast of characters" of all this in 1973 would not ever be repeated. I met Afrânio Coutinho the principal master of Brazilian Literary criticism, Professor Roger Bismut of the U. de Louvain at the closing of the congress, a formal dinner at the home of the President of Xerox of Brazil in his "house-castle" in Laranjeiras. Try to imagine the scene: a tiny Brazilian taxi crammed with seven erudite professors going to a party! I wish I could recall the conversation. The hosts were Sérgio Gregori and his wife, a niece of Henriqueta Lisboa of Brazilian literary fame. The house was in Parque Guinle; no more needs to be said. I met Vianna Moog of "Pioneiros e Bandeirantes" fame and Austregésilo de Ataíde, President of the Brazilian Academy of Letters who at that moment spoke of the major move of the Academy from the old 19th century building from the times of Machado de Assis to a new, rounded skyscraper in downtown Rio.

Brazil intervened once again: on the return to the hotel there was a wild taxi ride with a driver who got lost and we ended up in front of the cog train station at Corcovado, all ending with a 2:00 a.m. arrival at the hotel.

I forgot to mention that somewhere in all these festivities there was a diversion: a "show" at the "Club Canto" in Niterói by no less than popular singer Touquinho and the famous "sambista" Clara Nunes. Who would have thought! Lots of water under the bridge since then. The entire crowd was singing and dancing throughout the show, even the slightly tubby cultural attaché of Portugal José Blanc; indeed, he was not a bad dancer.

The next day we were all checking out of the hotel heading home when at the door of the hotel, Professor Hernani Cidade asked me if it was a custom to tip the bellboy in Brazil? I, more of a foreigner than he, said he was asking the wrong person.

Conclusion

There would be other congresses and beautiful moments in the professional career in Brazil eventually with several books being published and "noites de autógrafos." There would be two or three really fine conferences over the "cordel" or northeastern literature. And I cannot forget the "Fifty Years of Literature of Jorge Amado" celebration and the minor event of my book about him coming out during the commemoration in 1981. But never would these past days described be repeated nor the cast of characters. I was young, naïve and a new-comer in the middle of it all. Most importantly it was a life-long lesson on the comings and goings and doings of the Lusitanian – Brazilian academic connection.

Events After the Congress

Important or not was the moment on the bus after the Botafogo Tunnel and headed into Barata Ribeiro in Copacabana at rush hour: the driver lifted the floor gear shift off its place, stuck the whole thing out the window and adjusted his mirror, than clanged it back down in place on the floor and did not miss a beat!

Researcher and Folklorist Sebastião Nunes Batista

Sebastião Nunes Batista

Sebastião shared with me jewels of anecdotes on the old "literatura de cordel." He conversed telling of his father Francisco das Chagas Batista, perhaps the "cordel" poet who wrote the best of the long "histórias" or "romances" over the bandit Antônio Silvino a contemporary to his times. And Sebastião told of Leandro Gomes de Barros, the foremost poet of "cordel" coming home a bit "tight." He mistook his way and walked into the door and house of neighbor Chagas, adding one more chapter to the lore of the aforesaid poet. Only Sebastião could have told the story, his father a first hand witness to the fact.

Sebastião told of his own life: growing up in Paraíba state, then working on the railroad in Bahia state and where he had an encounter with the feared bandits of the times ("os cangaceiros"). Then came a time when he made a living under the guise of being a veterinarian in the backlands by virtue of the great knowledge he had of livestock. And, more apropos today, he was the "letter writing man," the "secretary of correspondence" at the Central Train Station in Rio de Janeiro (his real life role portrayed by the great actress Fernanda Montenegro in the internationally acclaimed Brazilian film "Estação Central" ("Central Station"). Sebastião became "the man with the typewriter" writing letters for the hillbillies at the northeastern fair of São Cristóvão in Rio. (One recalls a famous Mexican film with no less than Cantinflas playing a similar role, hilariously portraying the role with his double entendre and funny dialogue). This phenomenon of the "letter writer" was a great moment in Latin American popular culture! As mentioned elsewhere, Sebastião became invaluable as an informant of the "cordel" but really of Brazilian folklore at the august research center of the Casa de Ruy, and I was so fortunate to share a small part of his life. He took me to other folkloric places in Rio across the years, including to a session of Umbanda; I never made it to the "gafieira" or popular dance hall with him but sorely missed my chance at a real part of Carioca life.

By this time the traffic in Rio was getting to me as well as the air pollution and the infernal noise. I missed small town Colorado and my family. There was one small incident to report, not repeated in all the years in Brazil: on that final day on the big mosaic sidewalk on Copacabana Beach in Rio I witness a parakeet fight (think cock fight in the American southwest or Mexico or any number of Latin countries). The birds were yellow and red; the fight lasted about ten minutes. It was, I surmise, all highly illegal, but an exchange of money took place. This was the only time in Brazil I witnessed such a sight (I have told of a major cock fight witnessed in Juazeiro do Norte in earlier years, a bloody spectacle indeed.)

THE RETURN HOME

It was fourteen hours of air travel from Rio to Los Angeles where I missed the connecting flight to Phoenix, but eventually made it home for the reunion with Keah. All in all it was a short trip but crammed with impressions of a multitude of diverse aspects of life in Brazil.

BRAZIL 1978

INTRODUCTION

This time I had the good fortune and honor of going to Brazil on a study grant from the American Philosophical Society in Philadelphia. The goal was to consult once again the collection of popular literature in verse ("A Literatura de Cordel") at the Casa de Ruy Barbosa in Rio de Janeiro, specifically the chapbooks of the "Hell's Mouth" ("Boca do Inferno") of "cordel" poet Cuíca de Santo Amaro, "José Gomes Ele o Tal." I would return to Brazil and Salvador in 1981 to complete the research and would write and publish two books on the poet, the first at the Jorge Amado Foundation in Salvador in 1991 and later an anthology with introduction at Hedra Publishing in 2000. To save on costs, the international flight from New York was a charter; it was one of those cases, an old terminal falling into pieces due to overuse, a hot and humid day. I had to transfer to the international terminal, and there was a wait outside the national terminal waiting for the terminal bus, surrounded by bad humored taxi drivers, and a John Travolta type "hitting on" the girls on the bus in an accent 100 per cent New Jersey or New York.

I experienced "saudades" of Brazil still in the airport waiting in line to board the plane, an old jalopy D C – 8, watching all the Brazilians all in a hurry to board, why I don't know because the plane was late in boarding and taking off. The atmosphere on board was all Brazilian party time, everyone taking advantage of an open bar. Dinner was a small cut of some kind of beef and all, not comparing in any sense with the good ole' Varig Service.

Protecting the Country – Insect Spray in the Airplane Cabin

Upon arriving at the Galeão International Airport in Rio once more the Brazilians were in a terrific rush to grab the stuff from the overheads and rush out of the airplane perhaps knowing of the long wait in customs and trying to beat the crowd. This time it did not work. After much confusion all were herded back into the cabin and their seats, and a little man came on with a large can of insect spray "to kill mosquitoes" perhaps those coming from the United States without the proper visas. Afterwards the confusion and hurry came again, and we all ended up in the customs line together.

THE "NEW" GALEÃO

This was my first time seeing the "new" remodeled Galeão. It seemed huge and all made of steel and glass (it reminded me of the days in Brasília much earlier) with a very cold atmosphere, that is, with one exception: the "hot" sexy voice of the person announcing arrivals and departures on the p.a. system. This voice became famous to travelers to Brazil over a period of several years. Many of my students traveling to that country remarked on it as did I; we all imagined what a beautiful Brazilian body must accompany that 10+ voice. I used to try to mimic "the voice" in Portuguese language classes at ASU amid much laughter.

"Saudades" again – one still had to put up with the old bureaucracy at customs – the long lines, long waits, the employees in black suits, white shirt and pencil thin ties of the times, all conversing from their tiny booths, smoking, in absolutely no hurry to check and stamp the passports. Every entering passenger received a small slip of paper noting entry into Brazil and printed in capital letters: DO NOT LOSE THIS PAPER! Without it supposedly you could not get out of the country. During those years and perhaps twenty flights to Brazil I lived in fear of losing the damned thing. It never happened, but I still think of the possible consequences. It always brought to mind the frightening time in 1967 when trying to leave Brazil and having to get exit papers from the police in Recife, Pernambuco. You had to be "liberated" with proof of no taxes owed or having committed a crime. Only the political pull of friend Flávio Veloso's father, retired Admiral in the Brazilian Navy, builder of the Navy Hospital in Recife, got me out of that one.

DER "KRAUTHAUS"

Professor Adriano da Gama Kury, Director of the Philology Sector at the Casa de Rui Barbosa, to do me a favor, thinking of my being Catholic, had arranged lodging for me in Rio at the "Casa de São Bonifácio." I did not know where it was located and no one in the airport knew and there was no listing in the Rio phone book. After two or three hours of searching at the information booth in the airport someone found the "German Catholic Church" in Rio Comprido in Rio's north zone with the official name of "União de Caridade São Bonifácio." It was located a little beyond the end of the "Túnel Rebouças" connecting the north zone, going under the Corcovado and on to the Lagoa in the South Zone. It turned out to be a sort of hostel for German tourists in Brazil. So there I was, knowing no German in preparation for a stay in Brazil, and the commute to Botafogo and my work at the Casa de Ruy turned out to be a long one. After a few days I decided to make a change and as they say in Brazil "Saí da panela para o fogo" ("Out of the frying pan into the fire"). To be explained.

There is something to be added: seated on a park bench in a plaza near São Bonifácio, I felt a great deal of enthusiasm contemplating the scene: young lovers, young kids playing, old folks conversing, and card games. We were all surrounded by the dense traffic, pollution and noise. The racial makeup was blacker than that of the South Zone and the atmosphere was more like Recife or Bahia, my haunts in the Northeast.

A HAPPENING: THE BUS AND THE VIADUCT

There are several viaducts between Urca and Botafogo and one entering into Copacabana. I have traveled on them often over the years going "to work" at the Casa de Ruy Barbosa or to do research in the libraries in downtown Rio. Today a bus rammed into another bus and "jumped" the concrete barrier of the viaduct flying over the side and landing on vehicles below. There were several deaths. My recollections of riding these buses were that the drivers augmented their speed upon crossing the viaducts, getting up steam for the "straightaways" and curves of the "Aterro" to downtown. The moments caused me to remember the rote prayers memorized by a young Catholic boy while growing up.

A HAPPENING - A TAXI RIDE

On a taxi ride in those days I encountered one of the most entertaining drivers of my days in Brazil. In the beginning he was raving about the rogues and thieves who cheated his uncle in an investment. Then he moved on to tell how he wanted to go to the U.S. and drive one of those beautiful cars in the land of Uncle Sam. But finally he changed the topic to talk of a favorite theme in Rio: the women in Rio. He said, "They all want to screw here in Rio, but some want to screw more than others. They're all "fuckers.""

A HAPPENING - WATER HEATERS IN BRAZILIAN BATHROOMS

The Hot Water Heater in Rio

The process was as follows: you take a match and light the pilot light, you then open the hot water faucet, and that should cause the heater to catch, turn on, burn with the gas flames (provided by a portable gas tank) and slowly the water would warm up. Every once in a while you read about them exploding. My memories from the Northeast were the electric hot water heaters in the showers and people constantly suffering electric shocks, especially foreigners like me who were not accustomed to the "jeito" or way to turn them on.

A CHANGE IN RESIDENCE

As I said before, the distance, the isolation and the commute from Rio Comprido to Botafogo and the Casa de Ruy Barbosa for work led me to abandon the good Germans who adored eating soft boiled eggs in a cup for breakfast, something I never grew to appreciate not being able to master the technique of using a tiny spoon to crack the top of the egg, make a neat round hole in the cavity and devour the contents.

The search for a new place was not easy. By way of the classified in the paper – "room for rent, young gentleman" - I went to see several places, the first a run-down depressing place in Copacabana and then a tiny, dark and depressing apartment in the interior of an apartment building in Ipanema. But a few days later I found a room in a very pretty apartment if I'm not mistaken on the tenth floor of an apartment building in the back of Copacabana, but still only three or four blocks from Nossa Senhora de Copacabana, the main drag, and the beach one block beyond.

Dona Dulce's Boarding Apartment

The apartment was pretty with well appointed furniture, the owner Dona Dulce (her husband had been in management in the Banco do Brasil) and her daughter lived with her along with her husband Françoise (I never did discover what he did to make a living) and a teenage son who reminded me of the young guys at the "Chácara das Rosas" (the "Rose House") the boarding house I lived in in Recife years before. He had the great Brazilian name of Juca (perhaps the nickname of José Carlos), coincidentally the name of one of Chico Buarque de Holanda's hit songs of the period.

I did not notice at first, only later, the images of "Umbanda" in the apartment. Françoise was a practicioner of the same and later tried to explain it all to me. But that "winter" (June, July, and August) in Rio with its devasting rain storms and terrific winds was frightening when it hit the 10th floor of the building. One constantly heard doors slamming in the wind and occasionally the sound of glass breaking, the outside windows. On those nights I slept little; the window in my room faced the "morro" or hill directly behind the building and I was sure it would break as well. A good thing was that the infernal street noise of Copacabana was somewhat muted by the height of our apartment floor. But contrary to the folk wisdom of the guys in the boarding house in Recife in 1966 (the higher the floor the fewer mosquitos), we still had them on the tenth floor. It might have had to do with the intense tropical vegetation on the "morro" behind the building. All turned out well and I stuck it out for the time in Rio those few weeks.

THE BLACK MARKET AND
EXCHANGING DOLLARS

In those days due to the tremendous inflation in the Brazilian economy, the weakness in the Brazilian currency (I think it was still the "cruzeiro"), the black market for dollars prospered in Brazil. I ended up changing my U.S. travelers' checks in dollars at "PM Turismo" in Copacabana, and as famous English comedian Terry Thomas would say in the film "Mad, Mad, Mad, Mad World," it all was very "hush-hush." The business was all very mysterious, done in the back room, everyone whispering as the transactions took place.

On another occasion I actually traveled all the way to downtown Rio to a travel agency on Avenida Getúlio Vargas far from my residence in Copa to talk to the Portuguese manager who offered 20 "cruzeiros" per dollar, two more than the banks. But it was complicated: I had to receive my "cruzeiros" in a personal check from the manager, take the check to a regular bank on Avenida 7 de Setembro in the downtown and wait in line to actually get the cash. The speculation on the dollar was astoundingly high, so much so that it seemed like you always knew someone or a friend of someone living from the black market.

I should add that part of the problem was that I had traveler's checks in dollars. People told me, "Only idiots do that, the exchange is far less than in cash." There were other times when I succeeded in changing at hotel desks (I remember the Hotel Novo Mundo in Flamengo) and not have to risk carrying money, passport and all in the streets. I did think of a possible scenario: me, an obvious tourist, standing in line in a regular bank changing the traveler's checks and getting a wad of "cruzeiros." And this with the banks, as they were, with broad open glass doors and windows visible to all in the street outside, and each mugger or robber or pickpocket just drooling waiting for innocent gringo to walk out the door! Ha! Better the slightly poorer exchange at the same front desk of the hotel. I may have gotten a few less "cruzeiros" but was never assalted in that scary Rio of the times. Common advice from all the Brazilians was to take little money with you in the streets, just enough to get by, and even less to the beach. And whatever you do, don't ask someone on the beach to watch your stuff while you take a quick dip!

RESEARCH – CHANGES AT THE CASA DE RUY BARBOSA

The Façade of the Ruy Barbosa Foundation

The Research Team in the Center of Philology, Ruy Barbosa Foundation

The main object of research this time was to investigate and read the originals of the Bahian poet Cuíca de Santo Amaro, chapbooks located in the collection of the Casa de Ruy Barbosa in Rio de Janeiro, a familiar place to me due to study there in 1966-1967, 1969, and a little bit in 1973. The library now was located in the new Research Center, a modern, concrete and glass building in the back and overlooking the beautiful gardens of the Casa. I'll write more about this and the civil service in Brazil in a while. Professor Adriano da Gama Kury was the head of the Philology Sector, Sebastião Nunes Batista full time as informant and research on the "cordel," and the young Marco Antônio Nedu as well as Sérgio Pachá whom I would see later in California in linguistics in the Philology Sector.

An Aside. Marco Antônio Nedu spoke of the great irony of the Popular Literature in Verse ("A Literatura de Cordel") something "ugly and looked down upon" being housed in the great Casa de Ruy Barbosa, truly one of the more "snobbish" entities in Brazilian Culture. And ironically he spoke of the fact that the "cordel" actually added prestige to the Casa! My opinion: the research team of Manuel Cavalcanti Proença, Orígenes Lessa, Manuel Diégues Júnior and Thiers Martins Moreira were not so stupid in their endeavor of rescuing and initating the "cordel" collection at the Casa in the 1950s and 1960s.

In 1978 in the "Cordel" Sector things were going well: there was a "harvest" of new publications – anthologies, catalogues and an important volume of studies in 1973. It would be the following years in the 1980s that would be less productive for the Casa, this due mainly to the perennial lack of budget for research and publication. My own study on Jorge Amado and the "cordel" had been revised and corrected: "It should come out in 1979 together with a study by a French researcher." Ha ha. And old friends from 1966, 1967 and 1969 had moved on: Armando, Ana Maria, Kik, and Alice.

On the day to day work I was consulting the "cordel" archives, principally in search of Cuíca de Santo Amaro originals and it was fortunate to have Sebastião Nunes Batista across the reading table each day always ready to answer my questions about "cordel," Cuica and problems of language and interpretation. He was a master at all the above.

Lunch hour was at a small, modest working man's café across the street from the Casa, always "the plate of the day" for USD $1.50: turkey breast, rice and beans, French fries, vegetable salad, fruit salad for dessert and delicious "cafezinho." It was at one of these sessions with its great conversation that Marco Nedu commented that I should be "extremely exhausted!" It was an allusion to my being "um gringo simpatico, não feio e com dólar" and perhaps to some of those mythical "carioca" women alluded to by the taxi driver days earlier. Unhappily, or happily, this was not the case. Due to a moral code from my upbringing, traditionally Catholic, I remained faithful to my wife throughout those research trips to Brazil. That did not mean I did not appreciate the "carioca" scenery both on the streets and the beaches: the skin tight jeans, the low cut blouses or tops, and of course the beach attire, and just the beauty of the "cariocas" did not escape me. Today I think, was I stupid? As they say in Brazil, "Em compensação," ("on the other hand") my marriage goes well and I did not pick up any social diseases rampant in Brazil at that time.

CIVIL SERVICE – THE INSTITUTON
AND THE CASA DE RUY BARBOSA

Anyway, the Casa de Ruy, in spite of its fame, was and is a part of the civil service of the government and with that syndrome of the "civil servant," and besides that, with the problem that Ex-President Jânio Quadros tried to resolve in his short regime full of tension of 6 months time in 1960. The "system" so criticized by Jânio was well rooted at the Casa de Rui. Upon arriving at work, each employee had to sign the "livro de ponto" or attendance book. Many arrive late, leave early and take long "breaks." There is a lack of both furniture and necessary office equipment; I saw only old typewriters. And shelves had not yet arrived for the books ("They are on their way, but it will take a while," someone said.) Each functionary has a project to do, but no one seems in any hurry to complete it. The reason is there is a chronic lack of funding for publications. "Everything is at a standstill." It turns out that the "New" Casa de Ruy Barbosa spent all of its funding on the construction of the building itself, and nothing was left for operations. The building is handsome in the "new" Brazilian style of prefab concrete, steel and glass. There are three floors and a basement (incidentally where dozens of copies of my book in 1987 on Rodolfo Coelho Cavalcante ended up gathering dust with absolutely no plan or money for marketing!) The floors are dedicated to Law, Ruy Barbosa and Philology. Marco told me that salaries are quite low and there is no future there; he sees it all as temporary. Professor Adriano, director of the Sector of Philology has a full time post as well lecturing at the "Universidade de Santa Úrsula," admitting that the study of traditional Philology is "passé" in the Brazilian universities of those times. He makes his real living giving private classes in Portuguese (he is considered one if not the top teacher in Brazil of such materials), classes for the elite of Rio de Janeiro, the upper class young men aspiring to enter the Brazilian Foreign Service ("O Itamarati"). His record is second to none with the success rate of his students passing the incredibly difficult Portuguese exam for entrance.

There incidentally was a shiny new telephone hookup (we are still years before the cell phone), one of the most recent systems available, but there is great confusion on how to use it.

A curious aside: One of the female employees in a brief conversation with me about soccer great Pelé and his new blond wife, said "That dirty nigger" or the like. And there was the inevitable social type – a sort of "message boy" – a highly effeminate fellow. All seemed to accept him as just "one of the girls" and there was a nice birthday celebration with cake on one occasion. I always thought that Brazil was much more advanced in such matters than the United States at this time, <u>circa</u> 1978.

Researcher and Folklorist Sebastião Nunes Batista

Sebastião Nunes Batista – Friend, Mentor and Guide in Rio in 1978

Sebastião is now retired (with a very small pension from years of service as a public servant in the Ministry of Planning, or perhaps Agriculture, my notes fail to say) and is full-time at the Casa de Ruy, the result of persistence in studying at night for five years for a university degree in Literature. He mentioned, casually, that in all that time he never once met his official adviser, Professor Afrânio Coutinho, one of the "greats" of Rio's Academy at the time. It was simply the custom that the full professors ("catedráticos") sent their assistants to actually teach the classes, and as well, grade the papers! That's just the way it was. On the other hand, it was the "pull" of now deceased Professor Theirs Martins Moreira, former director of the research center at the Casa who encouraged and in effect enabled Sebastião to get into the baccalaureate program.

Like the good "nordestino" that he is, Sebastião still dreams of returning to the Northeast, in this case to João Pessoa his birthplace, but the job keeps him in Rio. He is separated "desquitado" from his wife; she and the two children live in Brasília. He gets along well with them all, but says "I simply could not stand to live with that woman." He has a small, modest apartment in the Glória District of Rio, and with the constant numbing inflation of life in Brazil, says it is worth ten times what he paid for it.

Sebastião's roots, in regard to Brazil's folk poetry, the poet-singer and the poet of "cordel," are the best! As mentioned previously, he is a relative of some of the most famous poet-singers of the Northeast and one of many sons of pioneer "cordel" poet Francisco das Chagas Batista, a contemporary and colleague of Leandro Gomes de Barros, still acclaimed as the greatest of all "cordel." Sebastião has family all over Brazil and is a walking encyclopedia of Brazilian folklore and especially the "cordel," a real jewel!

He left Paraíba in 1941, spent three years during World War II time in the state of Bahia, than a few years in Minas Gerais State and finally ended up in Rio de Janeiro. (He sentimentally reminded me of the adventures of my own father, his motorcycle ride of 1925 to the western United States where as a young man he worked on a small truck farm outside of Denver, a huge dairy in Washington State and later drove a combine for wheat in eastern Washington State driving a team of no less than 36 horses!) Sebastião worked at one time on a large ranch, pretending to be a veterinarian! Perhaps that knowledge was what enabled him to be a public servant in the Ministry of Agriculture in Rio for so many years.

He told anecdotes of the old northeastern fair in São Cristóvão in Rio's north zone where he was the "letter writing man" for so many years. He would write letters for the illiterate "hillbillies" at the fair, much in the style of the "Cartas Amorosas" ("Love Letters," a standard topic of old "cordel"). He had an encyclopedic knowledge of folkloric life in Brazil not just because of his roots, but because he really lived that reality. I met Sebastião in the 1960s and would be with him, often on a daily basis during those research times at the Casa de Rui in the 1960s through the 1980s until his death in 1981. He "died with his boots on," suffering a heart attack while giving an academic talk on "cordel" in Sergipe State. He was simple, honest, and a good friend in Brazil. I still miss him.

SEBASTIÃO NUNES BATISTA AND BRAZILIAN SPIRITISM

One day during lunch Sebastião introduced an unexpected topic – Brazilian Spiritism – and gave me a "class lecture" on the subject. The Batista family, like most in Brazil, was traditionally Catholic, but today are Baptists or Spiritists. He believes both in Kardecism and "Umbanda," the first as seen in Kardec's "Book of the Spirits" ("Livro dos Espíritos"). It is reduced to a belief in Reincarnation; the spirit of a deceased person can be "called" by the Medium, thus "communicating" with the believers who call for the spirit. Sebastião attends two different sessions: one Spiritist, the other "Umbanda." He believes in both (and we are speaking here of a Brazilian intellectual and very rational person), and comments that both are derived in part from Catholicism.

The Center Sebastião attends is in an old house in Flamengo. The floor was old wood and the walls had Indian bows and arrows and an Indian headdress something like a Comanche headdress we might know in the United States. There are images of Catholic saints, an altar with various images, and images of saints, including the "old black men" ("os pretos velhos"). The people attending seemed to be from the humble class. Upon entering there is a short old man who collects pieces of paper, the "prayers" (as "preces") which are requests for prayer written on small slips of paper. Then there is the "smoke" or purification of those persons wishing to "receive" or communicate with the saints. Yours truly was keeping his eyes wide open during all this witnessing of that "other world," and I was surprised to see Sebastião in the middle of it. He encouraged me to get a paper, write down a prayer request and be involved in the process. Out of insecurity and also the old Catholic belief to avoid such things, I chose not to, apologizing to my friend.

An aside: it turns out the entire family at my current boarding apartment in Copacabana is Spiritist but of the "Quimbanda" persuasion, mixed religion from the Orient, a "confusion" of things it seemed to me.

The name of Sebastião's Center is the "Centro Espírito Cruz do Oxalá" ("Spiritist Center of the Cross of Oxalá"). Here is a summary of the unfolding of events that night:

1. The "smoking" or purifying chant: cleansing the area of negative spirits, that is, of Exú, so that the other spirits can enter. The mediums are the first to be cleansed.
2. Purification by smoke of the persons present: preparing the "atmosphere."
3. The song of invocation (to the spirits Oxóssi, Xangô, Iemanjá, Cosme and Damian (all these are also saints in traditional Candomblé form Bahia or Xangô from Recife, "mainline" Afro-Brazilian cults). Then other spirits are called: the "caboclos" or indigenous saints: Mirambá, the "Cabocla Jurema (indigenous saint), the "Star Guide" ("Estrela Guia"), the spirit of the star that guided the Three Wise Men to the Christ child in the manger).
4. The principal saint of the "terreiro" is called "Caboclo Mirambá."
5. Each medium approaches the altar, bends and touches it gently with his forehead, a sign of respect and confirmation of his faith. Then the spirit takes possession of the Medium who is now making whispering and groaning sounds. Sometimes there is a stronger effect that shakes the person; this is called a violent "incorporation" when the spirit takes possession of the Medium. There may be a snapping of fingers by the Medium (now possessed by the spirit) who ritually cleanses the "aura" of a person-participant with one of the prayer slips, thus cleansing any "negative emanations" that the person may have absorbed previously. Cigars are used and their smoke effects this "cleansing" of the "aura." One Medium cleanses another. At that point the "public" is allowed to enter the altar area, each person assigned a number (according to the prayer slip filled out earlier in the evening).

The number also gives the right to the person to "take a pass" ("tomar passe"), in other words, to communicate with the spirit. This process was as follows: the Medium draws close to the person with the prayer slip. There is the greeting ("a saudação") when they embrace, then the cleansing of the person by means of the snapping of fingers by the Medium. The Medium, already possessed by the spirit, asks that "God" or another spirit cure the person or fulfill his prayer request.

Sebastião says that a person in the public audience who experiences fear during the session may indeed have "mediunidade" or the capacity to receive the spirit and to become a Medium. (Holy Mama! What that my case?) Sebastião spoke of things that may happen during a spiritist session: a glass of water turns over, letters of the alphabet get mixed up, or three or four persons may place there fingers over a glass and the glass vibrates and moves. My "guide" says that all these things are the results of negative spirits. A Medium must be present to guide the group on such occasion.

At this Center, Friday is the "Table Day" ("Dia da Mesa") a night of Kardec Spiritism; Monday is a "pass day" ("dia de passe") or Caboclo Spiritism; Friday is the night of the Old Black Spirits (spirits originating from black slaves).

So ended the evening and the explanation. All was very calm, another "class" given by my friend and mentor Sebastião, my guide to things folkloric and cultural in Rio in those times.

RETURN TO THE FAIR OF SÃO CRISTÓVÃO, MY "CORDEL" FIELD RESEARCH SPOT IN GREATER RIO

June 16, 1978. It all began in Copacabana with a long wait for Bus # 474 "Jardim de Alah – Jacaré" to take me to the north zone. The wind was whipping through the "canyons" of tall apartment buildings in Copacabana, but it was the quietest part of the week in the area, Sunday morning before everyone was up and out to the beach. Everyone, that is, but the "flat heads" ("as cabeças chatas"), the pejorative term the southerners used to refer to the "northerners" or "northeasterners" (that together with other terms like "pau de arara", "matuto", "caipira" etc.)

Finally the bus arrived at my stop already jammed with a noisy group of young "nordestinos" jammed in the back of the bus, all going to the fair, the principal diversion of the week. The bus collector who sits behind a turnstile at the rear of the bus by the rear entrance door (I can't help but think of the "folheto de cordel" by Mocó about the bus driver and collector in Rio and their difficult life) was shouting at each bus stop "We're empty, we're empty," even though the entire bus was full. An elderly passenger cussed the driver and the collector for letting so many people on. A turn, even a small one, caused the overcrowded bus to roll dangerously (I said to myself, "This is like a crazy carnival ride in the U.S.") I might add: on every city bus, by law, there is a placard in the top center of the front of the bus listing maximum passenger capacity. Ha ha ha. Really! It looked like we would turn over at any time. I was quietly repeating all those memorized Catholic prayers of my youth as we continued toward downtown, especially on the big curves of the "Aterro" or freeway between Botafogo and downtown. The drivers used to "race" on the Aterro keeping track of times, and some money was exchanged. There were a lot of changes since my last stay of 1973 – more roads with four lanes, more viaducts; all of Getúlio Vargas Avenue in the downtown is torn up with construction for the new subway. The result is that all the buses are detoured to small badly paved streets.

From the beauty of the beaches, parks and skyscrapers of the South Zone, through downtown, the bus now was passing through an area of slums ("favelas"), factories, and more torn up streets, the ugly part of the city. But "beauty is in the eyes of the beholder" – in the distance the brightly colored houses in primary colors almost appeared like abstract art, Cubist in particular! And Corcovado which reigns above it all was picturesque in the distance.

The crowd on the bus was predominately black or mulatto, poor, noisy, many already drunk, gross, and frankly, frightening (I thought I was back in Recife heading to one of the markets). One of them, climbing on board via the back door, spied me and figuring I was a typical tourist, shouted to the collector: "He'll pay." I refused and fortunately everyone laughed at the little joke.

The fair in 1978 is gigantic and surrounds the pavilion of São Cristóvão; there are hundreds of market stands and huge crowds. My friend Sebastião believes that it is the biggest "northeastern" fair in Brazil aside from the famous one in Caruaru, Pernambuco. The market stands are made out of wood with canvas tops. We saw food stands – corn on the cob, sugar cane drink, meat on spits, manioc flour, "roll tobacco," and an uncountable variety of fruit and vegetables. There were dozens of "lunch" stands with all the above. The air was full of smoke, a result of all the cooking on hot coals in the food stands. Another section of the fair held the clothes stands, shoe stalls, shoe repair stalls, and all kinds of "junk souvenirs." There were men everywhere selling wrist watches or trading them. The worst was the incredible noise emanating from the music stores and cafés and dance halls and amplified country trios playing northeastern country music – "forró." I left the market that day with a splitting headache from the noise.

But the main thing for me the researcher was the search for the chapbooks of "cordel" and its poets. I think that I saw more this time in 1978 than any other time before or after in my stays in Rio de Janeiro and a lot more wandering salesmen of "cordel."

The "Cordel" Poet "Azulão" 1978

The most successful poet seemed to be "Azulão," the poet I had met years before, the first time in 1966 and 1967 (he is detailed in "Adventures ..."). I came upon him singing "Rufino the King of the Rowdies" ("Rufino o Rei do Barulho") before a large, attentive and avid crowd. Now he was wearing glasses with thick lenses, bi-focals, holding the chapbook in one hand, perhaps only three or four inches from his face (definitely with a vision problem, one this author can relate to). He is singing the story-poem into a small microphone held in his other hand, covered with a white hankerchief. He is dressed in a white shirt with a narrow black tie, and is well shaved. His little portable sound system is efficient and set at a high volume so he can compete with the blare of the "forró" music stands. The speaker is tied to the branch of a nearby tree with a small cord. It is controlled out of a little box, perhaps the amplifier which seems old and very used.

He sang the poem in expert fashion and with stops for asides, comments on the poem itself, its characters and goings on, making wry jokes over what has occurred and perhaps what may come. The poem is from the "cycle" of the "brave outlanders" ("os valentes do nordeste"); his audience is almost all male and they laugh and carry on when the hero conquers his enemies. In intervals or pauses between the singing of the verse, Azulão and an assistant sell copies of the poem he is singing and sales are good! He runs out of copies!

An aside: Sebastião Batista believes that the "cordel" here in the northeastern fair of São Cristóvão far from being in danger of disappearing as the scholars fear, is in fact prospering!

I accompanied the "performance" with an open "folheto" in my hand thus easily following the plot, something much more difficult if I had not had the text in front of me, this due to a personal hearing problem and even more to the incredible noise surrounding us in the market. I found it interesting that the crowd, many in the crowd that is, bought the poem in spite of the fact that they had actually heard the whole thing sung in the performance. It proves that they truly like "cordel" and this story and wanted to take it home to family and friends and also for safe-keeping. People collect these things!

Later Azulão sang another story-poet of 32 pages from Editorial Luzeiro. The price for the public was not cheap, a "folheto" of 8 pages was 30 cents U.S., 16 pages was 48 cents U.S. and the long poem of 32 pages from Luzeiro was 60 cents U.S. (all a far cry from the price of about a nickel US for an 8 page poem in 1966 when I began collecting in the 1960s). The poets blame the increase in price on the cost of printing the chapbooks in the local printing shops.

Immediately to Azulão's left was the stand of the old poet who claims to be the first ever to frequent the fair in this plaza. Sebastião says the old guy came to São Cristóvão 45 years ago. He presented a sad case today – not being able to compete with Azulão, first because he had no microphone or sound system, and also because of the former's charisma. The old poet is from Paraíba state (60 to 80 percent of "cordel" people share this origin). Old, almost without teeth, I had a hard time understanding him because of the roar of the northeastern bands ("música forró") immediately behind his poetry stand. And Azulão just turned up his volume as well. The old man tried to "sing" a story-poem but finally in exasperation stopped. Sebastião noted that the fair today suffers greatly from "noise pollution."

The "Cordel" Poet Apolônio Alves dos Santos at the Fair in 1978

We then went to Apolônio Alves dos Santos' poetry stand; I would see him off and on in the years to come. He seemed young, very "simpatico," perhaps in his 50s and doing a good business. He said he appreciated my letter from some time back (was this for the questionnaire of 1979?)

We ended that morning at the stand of a man named Severino. He was selling the "folhetos" and "romances" of the famous old printing shop in Juazeiro do Norte, "A Typografia São Francisco," originally of José Bernardo da Silva in the 1950s and 1960s as well as others from the Northeast (nothing from Editorial Luzeiro from São Paulo). He had grey hair, was pretty overweight, had a moustache, and was on crutches that day due to "a bad leg." He complained of being robbed in the Fair the week before, losing all his documents, and the fact that the police "did nothing."

THE BRAZILIAN STEAKHOUSE ("CHURRASCARIA") IN THE NORTH ZONE OF RIO

After the morning in the fair Sebastião and I had the noon meal in a "churrascaria" near the Fair. They brought about ten different types of vegetables: cauliflower, beets, beans, onions, carrots, "aipim." Sides were spaghetti, French fries and rice. One is literally surrounded by plates of food on the table. The main dish, the meat itself, arrives via agile waiters with a spit with the cut of meat in one hand, a long knife which is enough to scare you in the other. Pork, chicken, "lombo de boi," etc. The meat was tasty but not as tasty as that at the "churrascarias" in the South Zone. We tried several cuts of beef, another more like roast beef but with a lot of fat. The price was good, $7.20 USD. It seemed like you had to stay very still to avoid the loss of an ear or your nose to that big, sharp knife of the waiter. It seemed like every five minutes a new spit and cut would arrive and "zas" they cut off whatever you wanted. Dressed perhaps in a white shirt and black vest, they reminded me of the ubitquitous Brazilians buzzards "flying" around the table.

Once again I was astonished to see the capability of the Brazilians to seem to swallow it all whole as if it were their last meal and only five minutes to devour it before the executioner would arrive to lower the guillotine! You had to see it to believe it.

And I also noted the agility and talent of the Brazilians and the dexterity of handling a toothpick when it was all over. There is a toothpick holder on each table. Speaking of this, the "gringos" always are deceived, thinking the "paliteiro" is a salt shaker. They pick it up, turn it upside down to "shake out the salt" and bang! They end with a hundred or so toothpicks all over the table and the floor! Actually it is a healthy custom and the Brazilians actually make an art out of using the toothpick. I suppose it is good to do such a good job on the teeth, but perhaps with a little more discretion. The diner, man or woman, uses their napkin or hand to cover their mouth, or perhaps even the tablecloth! I found it great fun to watch customers' eyes as they worked the tool beneath the napkin. (I used to do a hilarious imitation of this in front of my students in first year Portuguese class, thus explaining the "social mores" of the Brazilians.) But one scene topped it all, and I only saw it one time: a man pulled dental floss out of his shirt pocket and did a very thorough once-over on uppers and bottoms.

After lunch and an extra long wait for the bus, I had a bit of a fright. In a bar or "pé sujo" to the side of the "churrascaria" there were many "types" who seemed to be from one of the "favelas" or "morros" swilling beer from the large Brahma bottles; someone was playing the "berimbau" and some one else a tambourine and there was a lot of singing. I thought, "This is pretty folkloric! I think I'll get a picture." When they saw the camera and the obvious tourist, they demanded I take a group picture and buy a round of beer for the crowd. It turns out that I had spent all my cash at the Fair on booklets of "cordel" and had even to take a loan Sebastião to pay for lunch. I was for the moment broke! I murmured an apology and we split the scene. I never did find that photo and it could be in the confusion that I never took one. But I would like for whoever might read this to appreciate to what point a good "folklorist" might go in his fieldwork. Right then I was thinking of trading in my task as a folklorist for something a bit safer like Library Science or something of the sort.

HAPPENINGS: NEW STUFF DOWNTOWN

On our return we passed by the huge new Petrobrás Building, that is the national oil company (of such scandal in 2015, critics dubbing it "Petrolão" imitating the famous "mensalão" of just a few years ago, both huge payouts to congressmen for bribes and the like. The "mensalão" took its name from the monthly payments to corrupt politicians. Brazilians are used to this but that does not mean they like it.) The building is of flasy design of steel, concrete and glass, very modern in design. Next to it is the new Cathedral of Rio – a conical futuristic building which reminded me of John Glen's space capsule in the Mercury Program. The interior is very dark on a cloudy or rainy day, but if sunny in Rio it is beautifuly lit as the sun streams through the floor-to ceiling stained glass windows. Images once again are super modern; think Cubism and modern art.

We ended our foray with a "cafezinho" in what Sebastião says is the best such place in Rio. Nine cents USD but still double the price in 1973. You can accurately guage inflation in Brazil with the price of a "cafezinho" or an 8 page "folheto de cordel."

Sebastião Nunes Batista in "Cinelândia" 1978

SEBASTIÃO NUNES BATISTA IN "CINELÂNDIA" PLAZA, RIO DE JANEIRO 1978

The plaza had also taken on a new look since 1973, a beautiful large plaza in the center of downtown Rio with the famous mosaic sidewalks. The bad thing is Brazilians tore down the old Monroe Palace, the old Senate Building, a beautiful neo-classic edifice which matched the grandeur of the Municipal Theater, National Art Gallery, National Library and the old Brazilian Academy of Letters. There are open cafés on the entire side of the plaza, and a few movie theaters s well. As you sit for a coffee or an icy draft beer, you view the grandeur of Imperial Brazil of the 19th century but off to the south and west one sees the huge, concrete monument dedicated to the armed forces of World War II, one of the Generals' greatest triumphs in the time of military dictatorship. The people in the cafés seemed working class, most I would guess on breaks from the business and government buildings in the area. It felt a bit to me like perhaps being in Europe – Lisbon, Madrid or Paris.

It was here that I had the pleasure of meeting a good friend of Sebastião's, the film director Nelson Pereira dos Santos, he of the "New Cinema" ("Cinema Novo"), director of black and white "art" movies based on some of the best of Brazilian literature: Graciliano's "Vidas Secas" and "Memórias do Cárcere", Jorge Amado's "Jubiabá" and "Tenda dos Milagres" and João Guimarães Rosa's "A Terceira Margem do Rio". It does not get any better than these! I should add that all said about Cinelândia is that of the scene during the daytime. It changes character at night! I'll leave that up to the imagination of the reader.

OTHER MOMENTS OF 1978

The Men's Bathroom at FUNARTE (National Art Foundation)

The case in point is found at the National Foundation of the Arts in downtown Rio. At that time the National Institute of Folklore (the former "Campanha de Defesa do Folclore Brasileiro") was located in the same huge building, thus my presence to read their collection of "cordel." FUNARTE was headed by Manuel Diégues Júnior a prominent cultural anthropologist in Brazil and one of the participants in the collection of "cordel" for the Casa de Ruy Barbosa; his son, incidentally became more famous than the father, Cacá Diégues a major film director-producer in Brazil.

The urinal (or the urinals) must have been over six feet high; you could, if of such a bent, almost walk into one. It was the tallest and the whitest possibly in all of Brazil. And it was spectacularly clean. There were short, little ladies constantly about keeping it clean and shiny, independently of any man about actually using the one next door. I think it should have been placed on the "National Historic Register" or the like.

The reader may wonder why all the fuss? Thinking of a famous sociologist in Brazil, Roger Bastide if I am not mistaken, and his classic book "The Two Brazils," I am tempted to contrast this marvel of Rio, unfortunately not in the tourist brochures, with that other ubiquitous place, the "pisser" or "mictório" of the corner bars ("pé sujo" or dirty foot, no accident this name) all over Brazil. Any tourist in Brazil, or even the "cariocas" themselves in need, might be interested to know what they have missed in the "cidade maravilosa". One plans ahead, or if that is not possible, simply takes immediate advantage of a bathroom, even one not so clean, in Rio and in Brazil.

So it was I was in this environs at FUNARTE because of its relation to Brazilian folklore and the Institute of Folklore. By the way, the Institute's director was Bráulio do Nascimento, a fine folklorist and acquaintance and colleague in Brazil. I would in addition read "folhetos de cordel" in the collection of the National Library in the downtown as well. Years later I was both pleased and surprised to actually see a worn copy of my first book in Brazil, "A Literatura de Cordel," a rarity due to its small printing, in the library of the latter.

A Curious Aside: The famous (and infamous) Catete Palace ("Palácio do Catete") where President Getúlio Vargas committed suicide, located a few blocks from the beach in Flamengo, was being remodeled at this time but eventually would have a small annex with space for the new Institute of Folklore and its "cordel" collection (a good one I consulted at a later date). It is another Brazilian irony: such a famous, historic and beautiful building, the center of the Brazilian presidency before Brasília in 1960 now the place of such an insignificant matter to the general public – the "cordel." I think of it in much the same way as the Casa de Ruy Barbosa fulfilling a similar function – "cordel" alongside Ruy's library!

At any rate Braúlio received me well and shared that Brazilian custom of filling the foreign researcher's arms with publications, magazines and books, and now historic LP Recordings of the Poet-Singers of "Cordel." The latter included recordings, now rare, by the masters: Azulão in Rio and José Costa Leite in Pernambuco. The one thing he could not help me with was an avenue of publication; he said that FUNARTE did not publish in the area due to the fact that the Casa de Ruy and the Federal University of Bahia were fulfilling that need. So be it.

The "Frescão"

One has to know some Portuguese and to have spent some time in Rio in those days, and in addition appreciate Brazilian and Carioca ways and humor. "Fresco" can mean "cool," as in cool air. The augmentative "frescão" means a huge amount of the same, as in "freezing cold air." So in these days since my last visit in 1973 a new convenience arrived in Rio: the very large "Greyhound" type buses in the U.S. style available for travel from Leblon in the south zone, through Copacabana, on the "Aterro" or "Freeway" from Botafogo to downtown and all the way to the international airport, the Galeão in Rio's north zone. The buses were meant to have a certain luxury: comfortable airline-style folding seats, mood music a la "Musak," and a system of air conditioning that could freeze water! I noted the customers were, in the current parlance, "suits," business types or perhaps government workers, most living in the south zone and working in the downtown. They wore business suits, long-sleeve white shirts, nice ties, shiny leather shoes, and with ubiquitous "pasta" or briefcase to their side.

The bus's crew was also excessive with three full-time employees: a uniformed driver, a uniformed ticket taker (the customer entered through the front door, found a seat and the ticket taker would find you) and a uniformed, nice-looking stewardess. The fare of course was much higher than the standard city buses, perhaps three or four times as much, so that eliminated the "riffraff" with the possible exception of naïve foreigners in Rio dressed for sweltering hot, humid weather in their sandals, short sleeves and walking shorts, but with the requisite funds for the fare. I took the "frescão" upon occasion, but not much. I could only think of the "cordel" poem by Mocó during these times when he wrote what is really a sociological "gold mine," the story-poem relating the life of the bus driver and collector of fares on the "real" buses in Rio.

Now, Cariocas, perhaps those who did not ride said bus, were "wont" to also relate the "frescão" bus to a couple of slang terms in Portuguese, reader beware! Just coincidentally the word "fresco" in those days meant sissy, effeminate, or even "queer" or homosexual; by extension the word "frescura" was possibly something a "fresco" might say or do, but really beyond that in a greater use. It could be someone who is affected or pretentious or even worse, it could be something said or done which is absolute nonsense or foolishness. So, to make a long story short, the whole thing – the bus, the people who rode the bus – were referred to as one big "frescura." Pretentious to say the least!

The Literature Conference at the State University of Rio de Janeiro ("Universidade Estadual do Rio de Janeiro")

The State University of Rio de Janeiro is gigantic. I went to the conference by bus, the pretty scenery of Copacana, Botafogo and the boats in the bay, the "Pedra" da Urca, Sugar Loaf, Flamengo Beach on the "freeway" by the beach, Avenue Rio Branco in the downtown and later Maracanã Soccer Stadium. It was interesting to see the old docks at the port near old Praça Mauá and the many large cargo ships in the bay. All this was before passing into the North Zone. As I spoke on another occasion, Avenue Presidente Vargas is totally torn up with construction of the new subway system in Rio, but there must have been fifteen lanes of traffic near Candelaria Church.

The North Zone with the hills seen through the cloud or pollution and/or fog, the colorful "favelas" looking much like a Cubist painting, and Corcovado and the Christ Figure in the distance completed the scene.

The Literature Conference was similar to the one of 1973 I described in great detail in this book because it was my "baptism" into such matters in Portugal and Brazil. The present auditorium was nicely done and was quite large with a full crowd! There were conferences and talks, all with debate. I noted the formal language: "I invite to the speakers' table the Illustrious …" or "The Illustrious … is free to speak" or "I give the word to the Illustrious …." Once again I am astonished upon observing the Brazilian man of letters in action! The speakers seemed to me to be like peacocks displaying their tail feathers. I write of this not to criticize, far from it, but to contrast the scene to the rather "poor" one in U.S. academia and its customs. There were several such figures but once again the one who stood out was familiar from 1973 - Leodegário de Azevedo Filho. He dazzled in an immaculate suit, crisp white long-sleeved shirt with elegant cufflinks, and an elegant tie as well. He seemed to exude a certain "proud arrogance" (pardon the "Barroquismo"). He delivered his words of wisdom to the audience rapt with admiration and applause. He was acting as a "chefe da mesa," or "session head," but the "star" of the day was Eduardo Portela of the more prestigious Federal University of Rio de Janeiro and current Minister of Education in the country.

The theme was Jorge Amado (perhaps my favorite Brazilian author and one I was extremely familiar with, our connection to be described later). Portela's mastery and command of the Portuguese language was to be admired as well as that of other "Big Guns" of the literary-academic world: the oration, the peroration, the perfect pronunciation, the linguistic "turns of phrase," and the poetic imagery employed. It all seemed poetry in prose. Mr. Portela spoke applying a global vision of the total work by Jorge Amado in an eclectic style. I'm not certain, but the florid style may have had a touch of narcissism, but maybe not. After his discourse standard conference procedure was that there were two persons who "debated" his presentation, obviously junior assistant professors, and just coincidentally feminine. It is good to recall that they were talking of the Minister of Education of the ENTIRE COUNTRY! Not to take away from the moment, but he was fired six months later for "inefficiency." As I said, be it style, philosophy or just simple academic custom, NOTHING in the academic world in the United States can compare to it! Many years later as I muse on the moment, I am grateful to have had the chance to experience just a taste of it.

Rick's

In 1978 this was the Brazilian version of "fast food," just an incipient phenomenon in Brazil. It was indeed "fast food," but in the Brazilian style - "pratos à viagem" ("dishes for travel" a phrase I found funny). I found the place efficient far beyond the most extravagant dreams of Brazilian eating places. It was incidentally modest, plastic, but with reasonable prices and with good food. It was also convenient for me in those days of research in downtown Rio.

Reencounter with Vicente Salles

Vicente dates from my earliest days in Rio in late 1966 and early 1967 when I researched at the "Campanha Nacional de Defesa do Folclore" in modest digs across from one of the most famous buildings in Brazil at the time – the old Ministry of Education with the columns, window shades and the like of the French architect Corbusier, mentor of Oscar Niemeyer, all in downtown Rio. The "Campaign" was headed by renowned folklorist Renato Almeida

(I remember his chain smoking and cigarette ashes down his white shirt and dark suit) and Vicente was second in charge, one duty being putting together the quarterly folklore review. He was responsible for my first published academic article in 1969 in the highly respected "Revista Brasileira de Folclore." Now in 1978 he is the representative of Manuel Diégues Júnior and FUNARTE in Brasília the capital. He will be the future editor of the really classy review "Cultura" in that city.

On another occasion I was invited for a wonderful dinner at his home in Rio, met his beautiful wife, a violinist in the Symphonic Orchestra of Rio de Janeiro. My point in all this is cultural as well, case in point, the staple of life which makes most Brazilians go – the fiery hot, sweet Brazilian demitasse coffee or "cafezinho." Since my last time with Vicente in Rio he had suffered a heart attack, happily survived but with some changes; he admitted that prior to the heart attack he consumed on an average of twenty "cafezinhos" per day! And I daresay he was one among many! The "pick me up" was one of my greatest pleasures in Brazil from the very beginning and enjoyed to this day. There was a time when I perhaps drank six to eight a day. Also related to my research, Vicente would write one of the best books on an aspect of the "cordel" in those years, a book highly thought of and a prize winner in folklore circles in Brazil on the "cordel" variant in Belém do Pará in the 1930s, 1940s and the main source of what Brazilians "cordel" poets thought about World War II. Vicente was from that city and had access to the now rare story-poems of the era.

Shortly after the encounter with Vicente I meant another person added to my list of admired folklorists in Brazil – Raul Lody of Rio de Janeiro. Yet today he has the best study, a very long article which is poetry in prose describing in wonderful detail the old, classic "Feira Nordestina de São Cristóvão" of Rio de Janeiro.

Painting the National Library

The scene took place on one of those days when I was researching in downtown Rio consulting the various libraries and collection of "cordel" poetry. One day as I was having a late breakfast and drinking one of those "cafezinhos" in Rick's, the place located opposite the FUNARTE building and adjacent to the National Library I witnessed an unforgettable scene. For me it is the epitome of the Brazilian "jeito" or "quick fix." For thirty minutes I watched the following: two men were painting the National Library. They were on a scaffold hanging from the roof of the building and were painting the exterior wall below. But due to the architectural plan or design of the building there were many "indented" sections in the walls. Not being able to reach said wall with their paint brushes they found the "jeito:" they rocked the scaffold in a slow back and forth motion, first into the "crevice", then out. And so in that swinging rhythm back and forth, "whoosh, whoosh," they would make a couple of passes with the paint brushes.

It seemed to be in waltz time: Ta ta ta TA DA, paint –paint, paint –paint; Ta Ta ta TA DA, paint – paint, paint – paint. It was fascinating and held my attention for about thirty minutes. Even the house painters in Brazil are "dancers" and artists!

Tourism in Rio

Tourism in Rio, the Benedictine Monastery

Catching the bus to old Praça Mauá in the old port district of Rio, very run down in those years, I then walked to the old Benedictine Monastery ("O Mosteiro de São Bento") one of Brazil's most important colonial churches. It was founded in 1590 by the nobility on a large piece of ground in the old center of Rio and then donated to the Benedictine Order; the first monks came from the monastery of the same name in Salvador. An Aside: One of the most memorable times for me in Salvador in later years was one occasion when I went to the old St. Benedict's Monestery in Salvador and was able to attend the vespers: monks clad in their traditional brown habits with hood sat opposite each other in the old choir ("coro") of beautiful carved rosewood and sang the Holy Office. Construction on the monastery in Rio was done by slaves and the original architectural style was the "Maneirista" of the age in Portugal. The interior is all of guilded carved wood, either rosewood or perhaps mahogany done in the ensuing years, thus the church has Baroque and Rococó traits. Its beauty is astounding!

This was my second visit to the Monastery; the first time was as follows: in the boarding apartment where I lived in Rio for several months in 1967, the owners, a widow and her daughter, happened to have close connections to one of the Benedictine monks. They were able to arrange a special "private" visit for me. Being a traditional practicing Catholic (except for occasional lapses as a young man), I jumped at the chance which consisted not only in a private "tour" of the place with all the lights on (they often keep the church dark), but a place at table in the monks' refectory for the noon meal. The food was tasty but plentiful; we ate in silence save for the readings in Sacred Scripture by one of the monks in the dining room. This indeed was my first (and until now) last such experience. I am forever grateful to the widow, her daughter and to that Benedictine monk.

Candelaria Church 1978

After the Benedictines it was the turn of Candelária, a huge edifice on Presidente Getúlio Vargas Avenue, one of the two major thoroughfares in downtown Rio. Construction took place from 1775 until the end of the 19th century. The origin of the church is an interesting tale. In the 16th century a Spanish ship almost sank in the sea east of Brazil, and when the Spanish mariners were saved they insisted on constructing a chapel in thanks for their "miraculous" survival. Thus the "Chapel of Our Lady of the 'Candelaria'" ("A Capela da Nossa Senhora da Candelária") took place in 1609, the name coming from that of the ship "La Candelaria."

In serious need of repairs, the original chapel was converted into the large structure in 1775 and was inaugurated by no less than King John VI of Portugal due to the happy circumstance of the Portuguese royal family, the Braganças, residing in Rio after having fled Portugal during Napoleon's invasion in 1807. The Braganças had ceded to most of Napoleon's demands but he still invaded, using Spanish troops as well, in that year. When he arrived, the Braganças had already fled, lock, stock and barrel, to the colony and its capital Rio de Janeiro. This marked a unique and rather grandiose situation: it is the only time in American colonial history that the mother country is ruled from its colony! The Napoleonic War raged in the Peninsula, and only with the help of the British and Lord Wellington was Napoleon finally vanquished. So John VI de Bragança and the royals returned home but with a significant family change: his first son Pedro told Dad "I'm staying" (The famous "Eu Fico" speech so important in Brazilian History). Thus a Constitutional Monarchy in effect would rule Brazil with Pedro's young brother, a truly enlighted 19th century "benevolent despot," Catholic and Mason, ruling in Brazil until the end of the Monarchy marked by the end of slavery and the abdication in 1880. All this explains that the major architectonic style of the Candelaria was Neo-Classic. Not being an expert in architecture I can only report that personally Candelaria seemed cold and distant to me and I favored the Benedictine Monastery with its Baroque and Rococó styles. No comparison in terms of beauty!

For me it is a more recent event that ties my memory to Candelaria: the infamous massacre of street children outside the church in 1993 by the more infamous "Death Squadron" (" O Esquadrão da Morte"), probably off duty policemen hired to "clean up the streets of Rio" in a less than tidy way. Needless to say the event was reported in all the national media and even in the modest story-poems of "cordel."

In the visit to Candelaria in 1978 there was beautiful organ music inside the church, but one could not hear the words of the priest presiding at mass; it all seemed like a "silent movie" from the 1920s.

There was time yet for one more visit to Praça 15 and the old Metropolitan Cathedral where Dom Pedro I was crowned Emperor of Brazil in 1822. I then made a short visit to the "Igreja do Carmo" with its huge altar entirely in brilliant silver, by coincidence the church where my friends Henrique and Cristina Kerti were married.

Somehow in all this time and yet that day I repeated the old days and took the ferry boat trip from Rio over to Niteroi and back. It was fun even though I was alone. With a fresh breeze we saw the new Rio-Niterói Bridge (I chuckle remembering Luís Fernando Veríssimo's hilarious "crônica" about the toll bridge, no one ever having change, and the little guy in the toll booth offering "balas" or hard candy for change. The problem then just began: Do you want strawberry, raspberry, orange, apple? No one could decide on the flavors and the wait grew worse!) Also new was the "hydrofoil" or jet boat that crossed the bay in a hurry and with a lot of noise and without the "graça" of the old ferries. We saw huge cargo ships in the harbor and sea birds. I did the round trip, Rio-Niteroi, Niterói-Rio, a great excursion into the past.

The "Glória" Church ("Igreja da Glória), Rio 1978

The Author in the Sacristy of "Igreja da Glória" and Portuguese Tiles

Another day. This time the tourism was to the "Igreja Nossa Senhora da Glória" located in the "Outeiro da Glória" (The Glória Hill), a real post card of the city for its beauty. Built in a polygonal form like "Nossa Senhora da Conceição" in Salvador and in the Brazilian Baroque style (it always reminded me of the churches in Minas Gerais in Ouro Preto), it had carved wooden altars but without the gold paint; one just sees the wood. The main thing is that on all the interior walls of the church are the famous Portuguese tiles, "azulejos," most with scenes from mythology, the exception being the hunting scenes in the sacristy. It turns out that the Braganças, the Portuguese royal family, had a special love for this church and Dom Pedro's children were baptized there. It is a one of the few surviving jewels of colonial Rio de Janeiro.

After that visit I walked down to the Hotel da Glória (where I was lodged in that congress of 1973), but with something new – the hotel was recently purchased by the Japanese; all its signs and placards were in Japanese characters, and all the employees were Japanese. I thought I was in Tokyo! I would return several times in the future, ignoring the Japanese placards but thanking the owners for their good sense in keeping the old salons in colonial style in the time of Dom Pedro II, Emperor of Brazil.

A Day at the Beach in Copacabana

The "Budding Teenage Girls" on Copacabana Beach

The "Budding Teenagers" and the Author on Copacabana Beach

On one occasion I went to the beach with the two teenagers, young girls from my building, ah youth! It gave me the unique opportunity to find out a bit about adolescent life in Rio, the young girls and their "vida p'ra frente," "cool young life." The young ladies spoke of studying English, of the good social scene ("bons programas") in the restaurants, night clubs and discoteques. The beach "scene" was also "pr'a frente" with lots of skin to be seen! The now famous "dental floss" bikini had arrived and thrived in Rio. On a sunny day people were jammed like sardines on the sand (I have commented before of the sense of physical space in Brazil, something I believe essential to their understanding and enthusiasm for "movimento" on the beach. The more people the better! I'll never forget the many times when Brazilians would meet me and say "Você está sozinho?" You are all alone! There could be no worse fate for a Brazilian than that!)

A Beach Scene 1978

"Living Is Very Dangerous" ("Viver É Muito Perigoso" - João Guimarães Rosa in "Grande Sertão: Veredas")

Sebastião Nunes Batista tells me today of the death of a dear friend, Rodrigues de Carvalho who wrote "Serrote Preto" ("Black Sierra") an importante regional book in Brazilian folklore. The writer was run over by a car in that insane traffic in Rio; he being 75 years old at the time. Another more personal shock would come in later years when in 1986 my friend Rodolfo Coelho Cavalcante, the prolific "cordel" poet I would do research on in 1981 and publish a book on in 1987, died of the same fate. I do not have the details at hand and don't know if it was a bus, a truck or a car, but he was run over very near his modest home in the protelarian sector of Salvador, Liberdade. I'm worried about Sebastião's own health. He is suffering from vertigo to the point of having to take a taxi to and from work, not trusting the buses and fearful of fainting or passing out in the street. He is such a good person, good friend, hospitable, always quick to offer me hints in research at the Casa de Ruy. He really provides a great service to the Casa even working for two months two years ago without salary in one of their recent monetary crunches, gathering material for the "cordel" section. The lack of funding is chronic at the Casa and continues. Sebastião would die a few years later, after our time together, but "dying with his boots on" as we would say in the old west of the U.S. He was giving a talk on "cordel" at a conference, I believe in Alagoas State, and suffered a collapse and death at that moment. So it was that my worries in 1978 became reality later on.

"The Cowboy Mass" ("Missa do Vaqueiro")

I attended the play at the FUNARTE auditorium, a small place with a sparse but enthusiastic crowd; it was an important moment for me due to the passion of my research of folklore in the Northeast since 1966. Those years of "folkloric" vocation marked my life. The piece has its origin in the creation of the story-poet Pedro Bandeira of Juazeiro do Norte, Ceará, along with the help of a local priest and is the dramatization of a real life event – the death of a cowboy. The mass is reenacted each year in the Northeast to an audience of thousands. The presentation that I attended in Rio was based on the L.P. recording by the Quinteto Violado and is adapted to the stage. It began with an improvised song by a cowboy, similar to performances of the singer-poets of the Northeast; then they sang "Acauã" by Luís Gonzaga along with other northeastern songs. The hero, Ramiro Jacó, is a cowboy who dares to speak publicly of social conditions in the Northeast and is shot. The rest of the play is in the form of a folkloric mass, the mass of the cowboy with a lamentation and elegy to Ramiro.

To me it was beautiful music, emotional, with lyrics that I could almost totally understand (not always the case with the singer-poets in the markets). The entire mass was "sertaneja," the priest dressed like a real northeastern cowboy in an all leather outfit, even with leather cross.

The instrumentation was legitimate as well: a "violão" of ten strings, flute, drum, triangle and sound box accordion. The cast was excellent, strong voices, in high spirits; they made the audience remember the Northeast. It produced that Brazilian sentiment of "saudades."

Naïve Comments by a "Gringo" Observer on Brazilian Clothing and Customs in 1978, That Is, What to Wear in Rio

I found what seemed to be a situation of good taste. It is possible to determine the social class of most persons by their manner of dress and perhaps even determine their residential district as well.

The Men

They wear a short sleeved sport shirt not tucked in their "jeans" for informal use; the shirt collar is unbuttoned and open; hair is neither long nor short. Moustaches are common and beards are seen, but trimmed and much neater than the U.S. in those days. They wear leather shoes with the jeans, and often without socks. Comportment is still that of Brazil (and Latin America) and the "macho" look, as present as ever. The guys on the street, on the beach, stare fixedly at the girls, and still use the "piropos" when they or the girls pass by. The Brazilian social custom of the "air kisses" on both cheeks for girls and ladies they know (friends, relatives) still is in vogue. The tourist has to ask someone to explain the "code:" how many kisses, one cheek or both? I never did get it straight. And it seemed like everyone still smoked.

Comportment in the corner bars, the famous "pé sujo" is classic: it's very loud and there is lots of conversation, jokes and laughter. And the table is full of glasses of "choppe" or draft beer. An Aside: In my times in Recife in the early days in the bar with the guys from the "Chácara das Rosas" a glass could never be half full. They kept it full and the beer flowing from those big bottles of "Brahma Choppe." The difference between Brazilians and perhaps other beer drinkers was the "head" on the beer: on the beach you might get an expensive glass of beer only half full, the rest foam. One learned local expressions in order to get the glass nearly full of beer: "sem colarinho" ("without the collar) or "sem bigode" ("without the moustache").

At work in the office

Businessmen and civil servants of rank wear suits, even if a very modest cut for lower level people. The use of a necktie is required if it's the business world or upper echelon government. In that heat of Rio these businessmen and civil servants wore a long sleeved white shirt but never with the white t-shirt underneath that was the custom in the U.S. at the time. I am sure this was the custom and certainly had to do with the heat and humidity. Leather shoes and black socks were the rule.

On the Beach.

Men generally wore the "sunga" the tight fitting skimpy "racing suit," but you could see all styles including the "boxer" suit from the U.S. In later years this latter suit became the rage, then the surfer shorts, and all that was worn for the "Cooper" on the wide mosaic sidewalks of Leblon, Ipanema and especially Copacabana. (I'm told the word "Cooper" came from this use by the British in Brazil, that is, the stroll along the sidewalk which evolved into an exercise routine still much seen in today's Rio.)

The Women

South Zone.

Remember it's the tourist and naïve "gringo" commenting on all this. I saw lots of sports clothes used for the workout in the gym and perhaps for "capoeira" classes as well. It was not a bit sloppy, but nicely fitting and "chic." In general the women exuded sex and were attractive and for the innocent American very provocative! They wore stylish blue jeans, super tight and with famous name designer label if possible, tops or blouses also super tight, and if not showing a significant "décolletage" certainly suggesting it. Upa! It was interesting to see the number of young ladies from teenagers to 20s and on up that were almost "thin" by U.S. standards with nicely formed breasts and derriere to match. I asked myself in 2008: was it Ivô Pitangui's fame and the silicon industry that resulted in all this? The Brazilian woman even from the 1960s had always seemed to have larger breasts. As the saying goes in Brazil, "O prazer é meu." I am sure that emphasis in more recent years has been more advanced plastic surgery on the buttocks along with jean, shorts and the like already "padded."

An Aside: in a brief and fortunate moment in 2014 I was able to witness in Rio de Janeiro a recording session of a samba school I think from Niterói at the samba school construction area in Rio. All the main "passistas" or "star" samba dancers were there in costume and all their glory. I suspect plastic surgery was not unknown to these beauties!

In 1978 I did not see nearly so many obese or "sloppily dressed" women as in the U.S., but you have to remember we are in Rio and the South Zone! Climate, the beach and social custom rule! I believe the women know they are women, are proud of the fact, and most importantly know what is expected of them and that's the way they act. But it all seems very natural.

On the Beach

There did not seem to be a great number of "tangas" or string bikinis but still small bikinis. It was difficult for me to tell (in this book I've tried to place more beach pictures, but remember they are 1978 vintage!) The locals complain now that Copacabana is being "invaded" on the weekend by people from the North Zone; this trend is sure to grow with the expansion of the subway system and more buses. It is not "the racially prejudiced 'gringo'" who is saying this but the Cariocas who are now fleeing from Copacabana to at least Ipanema and Leblon but even the far away "Barra" beaches. Why? What was just said. I think I am right in saying this: the appearance of the young girl from the north zone (or even the "favelas" all over Rio) is markedly different even physically from their counterparts in the South Zone – differences in money to buy clothing or even plastic surgery and certainly the "chic" styles of the shops in the South Zone, and perhaps makeup or even nutrition may explain differences. This is the stuff of sociological treatises! The physical appearance of the shorter "nordestinos", "pau de arara" plays a role as well. All this may be idle speculation on my part.

Formal Clothing

I cannot comment because I never had occasion to frequent events that required it. In the restaurants and bars of the "luxury" hotels where I might go to drink a beer or a "caipirinha" it was the expected tourist attire. I am thinking of the Hotel Meridien or Othon Palace. I don't know where I told it or if I have told it yet, but one cannot forget an interesting phenomenon reflecting the Brazilian economy in 1978, inflation in the Brazil entering into the First World Economy – all told by the price of a beer on the rooftop bar at the Othon Palace. I can still remember getting into the elevator, climbing the many stories to the top, sitting down at the bar and ordering a bottle of Brahma beer for 25 cents USD. Just one or two years later the same beer was available for four or five dollars USD. Brazil had entered the First World!

But to summarize in a general way the South Zone seemed faithful to its reputation – highly sophisticated in style. The "carioca" woman seemed better dressed than ever. And foreign and especially European brand names seemed important.

The Present Moment in Politics, July, 1978

There is lots of talk and gossip about government and current politics. "They" say that the opposition party, the MDB ("Movimento Democrático Brasileiro") is going to come out well in the next state elections slated for the fall of 1978 (and in fact it did). However, the official government candidate in the next presidential election, indirect elections yet, is General João

Batista Figueiredo the candidate of ARENA ("Aliança Renovadora Nacional"), already the "consecrated" future general-president elect.

One still hears talk of Orestes Quércia. I recall when he came to the U.S. a couple of years ago, the "man of the future" in Brazilian politics on a junket-trip paid for by I don't know whom, when he unexpectedly ended up on the ASU campus and was directed to my humble office in the Language and Literature Building. I recall his "guide" and translator wanting to know about the "female" scene in Phoenix!

And the old timers Ulysses Guimarães and Magalhães Pinto are in the news. Everyone really knows that all is a charade, a political farse, in this supposed "Democracy." "Beforehand" censureship ("censura prévia") has disappeared, but the atmosphere created by the generals has not disappeared. Please recall these notes are from 1978, are a little naïve, the result of what I heard in the streets, conversations with Brazilian friends, and even talk from the newspapers. But perhaps as accurate as anything at the time! There is also talk that the old political leftist Leonel Brizola wants to return from exile in Uruguay. All the above took place before the atmosphere of "complete amnesty" which would only come in 1980 and once again stir the Brazilian political pot!

A Return to Sugar Loaf

A Happening – a Return to Sugar Loaf (Pão de Açúcar)

Eight years had passed since the last time I did this tourist excursion with Keah in 1970. The old "folkloric" red cable car, that same small one I had stood in balancing in the Carioca wind when the generators were cut off during floods in 1967, was now replaced by the shiny new, glass and plastic car still in service today (in 2014). Urca Hill ("Morro") was much improved for tourism with shops, cafes and even a night club, and Sugar Loaf Rock or Mountain itself had more modern facilities including rest rooms and cafes. What had not changed and was actually worse was the pollution combined with "névoa" or fog (people argue about this). The view however was the same – that incredible view of the "Cidade Maravilhosa."

Beach Behavior – Copacabana, Ipanema and Leblon

Beach "Comportment" Copacabana

Beach "Comportment" Leblon

Beach "Comportment" Ipanema

You arrive at the beach and with your feet make a nice "mound" of sand, you place your beach mat of straw on top of the mound, and you lie down with your head facing the sidewalk or "calçada" (which is the direction of the sun in the morning). In 1978 there are large groups of young girls, families and the like. And there are always crowds even in "winter" as long as the sun is shining. The beach can be empty during rainy cool weather. The water temperature is for a "Northeasterner" from Ceará, Paraíba, Pernambuco, or Bahia, frigid! But on those hot, scalding days of Rio's summers, it is indeed refreshing. The waves are terrific for body surfing (even the naïve "gringo" mastered this) and decent for board surfers if there is high tide. And it is still a marvelous scene to see the women of Rio de Janeiro on display!

A confession: This author has almost drowned twice, each time at the most famous beaches in Latin America, one time at Cancún and the other on Ipanema Beach in Rio. Overconfident of my swimming and body surfing skills I ignored the "red flag" warning one time, was dragged out by the undertow, panicked briefly, but somehow regained my common sense to swim diagonally and eventually drag myself up on Ipanema beach exhausted and lucky to be alive.

Back on the broad mosaic sidewalks people are walking, doing their "Cooper," and there is a real parade of baby carriages, some huge in size, and the nannies dressed all in white, caring for their charges. One sees people with all sizes and shapes of doggies possible. It is all together an unforgettable scene.

Professor Adriano da Gama Kury

Professor Adriano da Gama Kury and Wife Dona Wilma

Born in Acre and moving later to Rio, Adriano then moved to Natal where he met his wife Wilma who was one of his students (she by coincidence is related to the famous Jesuíno Brilhante of "cangaceiro" fame in Rio Grande do Norte State). Adriano then moved on to Brasília where he taught at the new experimental university and finally ended up in Rio as director of the Philology Sector of the Casa de Ruy Barbosa and part-time teaching at Santa Úrsula University. A main source of income was giving private classes to wealthy Brazilians trying to pass the infamous Portuguese Language Exam for entrance into the Brazilian State Deparment, "Itamaraty." Adriano's success rate and fame for the latter were well known in Brazil.

A "Cordel" Moment: Meeting and Socializing with Franklin Machado and Sebastião Nunes Batista

It was on a Monday. The poet Franklin Machado of São Paulo appeared today at the Casa de Ruy. He regularly provides the Casa with the new story-poems from not only São Paulo, but Rio and the Northeast. He was a close friend of Sebastião so the three of us repaired to a neighborhood "watering hole" and closed the place up a few hours later. Franklin's appearance is that of a Brazilian "hippy," – round "granny" style classes, a long straggly beard, beginning baldness, wearing a small leather hat that reminded me of the Greek fisherman's hat common to the times. He is also in Rio to pick up an album of woodcuts he has recently finished and visit his ex-wife and children; he and the wife are legally separated ("desquitados") and the family lives in Guaratuba.

Machado is a bit picturesque and a bit "looney" in the good sense, but most of all he is entertaining. Originally from Feira de Santana in the interior of Bahia State (and he would return to Feira years later to head the "Museum of the Backlands") he grew up listening to Rodolfo Coelho Cavalcante declaiming his story-poems in the market in Feira and even saw Cuíca de Santo Amaro in action just once or twice in Salvador. In Feira he had heard the poet Erotildes Miranda dos Santos declaiming his poems in the market. With a degree in journalism and later in law, he only began to do "cordel"when he moved to greater São Paulo after Law School, all under the advice and counsel of Rodolfo. Today Machado is in the midst of a sometimes bitter debate with the "traditional" northeastern "cordel" poets in São Paulo, in particular the poet J. Barros. The latter has called Machado "an interloper" in "cordel," because of his university degrees calling him "A Dr. in Cordel."

Machado says that Rodolfo once invited him to come to Salvador and succeed him as "King of Cordel" in that city. He spoke of Rodolfo' drinking problem, but also his astounding prolific production of story-poems (RCC would claim 1,700 story-poems over his long career, perhaps not too far off the mark). That night in the bar Machado "recreated" his routine, his "jeito" of selling story-poems in greater São Paulo, how he sells in the "plaza," etc. He recited many poems and in general kept the place "rocking" for three hours!

He had much news on "cordel." He believes that "cordel" is strong now in Juazeiro do Norte, Ceará, São Paulo and Rio, but is dying out in Pernambuco and Paraíba (its place of origin). He says the poets are mostly migrating to the South. The poet João Severo from Bayeux, Paraíba, died recently. The "House of the Children" ("Casa da Criança" a "cordel" publishing press) failed in Olinda; only Zé Soares and one other continue in Recife. Note: Since this date the famous José Soares as well is deceased, his story related to me by his son Marcelo in João Pessoa in 2005.

Machado spoke of a recent "cordel" congress in Brasília yet in 1978. He said it was good to see colleagues and friends but as congresses go, it was "weak." Maxado Nordestino (Machado's pen name) is a sort of Cuíca de Santo Amaro of today. I do not believe he has mastered the true art of the "cordel" poet of Paraíba or Pernambuco fame, at least not yet, but in regard to "performance" and as a popular type and journalist or commentator of the times in "cordel," he is following in the footsteps of Cuíca and other poet-reporters. He is a legitimate personage in "cordel," just different (college degrees, etc.) He believes he can play a role in the future in the "urbanization" of "cordel," in his words the "massification" of the same, thereby extending its life.

He believes the big publishing houses like Editorial Abril are amenable to entering the field, ("entrar no ramo") and he is certain that the small "traditional" printing shops employed by the poets will not be able to compete with them. An Aside from 2015: Remember Machado is talking prior to the era of the personal computer and printer to its side used by so many of the poets today. He was right, in retrospect, about the old typeographies but could not predict today's times.

So by the end of that sometimes raucous evening I felt like we had connected and that we would be good friends; I was right and we certainly hit it off. It is such rare moments that research is converted into life and vice-versa, something truly lived and no longer "library research" or "pesquisa de gabinete" as my mentor Luís da Câmara Cascudo scornfully called it.

A Tourist Moment – the "Gadget of the Day" by the Vendors in Copacabana

This is one of the many "bugigangas" or "gadgets" sold by the "camelots" in Copacabana. It is an example of the "small things" that make Brazil Brazil! It is a small perhaps five inch tall plastic figure of a little boy in walking shorts. When the customer pulls down the shorts, the little boy pees ("faz chi-chi ou mija") straight ahead for a foot or so. It draws lots of laughs and is the "hot" item of the moment.

Time to Complain – the "Normal" Negatives of Life in Rio de Janeiro in 1978

A common complaint is: When you simply want to walk down a side street sidewalk in the city and especially the South Zone cars block your way parked in all manner on the sidewalks.

I recall one idiot who tried to pass traffic from the right (the sidewalk) on the road to the train station in Cosme Velho near the Corcovado Railway in effect screwing up the traffic flow for everyone. The sidewalks in Copacabana are packed with parked cars; you have to "dance a samba" to avoid them, even to get from your building down the street.

And I must not forget to mention another "samba" step needed to avoid the poopy remains of the multitude of little dogs whose owners "take for a walk" and don't pick up after them.

The cinemas are crowded; people smoke inside and irritate everyone. The national "shorts" in the cinemas are boring and an irritant; it's all military government propaganda and folks hate it. A typical short: a governmet official is attending a ribbon-cutting for a military statue. As mentioned years earlier, there are no catcalls, whistling or booing at such moments.

There is constant incredible noise all around you: TV volume is set at the maximum. There is however a positive note on "propaganda" or advertising: it is a genuine pleasure while at the beach to hear the ingenious verses in song that the vendors use to sell their lemonade, etc. They are a work of art and such persons could make a living doing TV advertising in the U.S.

Meeting the Writer Orígenes Lessa and Maria Eduarda Lessa in 1978

I am with the writer and fan of "cordel" Orígenes in the small apartment on Prado Júnior in Copacabana. I was very well received; Orígenes said that he had heard of my work and seen some of it. (After this visit I sent him copies of most everything through the mail.) He is opinionated: He told me that he thinks that literary theory and criticism are the "greatest stupidity – pedantic that is" of those who have no talent for creative writing. He was very critical of the French professor of the Sorbonne, Raymund Cantel, showing off ("fazendo figura") and making "cordel" his personal property, giving talks and conferences, "ending up the owner of it all." Orígenes spoke to me of his collection of "cordel"and that it would go to the library in his home town of Lençóis Paulista, State of São Paulo. (I was familiar only in general terms with the collection, knowing it was part of the whole that the research team of the 1950s at the Casa de Ruy). He receives a small pension from a publicity agency he used to write for (the "Repórter Esso" article I first saw, seminal in the study of "cordel," is one such sample), but lives modestly from authors' rights from his very successful childrens' literature. He would like to spend his final years in the "art of writing." He moved from the apartment facing Copacabana Beach when he "changed women." Maria Eduarda, born in Portugal and whose father was a General in the Portuguese Army, is his current wife.

Orígenes says he has no regrets from past life lived. He writes childrens' literature, short stories and novels and is quite respected in Brazil. He will become a member of that august group in the Brazilian Academy of Letters in future years. In spite of his admiration for Manuel Cavalcanti Proença (my first mentor ever so briefly in Brazil in 1966) he believes Proença erred in his major study on João Guimarães' Rosa's novel "Grande Sertão: Veredas" ("The Devil to Pay in the Backlands," perhaps Brazil's greatest modern novel) when Proença claimed the novelist created the many place names in the novel. Orígenes says the places have been proved to be original, real and not inventions of the author.

He liked my idea on the relation of said novel to "cordel" and said that one day in the future it could prove to be more important than the linguistic studies on the masterpiece. Orígenes turns out to be very "anti-elitist." He met and knew Cuíca de Santo Amaro and interviewed him; he has some 120 of Cuíca's story-poems that I am going to read in the next few days. He insists that Cuíca was, however, a "bad character" who did however appeal to and stay on the side of the humble masses. He was with Cuíca only four or five times. (The reader may recall that this research trip to Rio has as its primary purpose to read the originals of the poet at the Casa de Ruy Barbosa collection and others in Rio. Origenes' turned out to be a "gold mine.")

Another Day

I'm back at the Lessas to read the collection. We had a lunch of cabbage, beef liver, "maracujá" juice, and "jacutiba", the fruit from Orígenes' small farm in Paraíba do Sul, a few hours drive from Rio. As mentioned, Maria Eduarda is Portuguese; they met three years ago when she was a receptionist at the publicity firm. She is religious, a Christian, but Orígenes has not practiced any religion for the last 40 to 45 years. He says he has been "reconverted" in recent years, this in spite of all the family problems, but not to any specific "flavor" of organized religion. He is convinced that spiritual beings exist, but that some are satanic in nature and one of their main results is mental illness. An aside, he would like to know the western part of the U.S., the Grand Canyon, and I offered my services as "guide" ("cicerone").

Orígenes has I believe the best collection of political stories in the "cordel" in Brazil. He has had good reception for his own writings since 1970 with literally hundred of thousands of volumes in total sales as the principal income for him. He has to write to live.

Suddenly Franklin Machado knocks on the door. He provides Orígenes with the "folhetos" from São Paulo, a private "business deal" between them. I felt sorry for Machado that day; he was depressed with his family situation. However he did have news of "cordel" (he is as well an informant for the current goings on at the Casa de Ruy and Orígenes).

Marcus de Atayde, one of my guides and informants on "cordel" in the mid 1960s in Recife by virtue of being one of the sons of the famous João Martins de Atayde, the "empresário do cordel" from the 1920s to the late 1950s, is in São Paul studying journalism and working in public relations at Bayer of Brazil. Orígenes opined about João Martins: he had a typography in Recife as early as 1911, had learned popular medicine in Amazonas State during the rubber "boom," returned to the Northeast, succeeded in acquiring lots and property and later "the entire district" near the old São José Market in Recife (Origenes exaggerates a bit here). And then he starts his typography. He never sold "cordel" or "sang" in the plaza but became a sort of "aristocrat" of "cordel." Origenes quotes him: "I am an illiterate who lives from literature." The fine poet Delarme Monteiro worked for Atayde at the printing shop and penned many of the story-poems attributed to the latter. Zé Bernardo da Silva of later Juazeiro fame also worked for Atayde at the shop, this before his amazing career in later years in the city of Father Cícero. Lessa said Atayde had several land holdings and plantations, sired up to 40 children, many of them not recognized by him. Atayde had great respect for Leandro Gomes de Barros and bought Leandro's huge stock of story-poems from his widow (I was perhaps the first to see that actual contract for sale between the widow and João Martins, a hand-written document shown to me by Marcus Atayde in 1966, thus proving the legitimacy of Atayde's operation, much doubted by nay-sayers over the years.)

A Cultural Moment: The "Première" of Chico Buarque de Holanda's "Ópera do Malandro"

A group of friends took the bus downton to see the première of "Ópera do Malandro" by Chico Buarque de Holanda. Curiously enough, it is not one of his works that I best appreciate. I remember the opening with the "classic" Carioca "malandro" or rogue, a handsome man, black as coal, dressed in a white linen suit (the "uniform" of the Carioca rogue) with a red carnation in his lapel. The play was highly praised in that time, but the truth is a problem in hearing kept me that night from understanding many of the lyrics on stage and also the speeches. A pity but a fact.

The Cultural Moment and "Gossip" about "Cordel" - the French Researcher in the Casa de Ruy Barbosa

I met the madame professor from the Sorbonne researching "The role of woman in the 'cordel'." She tells me that my small book of 1973 in Pernambuco was a "pioneering study on the 'cordel'" and circulated and was known. If reprinted it would quickly sell out in Brazil. (I tried to get the UFEPE to do a second augmented edition years later and nothing came of it. So taking things into my own hands I reprinted the 1973 book plus a large addendum with interviews with forty cordel poets and publishers via Trafford in 2015. It is currently available to the public; if I had waited on Pernambuco I would be in my grave.) She spoke in a very negative manner (what else is new at this point?) of Raymund Cantel – "He zealously guards his "cordel" collection, is dishonest," and according to her, "has done little with the Institute of Latin America other than enlarge his own image and position. And he never fulfills his promises to Brazil regarding the "cordel." We all know him well." Yikes!

End of the Trip, Tired and More Observations on Time in Rio

I noted the apparent "insolence" on the part of the waiters in the cafés, a "não sei quê" of resentment or anger on their part. They were to say the least, "carrancudos e fechados." At least that was the way they seemed to this underdressed "gringo."

It always happens to the person on the street: you have to stop while a car maneuvers in front of you in order to park on the sidewalk.

A Bumper Sticker: "Be careful of your gas! ("Cuide com a sua emissão de gás") – the design shows the rear end of a VW Bug ("um fusca") with buttocks!

I am still amazed at the quickness with which the Brazilians eat; I cannot imagine how they can possibly taste their food! They eat as if someone were to quickly snatch away their plate or as if the food were a pill they had to take! I eat quickly, but nothing in comparison. A case in point: one night at the Braseiro in Copacabana I was having a dinner of French bread, "arroz à grego" and barbecued chicken. A guy sat down at the counter and the following ensued: he gulped down a huge bowl of soup, a dinner salad that filled the large plate, an order of barbecued chicken and rice (the plate I was eating), and a filet mignon with French fries. And he finished before I did!

The noise level. You can't escape it. My room in the boarding apartment is on the 10th floor and you can still hear the street noise from below. The television is always at maximum volume and the same with the noise in the bars and open air cafes. Right now I am hearing the blaring sound of "Saturday Night Fever" in vogue at this time exploding outside my window.

A Pleasant Discovery

But there was a pleasant surprise …

View of the Beach

In 1978 it is possible to go to the top floor of the Othon Palace (the sun roof with bar, pool, and dance floor) with perhaps the best view of Copacabana Beach and even of Rio. I mentioned before: if you sit down at the bar you can order a small bottle of "Brahma Choppe" for 25 cents US! You don't pay cover or minimum. And in the evening there are snacks. By chance I met a Canadian, a representative of "Newsweek;" he travels the world and lives in hotels. He says the Othon is very good and not very expensive (relative to world prices), one person $40 USD per day, a suite for $350 USD. And it's not particularly luxurious or "super-luxury". He agrees that nothing could be better – sitting at a bar on the 30th floor with the best view of Rio and drinking beer for 25 cents.

Research Colleague Candace Slater – an Encounter at the Casa de Ruy Barbosa

Candace has news on "cordel." Apolônio Alves dos Santos has just delivered his story poem "The Death of Pope Paul VI" to the printing shop. The daughters of José Bernardo da Silva have 138 titles for sale in the old "Typografia São Francisco" of Juazeiro; there were only six when they took over.

Candace is finishing her classic book on the "cordel" (it will be "Stories on a String"). She has a research grant for one more year and will return to Brazil after a conference at UCLA. (I attended in 1979.) I appreciate her success and her work but at this moment in 1978 I'll be happy to return home and to my family. One might recall that I left Keah and baby Katie only one year old to do this research trip. I'm feeling homesick and just want to return to being a husband and father right now.

BRAZIL 1981 - JULY IN BAHIA

THE FLIGHT

The adventure began this time in the U.S. itself. I had a research grant to do research on the poet Rodolfo Coelho Cavalcante, a resident of Salvador da Bahia. But I wanted to take the family to Colorado first. Our daughter Katie was now only four years old. She and Keah would live in the travel trailer there while I was gone. The plan was to leave from Durango in Colorado, make connections in Denver and later in Los Angeles on the Varig flight.

With no advance notice, we found out after arriving at the airport on the morning of my scheduled flight that the previous night lightning had hit the radar control at the local Durango airport and the flight to Denver had been cancelled. It was bad timing since I had my head and heart all set for the trip.

The "jeito" of the air line was to substitute the regular flight with a charter on a small commuter plane to Denver. So it went. We flew low over the great Rocky Mountains with a marvelous sight below – flying just above snow topped craggy mountain tops. Even wth the unstable air, the two engine prop plane popping up and down, we made it to Denver. With little time to catch the connecting flight on the 737 to Los Angeles, I ran from the Western Airlines Terminal, my large suitcase in hand and to save time did the baggage check - in on the sidewalk outside the terminal entrance. All okay, I climbed aboard the 737 with no problem and enjoyed the flight. Upon arriving at the airport in Los Angeles I discovered my bag had not made the same trip and was somewhere in the Denver airport.

The international flight was a charter, so I could not miss it; the only solution was to climb on board, make the 4000 mile trip without the bag and hope that with a bit of luck the bag would follow me on another Varig flight. I found out the next flight of Western's from Denver to Los Angeles would only arrive after the departure of the international flight. So, taking a deep breath and having blind faith in the gods of international flights, and with an attitude a little unusual for me I took a "devil may care," "O que será será" stance (thinking of Chico Buarque's song in "Dona Flor e Seus Dois Maridos") and climbed aboard the Varig flight.

In passing, the experience in the international airport in L.A. was none too pleasant. The passenger terminal was absolutely jammed, the city a cloud of smog and even the waiting room with scarcely an empty seat to rest a weary body.

The Varig flight was great as always, or almost, a new D C - 10 coming from Tokyo. Upon entering the plane and looking for my seat, I saw only Japanese, all very serious, the men in dark business suits, all reading newspapers from Japan. The accustomed Brazilian "bagunça" ("craziness") on Varig was absent and I missed it. The in flight service was however the same, the menu in French. It would be a nine hour flight with a stop in Lima, arriving with a cold and humid wind (I remembered the "garoa" of Lima from the brief sojurn in Peru in 1967). Most all of the sleepy passengers got out to stretch their legs or perhaps to experience the Peruvian hospitality in the form of a "pisco sour," Peru's answer to the "caipirinha."

After our arrival at the Galeão in Rio and upon entering the area of the duty free international shops, this after successfully getting through Brazilian customs, I heard that familiar "pssst pssst" sound and an airport employee of some kind came up to me wanting to know if I would buy him a bottle of Scotch in the duty free shop (only international passengers of course could enter the store). I thought to myself, "I smell a good deal here." So I accepted his request, bought the Scotch and delivered it to him in the national passenger area (he had slipped me the cash a while earlier), all very "hush, hush." I explained that in exchange for the favor perhaps he could make a special effort to keep an eye out for my delayed luggage and get it to me in Salvador. The miracle, according to my friends in Itapuã was that just two days later the bag arrived and not missing anything. To my way of thinking it was another good example of the Brazilian "jeito."

MEETING OLD FRIENDS IN SALVADOR

Laís and Mário Barros, Itapuã (Salvador)

In Salvador I was able to get in contact with my friends the Barros in Itapuã, Pedra do Sal. We were friends during from the early 1970s when Mário attended ASU studying for an advanced degree in electrical engineering and he and Laís has an apartment in the same student complex where Keah and I lived. Their house was two stories, colonial style with a nice varanda and a fairly short walk to the beach. It turns out that Jorge Amado at one time had a house nearby and they had met. Mário was on a business trip to Japan, but Laís showered me with that great Brazilian hospitality. She even took me to Mesbla Department store where I bought a few articles of clothing to get by, hoping my bag would appear one day soon but not knowing for sure. Funny, I chose a t-shirt with the famous logo of the Playboy Bunny and I don't know what else. A bit out of character! But it got the job done; the bag would arrive in a couple of days.

Luís Raimundo Fernandes in Dona Hilda's Boarding Apartment, Ondina, Salvador

After dinner at the Barros, Laís took me to the place I had chosen to live in during this stage of Bahia, Dona Hilda's boarding apartment on Avenida Presidente Vargas in Ondina across from the "Club Español" on the "litoral" or ocean. The apartment was nicely decorated with a surprise – the large "carrancas" from the São Francisco river boats of days gone past. When she found out I had seen them and knew something about them and liked them, she tried to get me into a deal to buy from her and export them to the U.S. She was barking up the wrong tree; I had given up the business world idea long ago.

I made a new friendship during the stay. Luís Raimundo is from Rio, his father retired from management in the "Banco do Brasil," and Luís is working his way up the management chain, currently by doing computer work on the night shift in the bank in Salvador. He has a shiny new car, loves to get out to the beaches on the "orla" like Piatã and will take me along a time or two. I will spend some time with him in later years in Rio and meet his charming wife. He was hospitable and a good Brazilian. I would even spend a night or two at the family apartment of his father in Ipanema, but that story comes in volume III.

A few days later there was another encounter with the Barros, this time for a nice meal of "bacalhau à portuguesa" Portuguese style codfish stew. We tasted wines from Rio Grande do Sul (the Barros are "gaúchos da gema" from Porto Alegre.) Incidentaly it is to Mário Barros that I owe my introduction to the "crônicas" of Luís Fernando Veríssimo, my favorite modern Brazilian author and humorist and inspiration for this book!

RESEARCH – "O NÚCLEO DE PESQUISA DA LITERATURA DE CORDEL" IN SALVADOR

The Researcher Edilene Matos at the "Núcleo de Pesquisa da Literatura de Cordel," Salvador

The "Núcleo" was part of the Cultural Foundation of the State of Bahia, a new entity for me in this new phase of research in Brazil now centering in Salvador da Bahia. It will be important for future research and publications in Brazil. It was there I met the couple - Edilene Matos, Director of the "Núcleo" and Carlos Cunha, two persons absolutely irreplaceable for my studies but as well good friends in Brazil. They both would be mentors and friends and showed me incredible, kind hospitality in this and other stages of research in Salvador. They certainly contributed to the possibility and good success I would have in Bahia in future years.

Edilene was immersed in academia in the process of getting her M.A. in Literature at the Federal University of Bahia (UFBA) and later the Ph.D. at the University of São Paulo. She therefore was linked to serious literary criticism, but "married" to the idea of research on "cordel" in Bahia. Carlos Cunha was autodidactic, without a university degree, but a man of letters, a serious poet, and more than this, the guide or "cicerone" of many literary activities in Salvador for years – cultural promotions, book publication, and most important for me, a link to the world of popular culture ("folk culture" as well) and "cordel" of those years in Bahia. He told me once that neither Edilene nor he could be nor could become known as "specialists on 'cordel'" due to the latter not being taken seriously in intellectual circles in Bahia. But the man had knowledge second to none of the "cordel;" I will mention him many more times in passing in regard to this.

In the "Núcleo" as well I met Abílio de Jesus, a black man and one of the best typographers in the city, a skill much admired and still needed in those days. Abílio had learned and gained experience during the many years in the typography of the Benedictine Press, an historical entity in the city. He was an orphan, was raised, educated and given a technical education by the Benedictines themselves, but now was in charge of all printing tasks for the Cultural Foundation. He dressed always in white, an obligation of "candomblé" (the reader may be familiar with such a thing in the literature of Jorge Amado), carried himself with great dignity, had grey hair, glasses and a very pleasant demeanor.

A Professional Aside. My book on "Jorge Amado e a Literatura de Cordel" is currently at the press and Abílio is coordinating the printing. It is a co-edition of the Cultural Foundation of Baha and the Casa de Ruy Barbosa in Rio but paid for by my subvention plus that of the Bahia entity. A "diplomatic" problem has come up: the choice for the cover illustration of the book. The Casa wants it in the "old" style of theirs: the book cover would have an illustration of a snake (an old woodcut from "cordel"). No one at the FCEB likes it and all want me to express my negative view of "the snake;" I did it and there was a very happy change. The cover will have a woodcut by a famous artist in Bahia, Calasans Neto, a friend of Jorge Amado's. The cover shows Jorge with a placard in each hand, all in the style of the woodcut, one of "Teresa" ("Teresa Batista Cansada de Guerra") and the other of "Tieta" of "Tieta do Agreste."

FIRST CONVERSATION WITH CARLOS CUNHA, FUTURE GUIDE TO "CORDEL" IN BAHIA

First Encounter with Carlos Cunha, Future Guide for "cordel" Research
in Bahia, Edilene Matos and the Artist Sinésio Alves

Carlos is someone I got along with very well, and when I left Bahia in 1981 I considered him a good friend (but other "más línguas" told me he was a "snake in the grass," "a bad dude"). I only know he treated me well, always. Like the "pícaro" Lazarillo de Tormes says in the famous novel at the end of the book when folks speak disparagingly of him and his "wife," he says (paraphrasing) "If there are negatives, so be it, but I don't want to either hear of them

136

or talk of them." The only sad note was that later on perhaps in 1985 there were times when I was in Salvador, had good talks with Carlos over the phone, but he would never show up for our planned get togethers, always offering excuses. The last time was 2005; others told me that he was in a depressed state and I was not the only one with similar treatment. But for years when he was Executive Director of the Academy of Letters of Bahia he always received me and treated me well. What do I know? I do know that it was Carlos who encouraged me to write directly to Jorge Amado and treat the question of the publication of my book on Cuíca de Santo Amaro at the Jorge Amado Foundation in Salvador, this when nothing else seemed to be working in regular channels. I did so, Jorge responded, and the book came out at the foundation in 1990!

Back to July of 1981. Carlos told me that "cordel" was a hobby and he had been "researching" the local scene for years, especially the case of Cuíca de Santo Amaro. He shared various documents with me, and I left the first draft of my study on Cuíca with him, the result of the initial research at the Casa de Rui in 1978 and be that as it may, it all came out well years later in 1990.

His stated reasons for not writing over Cuica: since Edilene was the director of the "Núcleo de Pesquisa da Literatura de Cordel," part of the FCEB, it would be considered a case of nepotism, and, besides, it would be very much looked down upon for a "poeta da vangarda" which Carlos was to a small extent, to "lower himself to deal with folk literature" in the milleau of "academic literature" of the period. Edilene, head of the Núcleo, was however preparing a book on "Cordel in Bahia" (Cunha did not tell me anything about that at the time but only later when indeed two small monographs she wrote came out on Cuíca. The fact is that it made no difference at all since the approach or "enfoque" was so different.) As I write this I can only recall the "viper pit" of the local literary scene described by Jorge Amado in "Tenda dos Milagres" – poets, novelists, publishers, women and love affairs, etc. and I felt like I was being dragged into a much less significant but equally poisonous scene in 1981. Cunha did say after seeing my manuscript on Cuíca, "How is it possible for a foreigner to come up with this stuff?"

Changing the subject, he said my book on Jorge Amado and the "cordel" would be ready in September and I should come for the autograph party. We shall see.

For the past five years or so Carlos had been working in the publishing of "literary supplements" for the newspapers in Bahia. As I said before he would be the principal source, my guide on "cordel" in Bahia treating both Cuíca and Rodolfo Coelho Cavalcante. He repeated, "It is incredible that a North American can come here and teach US about Cuíca; you have more story-poems on Cuíca in your study than even I know of!" He counseled me in 1981 to not mess with the manuscript and that certainly the FCEB would want to publish it. This was in 1981; in 1984 I was still waiting.

For better or worse, Cunha gave me the typed original of Rodolfo Coelho Cavalcante's auto-biography, a document which would be priceless for my future book on the poet. Seems like a good turn to me.

More about Carlos. He is auto-didactic, from Propriá, Sergipe. He tried life in Rio and it did not work out, then in Recife and finally in Salvador. Without a university degree, this definitely hurts him in terms of salary and prestige. But he can't face returning to school (a decision Edilene can't accept). There is no doubt he is extremely intelligent with a pragmatic "street education" and "on the job training" in journalism. He deals with the principal writers and journalistic circles in Rio and São Paulo. He is a former director of the FCEB; he left that post and is now the head of publication. This is his second "marriage" as well as the same for Edilene (the two children are hers by the previous marriage). Carlos says the first marriage for both was with "bourgeoisie" folks and that he and Edilene are more emotionally linked to the intellectual, literary, poetic life.

He does not have a driver's license or drive, but he knows the old city like no one! I went on more than one outing with him, walking very rapidly, to several stops in the old downtown, picking up books sent to him from all parts of Brazil. He sells them to bookstores, second hand bookstores or trades them for others he really wants. His home library is amazing. He says he does not want a telephone in the house because it will "take away the calm" ("Vai tirar a calma"), but I was there when the new phone was installed, a major event. He could not seem to get off it. Oh, Edilene "corrects" his "Sergipano" Portuguese!

He was very nervous during the taped recording and interview I did with him on "cordel," an excellent interview by the way. He lives with the TV or radio at maximum volume, proof that he is very Brazilian indeed!

The Artist Sinésio Alves at Work

Sinésio Alves Working – Jorge Amado and Cuíca de Santo Amaro

Sinésio enters this story for several reasons, principal among them he was the cover illustrator for the "cordel" story-poems of Cuíca de Santo Amaro during most of Cuíca's career. I'll write more in Volume III of "It Happened in Brazil" when we get to the publishing of my book on Cuíca at the Jorge Amado Foundation finally in 1990 in Salvador. I met Sinésio in Carlos and Edilene's house in 1981 and we had some great moments.

Sinésio told of his friendship with Cuíca, the "way Cuíca carried on," the day-to-day process over the years of Cuíca writing a story-poem, rushing to Sinésio to do the cover illustration, always in an incredible hurry, taking the result to the printing shop and declaiming and selling the "folheto" in the streets the next day. Samples of these covers are in the background of the image of Edilene at the "Núcleo."

I recall the artist's retelling of their "daily" life together: the poet would arrive for their meeting, putting his hand in the pocket of Sinésio's shirt, taking out a "cruzeiro" bill or two, and saying "It's just a loan ole' buddy, I'll pay you tomorrow." The friendship allowed for such things. Sinésio like no one else knew details of the "scandalous" life of the poet and told many things. Some of the anecdotes would appear in my book in 1990. After Cuíca's death, Sinésio became known as a coveted artist for carnival decorations, and he even arrived to the point of decorating the President of Brazil's house, the Casa da Alvorada, for a carnival party in Brasília.

But he told some sad stories as well, but not with a sad face or demeanor. Now with certain stability in life as an artist, with a new car and a nice house, he told of one night when thieves got into his house, wrecked it and the car. (I remember he told all this very matter of factly, not emotionally at all). After our last encounter, to be told in the next book of this series, I never saw him again, but I maintain until this day, THIS is the person who deserved a book. I lament the fact I never had a chance to do it. For any old time researcher of Brazil linked to popular culture or folklore, Sinésio would be one of the salient personages of those times. But, small consolation, I have several caricatures that he did rapidly in Carlos Cunha's house on one of those occasions, including one of me and the poet Cuíca! Treasures guarded yet today.

THE "CORDEL" POETRY STAND OF THE "BRAZILIAN ORDER OF THE POETS OF THE 'LITERATURA DE CORDEL'" IN FRONT OF THE "MERCADO MODELO" - ALL CREATED BY RODOLFO COELHO CAVALCANTE

The "Cordel" Poetry Stand in Front of the "Mercado Modelo" in Salvador

The singer-poet ("cantador") Bule-Bule was there, and Rodolfo Júnior, oldest son of the poet. And then Rodolfo arrived, a very important person for me in the future. Cunha had warned me, the poet's thought process was "disperse," his thoughts and his speech confused. No matter; it was then that I met the poet I had been corresponding with since 1966, some fifteen years before. At that moment with the tremendous noise emanating from the inside and outside of the market, it was a shock just to try to understand his conversation. I might have gotten 25 per cent of what Rodolfo said. I left frustrated and disappointed, but things would improve in future encounters. There was more to the shock: Rodolfo had few remaining teeth, he was extraordinarily short (I should have known, he being a good "nordestino), he was "branco," poorly dressed, a frayed shirt, but wearing a suit and tie. He was an egotist fulfilling the image held by most. He was a beer drinker in spare moments at the market and thus the "disperse" talk indicated by Cunha. I got the idea Rodolfo divided the time between his duties at his poetry stand and frequent "beer breaks" inside the Market. By the way, he had a "cordel" poem at the time: "I Used to Drink, I Don't Drink Any More." I would be with him a lot the next few weeks.

THE ABPC CONGRESS

In those days of 1981 the Congress of the Brazilian Association for Scientific Progress was a huge event, important taking into account the atmosphere created by the military government in Brazil. I went with Carlos Cunha, my main guide during this stage of research in Brazil; the moment made me think of "Tenda dos Milagres" and the satire of Jorge Amado on the intellectual and literary atmosphere in Salvador. In the novel a writer-researcher from North America will make famous the book's protagonist Pedro Arcanjo when the latter is so unappreciated in his home turf of Salvador. It was just a thought.

The organization and the event are a "political phenomenon" – the only way people can participate in the political process under the present regime during the military dictatorship. I had never seen up to this point the so open appearance of the Left in Brazil, an openly Marxist approach. I also witnessed a manifestation of "black power," this for the first time in Brazil, and a sign of things to come, with a showing of the racial conflict and changes in the racial climate and politics to come in Salvador. Incidentally, there was a group representing the "cordel" of the times, the people from Juazeiro do Norte from the Typography formerly run by José Bernardo da Silva, and also with woodcuts by J. Borges.

I saw a lot of literature using the format of "cordel," but by students, totally politicized in regard to workers' rights. What is happening is that the students are "borrowing" the "cordel" format in their protest literature ("Literatura de Contestação"). The format is cheap to produce (mimeographed) and is a good way to take their political message to the poor, students and intellectuals, reflecting principally class struggle in Brazil.

ENCOUNTER WITH RODOLFO COELHO CAVALCANTE IN THE "MERCADO MODELO"

Encounter of the Author with Cordelian Poet Rodolfo Coelho
Cavalcante at the "Mercado Modelo" in Salvador

Rodolfo was drinking beer in the café in the rear of the ground floor of the Mercado and did not seem to be particularly alert. I took photos of Rodolfo with the "Gold Medal" he had just received from an organization of "trovadores" or middle class dilettante poets, the poet being extremely proud of the honor. Later Rodolfo was highly criticized by other true "cordel" poets asking "Where is the gold?" The poet, incensed and a bit righteous, responded, "What gold? Since when have you ever heard of a "cordel" poet with any gold? It's symbolic gold!" I bought some story-poems and we put the next Sunday on our calendar for my first in depth interview with the poet at his house in the proletarian district of "Liberade" in Salvador. Rodolfo reminded me to not forget the "present" ($). The interviews would be very important in the book I would eventually complete on the poet, ""A Presença de Rodolfo Coelho Cavalcante e a Moderna Literatura de Cordel," probably the result of one of the most serious research efforts on my part in Brazil and the most poorly distributed!

Later that day there was a long session with Carlos Cunha, really acting as an informant for my research on Rodolfo, detailing his entire history:

How Rodolfo was influenced by intellectuals outside the "milleau" of "cordel," by Kardec Spiritists, by the middle class "Intellectual Troubadours" of Luís Otávio, all resulting in a poetic language by Rodolfo unique in "cordel."

How Rodolfo constructed his "empire" and is in total control and command of it.

How Rodolfo came to be known and accepted and invited as a "professional troubadour" in the least expected social circles.

How Rodolfo feared the sharp tongue of Cuíca de Santo Amaro, his contemporary in "cordel" in Salvador, and did not want to compete with him.

An Aside. Cunha's attitude toward Rodolfo is very negative, but just the same he admires what the man has accomplished. He says that the entire city of Bahia will "be in mourning" when the poet dies because Rodolfo has an incredible notoriety in the city (The irony: Cunha's prediction came true with the poet in 1986 and the emotional outpouring of the "Povo" and the intellectuals at his funeral).

How Rodolfo organized his most recent entity, "A Ordem Brasileira de Poetas da Literatura de Cordel" and how he operates as its "benevolent dictator." He names the officers and launches new poets. He in fact is the "empresário" in a dynasty that he personally created.

Another Aside. Rodolfo wants me to write down my name and how it might rhyme in Portuguese; he is planning another of his "homages", his way of earning money. I'm happy to donate money but want nothing to do with his "homages."

How Rodolfo is very confused these days, in part due to his drinking. How he mixes up "facts" in one interview and changes them in the next, so that it is practically impossible to interview him. I do believe I overcame this in several taped interviews at his modest house in Liberade, almost all taking place in the a.m. and with no drinking whatsoever; see the aforementioned book by Nova Fronteira in 1987 through the help of Orígenes Lessa.

GUIDO GUERRA – WRITER AND PERSONAGE IN BAHIA

Guido was very well known as a short story writer and novelist in Bahia. He has the reputation of being something of a literary "gadfly," in the style of Mencken, and is also a bit of a rogue in the picaresque tradition. Biting tongue, biting humor! He suffered from a sickness; I never got the name for it but I know his was a constant battle to get the funds for the high priced medicines. My own image of him was that of a "Literary Cuíca de Santo Amaro," quick to satirize events in the city. One needs to recall that even though a city of almost one million inhabitants at the time, Salvador had a smaller town atmosphere. All the intellectuals and artists know each other; there is lots of gossip and the tradition of the literary epigram ("epígrama") the four line stanza of high satire, continued in the city in the person of Guido. He seemed full of "malandragem" or "roguery;" a case in point was when he remembered and told of the poet Cuíca when the latter wrote a story-poem or threatened to write one of a journalist in a homosexual act (in Guido's vulgar but colorful expression, "deu a bunda") with a politician. The result: Cuíca was beaten up for his actions. Guerra seems to have scurrilous stories about everyone. He did have a bit of advice to me about my writings: get in touch with publishers in the south (Rio or São Paulo) that are bigger and more financially viable and forget about the "local" Cultural Foundation of the State of Bahia in Salvador. When I talked to Cunha about this, he not unexpectedly defended the Foundation saying that its publications do reach the major libraries and intellectuals. Personal interests? Could be. Due to some good fortune later on, I was able to enter into contact with the press of the University of São Paulo and Ateliê Editorial in the 1990s and it turned out well. Guerra's advice was correct.

REENCOUNTER WITH PORTUGUESE FRIENDS IN "A PORTUGUESA"

Reencounter with Portuguese Family at the "Portuguesa" Restaurant

Dona Miquelina in the Kitchen

For old times sake I found and went again to the old restaurant "A Portuguesa" on Avenida 7 de Setembro near Piedade Plaza from the old days of 1966 in Salvador. The restaurant is now located where the old boarding house was in 1966. The owners were the same, Dona Carminha Bastos, her daughter Miquelina and her husband Dom Amândio (their beautiful daughter Conceição whom we all had a crush on in 1966 is 27 years old, married with three children. She married Hélio one of the young Portuguese immigrant-businessmen who were in the restaurant in 1966 and dealing in textiles in the lower city.) The Bastos were surprised to see me but did remember me and gave me a warm welcome. They were impressed in my improvement in Portuguese since 1966; perhaps it had improved a tad.

The original restaurant to the side of Barra Beach (an excellent location) was rented; the property was sold even though Carminha had a lease for five more years. The owners were forced to give her in exchange for giving up the restaurant location an apartment in the same building. So that is when the Bastos converted the old boarding house on Avenida 7 into the new restaurant. And Amândio no longer has his gas stations. What did not change were the menu and the tasty food: delicious soup, beans, rice with meat in it, potatoes, chicken, a mug of Portuguese wine, fruit salad for dessert and wonderful "cafezinho." My bad luck – they leave tomorrow for two months in Portugal, the annual vacation, and will close the restaurant for that time. They will only be back in October.

A GREAT MOMENT – JORGE AMADO'S BAHIA IN THE "MERCADO MODELO"

Young Waitresses at the Old "Camaféu de Oxossí" Restaurant in the "Mercado Modelo"

I had a nice conversation with Camaféu de Oxossi, a very black man with his accustomed large straw hat, owner of the restaurant on the top floor of the market with a veranda overlooking the bay. He had been a minor character in many of Jorge Amado's novels and actually one of the narrators of "Teresa Batista Cansada de Guerra." I was drinking beer with him and Rodolfo Coelho Cavalcante, the two well known "popular characters" ("tipos populares") of Bahia

149

of that time. It seemed like Camaféu and Rodolfo were trying to outdo each other in telling the best stories from the old days or perhaps the best lies to impress the "gringo." I just wish I could recall them (unhappily there are no notes). It was truly an unforgettable moment, this due to their importance in the popular and folk scene of Salvador at that time. Both soon would be gone and a bit of Bahian popular life with them! Today in 2015 as I write this, I marvel at the good fortune that I had over the years just being in "the mere presence" of these important figures of popular life in Bahia.

MR. FERRO, ENCYCLOPEDIA SALESMAN AND TEACHER OF ENGLISH GIVING CLASSES TO THE GOVERNOR'S WIFE

Mr. Ferro in front of "A Portuguesa," Barra Beach, Salvador

He was a good ole' boy and our acquaintance goes back to 1966 and the boarding house restaurant "A Portuguesa." He was the epitome of the Portuguese gentleman, born in the old country and a migrant to Brazil. He is currently giving English lessons to the governor's wife.

I confess however that when he spoke English to me I did not get one word! Perhaps it was my hearing. It was common in those days to hear this complaint from Brazilians: the professors of English themselves can't speak the language! What do I know? I only know that the "business" of teaching English was beginning to boom in those days, witness the English Institutes like Yazigi or IBEU ("Instituto Brasil – Estados Unidos") and many others charging a healthy fee for their services. Knowing a little English automatically offered a raise at work or in many cases the job itself. I have told, and it bears repeating, that in 1966 in northeastern and northern Brazil with air lines like Varig, Paraense, Cruzeiro and others flying old D C – 3s, a third class cheaper ticket into the interior, a prospective young male flight attendant knowing a bit of English was in demand. Not intended to be a criticism, just a comment, the old jalopy airplanes still did pre -flight announcements in Portuguese and English and maybe even French, a bit "over the top" for the times. I never understood a word of the English.

DINNER AT THE HOME OF CARLOS AND EDILENE AND CUNHA'S "SILVER TONGUE"

Carlos spoke of the lack of researchers, or at the least serious researchers, on popular or folk culture in Bahia. He says my book on Jorge Amado will impress the local intellectuals, and beyond that, the coming book on Cuíca de Santo Amaro. He insisted that I send the completed manuscript on Cuíca to him by February of 1982. I did it and now we are in August of 1984, and "nothing!" Be it flattery, be it sincerity, Cunha did possess that "silver tongue," as we say in English, and the talent to make anyone feel extra good about themselves! I know because I saw him in action with the poet Rodolfo and others, myself included. Be that as it may …

MEETING THE WIDOW OF CUÍCA DE SANTO AMARO – THE POPULAR POET OF "CORDEL" AND CORDELIAN "HELL'S MOUTH" (CURRAN'S TERM) OF BAHIA

Maria do Carmo Widow of "Cordel" Poet Cuíca de Santo
Amaro at the Door of Her House in Liberdade

As mentioned, this phase of research combined further research on Rodolfo Coelho Cavalcante and on Cuíca; I would eventually publish books on both of them. Cunha took me one day to a very poor working man's district in Salvador where I met Dona Maria do Carmo and did a short interview with her (along with the "present" I gave her, some badly needed and much appreciated cash). See the photos and the interview in the book on Cuíca by the Jorge Amado Foundation in Salvador. The house was very poor in a proletarian sector of the city; the widow survived by doing laundry to bring in a little money. Her comments are in the book (to be treated in Volume III of "It Happened.") There are several grandchildren, many small children wandering about the house and street in front; the family seems to be living on the edge of misery. Carlos visits frequently, always bringing presents: clothing, food, etc. All Dona Maria's comments on her deceased husband will appear in my book "Cuíca de Santo Amaro – Poet Reporter of Bahia."

The Cemetery and a "Pauper's Grave" Like That of Cuíca de Santo Amaro

THE CEMETERY AND THE "COMMON GRAVE" OF CUÍCA

Cunha took me to this part of the cemetery; a "pauper's grave" being the final resting place of the poorest of the poor of Bahia. Cuíca de Santo Amaro was buried in one of them. But as is the custom in Bahia, a large entourage of citizens, politicians, journalists, and probably a few enemies accompanied his funeral procession.

LAST DAY IN BAHIA, JULY, 1981

I was once again with Mário and Laís Barros and there was a delicious shrimp dinner in Itapuã. Good friends, they always treated me well over all those years. Thank you. And thank you again.

I left Salvador with mixed feelings, but on the whole feeling good about it all, this due to the certainty that the book on Jorge Amado and the "cordel" was truly set to come out, and during the Commemoration of 50 Years of Literature of Jorge Amado in November (it really happened, one of high points in my career).

And I left with the promise from Cunha that the book on Cuíca would come out at the Cultural Foundation of the State of Bahia, but it ended right there, a promise! It would only be resolved years later. And I left with new material on Rodolfo Coelho Cavalcante, the manuscript not yet written, but well in progess. And with good feelings of friendship with the Barros, and with Carlos and Edilene. It was a great success, I thought then, of that time.

THE RETURN TO RECIFE – MEETING MÁRIO SOUTO MAIOR

An Encounter with Mário Souto Maior

Mário was one of the intellectual "heavyweights" in Recife at the time. He was a specialist on northeastern culture for years as a researcher of the team at the Instituto Joaquim Nabuco de Ciências Sociais (years later it was converted into a "Foundation"). One might recall that the Institute was founded by Gilberto Freyre of "Casa Grande e Senzala" ("The Masters and the Slaves") fame. Mário therefore had many possibilities for publishing his work (many books), the most recent being "The Dictionary of the Swear Word." He is a big fan of "Ham Radio" and communicates with the world. He has a copy of my old book "A Literatura de Cordel" from 1973, now a "rare book." I believe he did enjoy finally meeting me and it was certainly mutual! He was one organized intellectual with files on 300 intellectuals in Brazil and the world with whom he corresponds! He may write the preface for my new book at the UFEPE. Ha ha.

SOCIAL LIFE WITH FLÁVIO VELOSO

Flávio Veloso in Olinda

Flávio and Fiancée Alice in the Patio of the "Chapel of Gold," Recife

It was wonderful to be reunited with Flávio who had helped me out so much in my first tenure in Pernambuco in 1966. This time I actually played the role of "chaperone" as incredible as that might sound in 1981. His fiancée Alice was twenty-one years old and could only go out with Flávio with "accompanyment." Parents' rules! We went to the Hotel 4 Rodas in Olinda to the "Bar Piano Lounge" and later to the "Trago Violão" in Boa Viagem; the atmosphere was decidedly not northeastern – the music was calm, quiet, and the places were expensive. The new good news is Flávio and Alice have set a date for the wedding!

On another occasion Flávio took me to see his new apartment in Olinda. The building faces the beach; his apartment has four bed rooms, two large living rooms, three baths, and rooms for maids. There is a varanda up on top with a view of the beach and ocean which is impressive. I recall seeing "jangadas" and "wind surfers" in the surf that day. He has three slots in the underground garage for two cars and a small boat.

Later we went to see one of the truly beautiful historic sights of Recife – "A Capela de Ouro" ("The Golden Chapel") in the old city center.

Paintings on the Ceiling, the Chapel of Gold

The Suffering Christ, the Chapel of Gold, Recife

AN ADVENTURE AND "MISADVENTURE" IN JOÃO PESSOA

Flávio was going on business to a sugar cane plantation in the area and I tagged along, he leaving me at the Federal University of Paraíba (UFPB) where I could consult the Library of Popular Literature in Verse ("A Biblioteca de Literatura Popular em Verso:"). On the trip I saw once again the undulating hills of sugar cane on the huge plantations between Recife and João Pessoa, land that I had seen when I traveled by bus in 1966 and 1967.

The "Library of Literature in Popular Verse" was excellent; I saw the entire list of holdings as well as a copy of the same of the collection of the University of São Paulo (which I would consult in person a few years later) and in addition, that of the University of Lisbon. The director was Neuma Francisca Borges, friend and research colleague since 1970 and a later congress at UCLA (I had not recalled but evidently I had suggested her name to Professor E. Bradford Burns as a prominent researcher and was thus indirectly "responsible" for her invitation to the same, a good thing for her.) Neuma did not forget; she returned the favor twice, the last time a congress on "Cordel" in 2005. Sadly, Neuma passed on a little later, and I on the occasion was feeling very alone because this was just one more of the old friends and research colleagues of "cordel" that disappeared over the years. As a matter of fact, Neuma was ill in that time before my arrival in 1981 – ulcers, forty days of bed rest and a milk diet of twenty days!

The big new event at the Library during my visit was the "Dicionário de Poetas Populares e Poetas de Bancada" by Átila de Almeida and João Sobrinho, yet today a major work on the "cordel." I would only get a copy years later, but from the hands of the author. I forget as well, I wrote a review of the book for the literary magazine "Chásqui" and somehow the authors in Brazil saw it and thanked me profusely. "What goes around, comes around" we say – I should have been one of the believers ("adeptos") of Kardec Spiritism and its motto, the same but in finer words. At any rate I was able to get some important story-poems for my future book at the University of São Paulo, "História do Brasil em Cordel," especially over Lula and Collor de Mello in their campaign for the presidency.

That is when the adventure began. The library closed for the day, but I had agreed with Flávio to pick me up there that afternoon. But day turned to night and I was left absolutely alone in front of the library waiting in the dark. It was located on the outskirts of the city. No one, but no one was around and I must have waited two hours. It was a bit scary. No sign of Flávio so I walked to the street, then the highway, flagged down a car and hitchhiked to the inter-urban bus station in downtown João Pessoa. I was actually climbing the steps to the bus for Recife when Flávio showed up and he was quite upset I had not waited at the university! No apologies on my part were in order. Alone in that darkness, the "gringo" on their turf, I was as the thieves say, "filet mignon." Fortunately we both got over it.

AN OUTING TO GRAVATÁ TO
THE WEST OF RECIFE

Outing to Gravatá and the Pitú Distillery

I accompanied Flávio and Alice on a trip of one hour and a half by car to the west of Recife to Gravatá, beyond Vitória de Santo Antão, and later, after the sugar cane zone, now in the "agreste" or pasture zone, a land with many hills and dryer. One of the major sights along the way was the huge distillery of "Pitu," perhaps the sugar cane rum ("cachaça") most famous of the Northeast with memorable outdoors advertising – a huge green bottle with the "Pitu" on its side.

Gravatá is known, being a very dry climate, as an old place for the tuberculosis sanatariums, this in past days. It now has country bungalos for city dwellers of Recife wanting to get away from the noise and traffic of the city for the weekend. We went to a "pool party," in effect a goodby party for the consul from Czechoslovakia after five years of service in Brazil. Czechoslovakia sends heavy equipment and machinery to Brazil in exchange for prime material, i.e. agricultural goods. An Aside: the family that was so good to me in Rio de Janeiro in 1967, the Ferro Costas, had connections to concrete factories in Belém do Pará with dealt with Czechoslovakia as well. The consular territory is the north and northeast of Brazil. He seemed to be a nice fellow, "a nice commie" I wrote. Duty includes a luxury automobile and he will move to another post in Latin America.

The party was at the vacation home of Antônio Azevedo, a garrulous type who tells lots of jokes, a sort of "life" of the party. He told jokes about the U.S. and of the recently fired General Golberry, the chief of staff for the military regime for the last seven years, the " man behind the president," a very powerful personage. In 1980 Golberry had declared himself to be in favor of the political "opening," but with recent events folks are now fearful that the political "opening," so desired after all the years of dictatorship, may be delayed or not happen at all. There were many jokes about him and as they say in Brazil, "a política estava fervendo" ("Politics are boiling over"). There are promises now for the future election of a president, but only an "Indirect" election and to be arranged for 1984. Later President Figueireido said "no" for 1984. To be continued!

REENCOUNTER WITH ARIANO SUASSUNA

Reencounter with Ariano Suassuna

I believe our last time together was in 1970! Anyway, I found myself in the home of the famous writer and intellectual, a house replete with tropical gardens, the entire front façade in blue Portuguese style tiles. The living room was an "art museum:" a weaving by Ariano himself with its design based on his novel "Rock of the Kingdom" ("A Pedra do Reino"). We had a very pleasant conversation – he seemed genuinely happy to meet me again (my contact with his sister Selma in Tempe and the lunch at Keah and my house in Tempe did not hurt). For years Ariano has been writing a column in the "Diário de Pernambuco" I think the oldest newspaper in all Brazil. He says he is ready to stop that activity now; he is not writing any new works of literature and says he is simply tired! He spoke of the "Movimento Armorial" created by him in 1970, a literary-artistic movement now faded away, but which lasted for ten years. Ariano says its objective was to continue the movement of Tobias Barreto in the northeast - Recife in 1870. The musicians in one of its best known facets, the Quinteto Armorial, had moved on to João Pessoa in 1977 and then folded.

He told me that my small book of 1973 was now a basic book for anyone who wanted to know about the "Literatura de Cordel." He says he has read the second edition (the manuscript I sent to the UFEPE press at his suggestion) and really enjoyed the interviews with poets and publishers therein and that Moacir Dantas is indeed going to publish it. This was ironic in 1981; it never happened.

Ariano's family has grown up; the children are now in university or graduated. Ariano has lost some hair and his hair is turning grey now in the neighborhood of fifty years old. He teaches cultural history in the graduate program of the UFEPE and enjoys relating erudite classic literature to popular culture. It would be about this time or a little later that Ariano invented his "aulas-relâmpago" which made hime famous via television throughout all Brazil.

He donated his personal collection of the "literatura de cordel" to the University, and "It looks like it has disappeared." He seems thoroughly disgusted in regard to this latter matter, and he should be. Ariano is truly disillusioned in regard to the collection. He believes, now, he should have just kept it at home. (This author ponders now in 2015 a similar decision.)

By the way, the novel "O Romance da Pedra do Reino" has just been translated to German and Ariano is happy about that.

MEETING MARK DINEEN – WHAT'S NEW IN "CORDEL" AND THE RESEARCHERS

Mark was originally from London and Oxford and would become one of the quality researchers with books on the "cordel." I note that it was he who made contact with the older fellow, in this case, me! Friendly and a pleasant sort, Mark was researching the "cordel" now in 1981, along with the Northeast and the "Movimento Armorial." His news and hints are as follows:

He met Átila de Almeida in Paraíba (I had not met Átila at this time) saying that the Paraíban owned a collection of some 7000 story-poems of "cordel" which in the future would be one of the most important collections in Brazil. This all happened after his death with the collection being donated to the Regional University of the Northeast in Campina Grande, Paraíba, where I would see it in 2005. I should note that I met Átila later on a very short research trip to Campina, enjoyed great rapport and conversation with him in his home, perused very rapidly his extensive collection and was allowed to take some 20 or 30 important story-poems to my hotel which I copied, hand written notes, spending most of that night, and returned the following day. Átila did make good on a promise, Xeroxing said "folhetos" and mailing them to me later. They became an important part of my future book "História do Brasil em Cordel" by the USP in 1998.

More news from Mark. Candace Slater is now in Juazeiro do Norte, Ceará, doing the field research for her future book on Father Cícero, a book I would review for an academic journal in the U.S., another of her "masterpieces." Idelette Mozart is in Paris and has finished a huge dissertation of two volumes on the "Movimento Armorial." Franklin Maxado is in São Paulo, living precariously from the "cordel" with a tiny shop and apartment in that city. Abraão Batista is a professor and does "cordel" in Juazeiro do Norte. Pedro Bandeira is a businessman in Juazeiro, a "shaker and mover" amongst the singer-poets there.

Mark believes there are two modalities of "cordel": the traditionalists like Rodolfo Coelho Cavalcante, Manoel Camilo dos Santos, etc. and the new wave like Franklin Machado, Abraão

Batista and J. Borges. He says that the new ones are more "commercialized," less "pure" in regard to rural roots. I don't know if I agree with this, particularly in regard to Abraão Batista or J. Borges. Mark believes that the link between "cordel" and erudite literature comes from way back – at the least from erudite writers Mário de Andrade in the 1920s and before that with José de Alencar and Franklin Távora in the 19ᵗʰ century. (I must add that I had written of all this previously.) Mark spoke of the "Casa de São Saruê" in Rio, the "private" museum of Umberto Peregrino (whom I would meet a few years later). He is a retired general with connections to the present military regime. He is a "force" in Rio in 1981. Mark and I would remain in contact, trading letters over the years.

The "Bolt of Lightning" News Item in the "Diário de Pernambuco", August 9, 1981

Ariano Suassuna announces that he is abandoning literature! It was a "bomba" in Brazil. Disillusioned and saying he "needs to rest." It turns out that I was with Ariano the preceding evening at his house in Recife, the night before the "bomb" and he had spoken of this in our conversation.

ONCE AGAIN, THE FRIENDSHIP
WITH FLÁVIO VELOSO

I passed the last night in Recife at a nice dinner at the Veloso's house – "churrasco de bife de boi, arroz, batata frita, cebola, cerveja," and that night as well Dona Dodó's Shrimp Soufflé (a creation of the maid and cook from my days way back in 1966). By chance there was a funny link to Arizona: the family dog's name was "Apache." Later on an outing Flávio took me to Brasília Teimosa, the worst "mocambo" or "favela" in Recife, this in order to get to the "Yacht Club" of Recife which is located on a sea arm which follows the coast up to the port of Recife.

Finally …

I had been busy in Recife; it was a good stay and I saw lots of old friends. I made the contacts that I had planned, except with the poet Marcos Accioly, the head of the UFEPE, and the folklorist Liedo Maranhão, but not without trying. This would have to wait, and I would have to wait to see how Moacir Dantas at the press and the UFEPE would treat me in regard to a second edition of "A Literatura de Cordel," my first book in Brazil. I did everything I could and it would not turn out well. Psychologically that was difficult, but on my departure, the world seemed rosy and with lots of possibilities.

THE RETURN TO RIO DE JANEIRO, AUGUST 10, 1981

There was an encounter with the folklorist Théo Brandão at the José Olympio bookstore in Rio. This publisher at that time was still the best in all Brazil for the literary works of the Northeast, the publisher of the novels of José Lins do Rego and the poetry of Manuel Bandeira. So I met Théo again, the first time had been at that congress in Niterói in 1973. Now rather aged, he was still researching and writing; he is doing a Brazilian version of the Stith Thompson Index, famous in world folklore. He seemed happy to see me; I noticed that on this trip it was the case with many of the writers with whom I came in contact; I was beginning to carve out a "niche" in my research area.

MEETING IVAN CAVALCANTI PROENÇA, SON OF MANUEL CAVALCANTI PROENÇA, RESEARCH ADVISER IN 1966

Ivan knew of me via Dr. Doris Turner my professor of Lusitanian and Brazilian Literature at Saint Louis University in the 1960s. He was quite interested in my study on João Guimarães Rosa's "Grande Sertão: Veredas" and the "Literatura de Cordel." I took the manuscript to him and the plan was: he would read it, make a decision, take it to the editorial council of the publisher, in twenty days they would make a decision, and the contract would be signed with me receiving ten per cent of the published copies. Nice and tidy! He also wanted me to send him the study in Pernambuco (the possible second edition of the 1973 book) in case it did not come out there. He asked for a biographical note for the leaf of the book. If all this had taken place around that time in 1981, it would have opened many doors in Brazil. None of it happened, another unfulfilled promise and I never really discovered why.

There would be another encounter with Ivan years later and much happier. At his apartment in Flamengo we talked of Jazz from New Orleans and his love of this music. He allowed me to peruse his "cordel" collection, and I took a few notes on the few that I had not seen before for the future book "História do Brasil em Cordel."

THE RETURN TO THE U.S.

I returned with high hopes for the future professional life – the book on "cordel" promised in Pernambuco by the end of 1981, the book on Jorge Amado in Bahia, this one for certain the end of 1981, the promise of future publication of the book on Cúica de Santo Amaro in Salvador, and the promise of publication of João Guimarães Rosa and "Cordel" at José Olympio Publishing House. Fantastic! So with all this grist in the mill I decided that fall to apply for promotion to the rank of Full Professor ("Catedrático") at ASU, all in good faith. Well, the book on Jorge Amado came out in November of 1981. I sent the manuscript of the book on Cúica de Santo Amaro in 1982, but nothing happened. Pernambuco reneged on the second volume of "A Literatura de Cordel" and José Olympio as well. I did get the promotion but that "starry" promised future would be a few years coming.

BRAZIL, NOVEMBER, 1981 – THE COMMEMORATION OF FIFTY YEARS OF LITERATURE OF JORGE AMADO" AND THE PUBLICATION OF THE BOOK "JORGE AMADO E A LITERATURA DE CORDEL" – A GREAT MOMENT IN MY PROFESSIONAL CAREER

INTRODUCTION

The reader will have to pardon me in these personal notes. This was something that happens seldom in one's life, at least in mine. This was a very special trip. They are celebrating in Salvador ("the city of the festivals" – they know how to give a party) the "50 Years of Literature of Jorge Amado," at that time Brazil's best known and best selling author within and outside of Brazil. The sponsor is the Cultural Foundation of the State of Bahia. My modest book, "Jorge Amado e a Literatura de Cordel" is slated to come out during the celebration, the only such book chosen. It was a big moment in professional life.

HOW IT HAPPENED

The book was a sabbatical project in 1975. In order to do it one needed a broad understanding of the "literatura de cordel" plus a vast reading of the works of Jorge Amado, nearly twenty novels at the time. It required little research aside from this, but produced a unique "reading" and "approach" to his works. I had sent the manuscript to the Casa de Ruy Barbosa in 1976; it was quickly accepted for publication, the Portuguese corrected by Adriano da Gama Kury, and then "put in the drawer" ("engavetado") until this event. Edilene Matos, one of the planners for the Event, was desperately combing the archives and catalogues for a book related to the event, saw the title listed in the "forthcoming" catalogue of the CRB and negotiated an agreement for co-publishing. In the end, it was lucky for me, but in my defense was the result of long persistence in my work.

THE FLIGHT

I arrived quickly enough in Los Angeles from Phoenix for the international flight but there was a delay of two hours and a half due to air traffic at the huge airport in Mexico City. We ate dinner once again in the plane on the tarmac of LA International. All proceeded smoothly to Brazil and Rio where I got the "green light" at customs in the Galeão, but even then almost missing the flight to Salvador. I was rewarded on my ride on the "frescão" into the city with the beautiful "orla" or long series of white sand beaches outside the city, the beautiful green-blue sea, the tall palms but the hot and humid air arriving at the Grande Hotel da Barra where I spent the first night.

The Cover of the Book "Jorge Amado e a Literatura de Cordel"

Old friends Carlos and Edilene met me at the hotel with a copy of the book in their hands. It is difficult to put my happiness into words. The light purple cover sported a woodcut by Calasans Neto (a famous artist in Bahia, illustrator of the books and good friend of Jorge Amado) done as I understand as a favor to his friend. Carlos already had sent invitations and announcements of the book everywhere in Brazil. November 6th will be the big day in front of the "Banca de Folhetos da Ordem de Rodolfo Coelho Cavalcante" in front of the Mercado Modelo and a few days later there will be the autograph party for my book in the Itaguemi Shopping Center (the newest and most luxurious in Salvador at that time). There have already been "notes" in the main Salvador paper "A Tarde;" Cunha is "doing his thing," this is exactly what he does in Bahia to make a living. A master of public relations!

Carlos and Edilene. Carlos is back to work at the Cultural Foundation of the State of Bahia directing the distribution of its books. Edilene had been through a down phase of sickness, but she is fine now with a new hair do and really pretty. Cunha now has shaved his moustache and is a bit heavier. Caroline's kids – Caroline has a broken tooth and Bruno has a new puppy dog, a Black Lab.

CARLOS CUNHA "IN HIS GROOVE"

He says my book "is solid, true and unpretentious" (the truth). It will have little to say to the literary theory people, but it is the first book to truly link Jorge Amado to the poetry of the masses. Cunha sys that Alfredo Machado of "Editora Record" in São Paulo (the publisher of all of Amado's books in Bazill) may perhaps be interested in doing a commercial edition of my book which should sell up to 30,000 copies! It never happened. He is hoping for a big crowd on the 6th. He says once again that the Cultural Foundation is ready to publish my book on Cuíca de Santo Amaro (in preparation). He says that others will use my book as a point of departure for studies on Jorge Amado.

So this indeed Cunha in action with the ole' "silver tongue, but for a farm boy from Kansas, I took it all in. What follows is the diary of the days of the Commemoration.

NOVEMBER 1.

I took photos of the Hotel da Barra and then moved to the Hotel Bahia do Sol (arranged for me by the Foundation for those days), had lunch in the near by Restaurante Itália, went for a walk in the old Parque Velha, and then took presents to Dona Hilda from the boarding apartment of July of 1981.

NOVEMBER 2

I was with Carlos, Edilene and the kids on an outing along the "orla" swimming on the beach and tasting the local Bahian favorite, the "acarajé." Later at their house I saw on television an interview with Jorge Amado in the garden of his house in Rio Vermelho. He wore a "Hawaian" style shirt, spoke of the Commemoration to come, of the "cordel" and the singer-poets in my book. He showed a copy of the book to the TV people saying "a North American Professor is coming for the autograph party." He said that it is a thesis translated from English (Jorge's mistake; I always wrote my original manuscripts in Portuguese but of course with corrections at the publisher). It turns out this interview appeared on national television. If you are familiar with "Tenda dos Milagres" ("The Miracle Shop") it might make you recall, just a tiny bit, the story of Levinson's time in Brazil. Well, not really. But it is a nice fantasy of mine!

It was an emotional moment for me because this was the first live interview I had ever seen of Jorge, even on television, and in one sense it was like being introduced to him after a reading of his works over a span of some fifteen years since 1966. He seemed very dignified to me now, around seventy years old, wonderful silver colored hair, and with very calm, "measured" speech. An Aside: Amado told me that Théo Brandão the reknowned Brazilian folklorist, an acquaintance and research colleague of mine, had died this last September.

That night in Cunha's house, Carlos had me sign a copy of the book for "July" the society columnist for "A Tarde." The point was to create more publicity for the book. Cunha is a master of such things and is really in his groove ("está na sua!").

Jorge Amado and the Author in Amado's Home in Amaralinha

DAY 3. WITH JORGE AMADO

I took a taxi to Jorge Amado's house, all this set up by Carlos Cunha. The house is some two blocks from the beach and is more or less in a calm neighborhood. The large wooden entry door is in the form of a wood carving by Calasans Neto in a tropical floral design. (I should have said to the reader that Jorge Amado's story is long, complicated and controversial. I daresay that Wikepedia will tell most of it.) So the door opened and I was introduced to Jorge, to his son João Jorge, to Jorge's famous wife Dona Zélia and to João Jorge's wife. From the very beginning I had an excellent impression of Zélia; she seemed friendly, hospitable, pleasant and a good "mãe de família." An Aside: One should see her own literary presence and also that as a fine photographer. I get a kick out of the irony of her best known book detailing family days and early days with Jorge, "Anarquists Thanks Be to God."

They were all in a flurry of activitiy, busy in the preparation of literally hundreds of copies of Jorge's novels and their many editions for the official catalogue of the Commemoration. But they gave me a lot of time and were extremely gracious and courtesous when they did not have to be! Jorge was dressed in a red short sleeved shirt, appeared a bit overweight, with a healthy head of silver colored hair, and appeared to be in his 60s. His appearance was "imponente." He was extremely tired, even exhausted with the work, he yawned several times, but excused himself due to the lack of sleep. (I surmise one "50 Years" celebration was enough!) They are all in the middle of preparation of an exhibition of his books in the Teatro Castro Alves.

Then came a dose of humility. He said he had read my book and liked it, but gave no details. Finally I just asked, "Did I get it right?" He said, "Yes you did."

He spoke of a letter I had written to him some time back that he received quite a bit later, forwarded to him in Portugal, and even then in the middle of a post office strike. He has an idea for a new novel but has little time to dedicate to it. He told stories, and Zélia chimed in, about Cuíca de Santo Amaro. He liked the poet even though he was a "chantagista" ("blackmailer") and "sencacionalista" ("sensationalist"). Zélia told of a time when Cuíca had denounced a book written about Bahia, but had praised Jorge's ("Bahia de Todos os Santos") no doubt because the poet appeared in it.

He seemed interested in my sabattical leave and asked many questions; I spoke of my previous work, of Doris Turner (who knew him), of my research on the book on Cuíca and plans for the book on Rodolfo (without realizing or knowing that Jorge would repeat much of the conversation in interviews for the press and television, thus my private plans for Cuíca and Rodolfo ended up "out there and known," not necessarily a good thing. They rob ideas in Brazil!) He liked my thesis on Rodolfo, agreeing of my view of Rodolfo as an "empresário" and "traditional moralist."

He spoke in great detail, very knowledgeable about "cordel" (especially in the years of the 1940s and 1950s) and the role of the Casa de Ruy Barbosa in collecting and publishing. I spoke of the "Núcleo," of Edilene and Carlos' good work. Amado is quite familiar with the history of the "cordel" woodcut artists as well, Minelvino Francisco Silva in Itabuna and the "cordel" in Pernambuco and Ceará.

We spoke of mutual friends: Manuel Cavalcante Proença, Théo Brandão and so forth. He said that there were requests for interviews with me, wanted my address and phone at the hotel, and he would them send them on to me (the boy from Kansas was not quite able to believe what he was hearing and from whom).

He invited me to the luncheon after the Commemoration at Camaféu de Oxossi's restaurant in the "Mercado Modelo." (Cunha has been repeating that my book is the only book to come out during the festivities.)

Smaller matters.

The Amados' have two small dogs, both "Pugs." They served me Scotch whiskey, "cafezinho" and cake! And we watched a videotape of the recent filming of the "telenovela" "Gabriela" with Sonia Braga. The encounter must have lasted an hour and a half, generous indeed, I don't think anything is going to "top" this experience!

DAY 3. THE BOOK IS READY

The book is ready and my copies are waiting for me at the Cultural Foundation of Bahia. Knowing that in Brazil one "strikes while the iron is hot," I took a taxi there and picked up my share (or a good part of it), one hundred copies! (I would pack them all home in the suitcases from Arizona). And I took them all to the hotel. Afterwards I went with Cunha to the "Livraria Civilização Brasileira" and met its owner Dmeval Chaves; it was he would sponsor and organize the "lançamento" of the book. The price is set at a modest 300 cruzeiros.

Rodolfo Coelho Cavalcante in front of the "Mercado Modelo" with the
Banner "Thanks to Jorge Amado" ("Gratos a Jorge Amado")

I went to the "cordel stand, the "Banca dos Trovadores", in front of the Mercado Modelo for
an important meeting with Rodolfo and Carlos Cunha. I witnessed "the master" preparing the
scene: how he speaks very calmly and carefully to Rodolfo because the latter "anda confuso."
He gently orders Rodolfo to arrange for a big cake to present to Jorge in the name of all the
"troubadors," and suggests to the old folk poet to sing "Happy Birthday to You" ("Parabens
p'ra você") and present the cake to him. Cunha explains that the singer-poets ("cantadores")
present should improvise verse about "Gabriela" and not the mayor or the governor! And he
tells Rodolfo to prepare a speech, write it down, nothing improvised on the moment, and no
"foolishness." Rodolfo loved hearing it all, being in the middle of everything, the flattery, the
moment, of being important. It really is a sight to see Cunha in action; Rodolfo's eyes shone
with excitement envisioning all the possibilities. Really, he had not realized before this moment
the importance and "grandeur" of the Commemoration inSalvador.

An Aside: News of the Moment. Rodolfo has a new invention: "The Club of the Troubadors
of Rhyme," returning one more time to those folks – the middle class "troubadour" poets of
Brazil not related in the slightest to "cordel." Cunha asks Rodolfo to make up another of his
many "diplomas" (he used them to garner donations and support for his myriad activities at
the time) and name it and give it in honor to Zélia Amado as "Godmother of the Troubadors"
("Madrinha dos Trovadores"). Cunha really is a master of public relations; he would be a great
success at the right time and place in the U.S.! He was asked to do a Literary Supplement for

the occasion, but realizing he could not get the major voices of literary criticism to "come aboard" (he did not explain the reason, but Jorge Amado was never accepted by the "crème" of the "litterati" in Brazil, this in spite of his huge national and international success, a long story with several threads) refused the task. Cunha says he has never had a "9 to 5, 40 hour a week job," and never needed it; he has always done just fine through free-lancing. After the Commemoration he will return to the Cultural Foundation of Bahia as "publishing chief" ("chefe de editoração") with his main task the marketing and distributing of its books.

Carlos Cunha also is a poet, of the "modern" wave and really directs "the book situation in Bahia." He shared some of his ideas on literature and literary criticism; he is against the "formalism" of the moment and believes there should be a "Brazilian model." He does not understand certain aspects of Edilene's work and sees the university as a "deformation" of the Student of Letters, this due to the currently accepted version of literary criticism. He is fearful that Edilene will end up right in the middle of "this fad". She did to some extent, perhaps as a practical way to survive in academia, but always maintained her interest in the "literatura de cordel" of Bahia; her books are the proof.

THE SAME DAY. INTERVIEWS ONTV

I was called out of the blue to appear at the Foundation for an interview with Channel 7, TV Itapoan, and it ended up ten minutes in length. There was no time to get nervous, it all happened so quickly. I saw the interview later that day on television at Carlos and Edilene's house; it appeared on national TV as well. To speak honestly, my Portuguese was pretty good with only one error to note: instead of "dívida para com o povo" I said "dúvida para com o povo." Uh oh. But I think most folks took it in stride. Tomorrow there is supposed to be a "collective interview" for the Bahian press at the Foundation. It all seems surreal to me right now.

The Author and Geraldo Mayrink, Reporter from "Isto É"

THE SAME DAY IN THE P.M.: THE REPORTER FROM "ISTO É"

Back in the hotel room I received a call from the journalist-reporter from "Isto É," a national news magazine a bit like "Time" or "Newsweek" in the U.S. The reporter was on special assignment in Bahia to cover the commemoration. The call was due to Jorge Amado's suggestion himself! Alone in my hotel room, the phone rang and "Alô, é Geraldo Mayrink quem fala da "Isto É" querendo entrevista." I only knew vaguely of the magazine, my error, and ran out to the street to buy the latest copy at a newsstand and have a quick look at it. My feelings at that moment were of surprise, feeling very flattered, and also thinking it all a bit funny. "I can't believe that everything is happening and if it's all serious and not just a joke or trick." I thought, "Soon I'll be back at ASU in the office and classroom, normal day to day life, but let's live the moment, a little like Segismundo in "La Vida Es Sueño" when he struggles with reality and dreams and says "But while we live, let us dream" or something like that."

The interviewer and journalist Geraldo Mayrink is a true professional and good at what he does. He arrived with the photographer, both on assignment in Bahia to cover the big event. Here is how it went: Mayrink, the good reporter, is quite calm and methodical, and the photographer is snapping photos the entire time. It all came out as planned. The cover and principal article of "Isto É" that week was the "Commemoration of 50 Years of Literature of Jorge Amado with a picture of Jorge taking up the entire cover. Yours truly appeared later in the article with a photo and a half page of text from the interview, incidentally sharing the page with a photo and note on Bahia's famous governor and "shaker and mover" in the region Antônio Carlos Magalhães.

I can say I gave a good interview during about thirty minutes of questioning. I spoke of Jorge Amado, my own up-bringing and background and interests in Brazil, Portuguese and Brazilian literature, of the "Núcleo," Rodolfo Coelho Cavalcante and his poetry stand in front of the Mercado Modelo, of my interest and research on Cúica de Santo Amaro and a possible approach to him, but especially of the character and generosity of Jorge himself. I noted the considerable time he had spent with me, the generosity of sending reporters from TV and the press my way and his opinion on my modest book.

Mayrink's comments after the interview were revealing: the whole thing of relating "cordel" to Jorge's books was all new to him, but he was happy to meet me and learn of my work and the importance of the "Literatura de Cordel." He appreciated my approach and point of view. An Aside during the Interview: Mayrink mentioned that no less than Mário Vargas Llosa would be in Bahia representing the media from Peru for the commemoration. Wow!

I wrote in the diary: "I may be hard to live with after this." The "high" lasted just a short time because that night I found myself alone for dinner at the hotel. I came down to earth in a hurry! Why? I think because there was no one to share it with. So I spent the evening writing all these notes I've just written, and that Keah and I would share later in Arizona.

Encounter with the Artist Sinésio Alves at Carlos and Edilene's House

Sinésio Alves and the Mockup of Cuíca de Santo Amaro

There was another meeting with Sinésio; the image shows him and the cardboard mockup of the "cordel" poet Cuíca de Santo Amaro to be seen years later in 1990 on the occasion of the autograph party for my book on the poet.

FINALLY SEEING THE MOVIE "TENDA DOS MILAGRES" BASED ON THE NOVEL OF THE SAME NAME BY JORGE AMADO

I saw the movie in the auditorium of the Cultural Foundation and it was a very emotional moment for me because I believe that it is Jorge Amado's most important novel, not necessarily his most entertaining, but the most important in the sense of thesis. I was able to catch very little of the Portuguese due to the horrible sound system; it was for an auditorium and not a movie theater. But I knew the novel so well that I could follow the film and truly appreciate it. It comes down to the fact that the totality of Jorge's novels and northeastern popular culture has been part of my life for so many years, maybe now a part of me. In one sense this is a consoling fact to a negative fact – the loneliness I felt so many times in these research trips without family and U.S. friends. I will enjoy it all when I get home to Arizona and realize what has happened. I am also realizing that this event and these days are something that may happen once in a lifetime; there is only one "50 Years of Jorge Amado's Literature" and only one book I'll ever do about him.

Philosophizing: looking at the past years I think I always remained faithful to a vision of what was possible for me being guided by I don't know what, but in the end coming out well.

Returning to the film: it had good color, good photography and followed closely the plot and many "flashbacks" in the novel. And it succeeded in showing Amado's thesis, misegination in Brazil. An aside: "cordel" did appear in the film, so my own thesis about it held up well.

ANTÔNIO "THE BARBER" IN THE "NÚCLEO DE PESQUISA DA LITERATURA DE CORDEL"

He says he has just read my book on Amado and literally gave me a big embrace, praising the effort, genuinely it seems. I have a short note from then to remind me of these moments when difficult times come. I remember well writing the book on Jorge at our house in Tempe, Arizona, in 1975; the words in Portuguese came easily. Could it be someone was helping at my side? The same thing has happened with almost all my other books up to now. Antônio is a humble person of humble class and means, uncomplicated; I find his opinion to be pure and genuine. And I'm proud of the moment.

AT THE "MERCADO MODELO" WITH RODOLFO COELHO CAVALCANTE

There was an unexpected encounter with Rodolfo Coelho Cavalcante and Camaféu de Oxossi. The latter is famous, a "popular type" in the Market, in Bahia, and is a long time friend of Jorge. He appears as a minor character in many of the novels and as one of the popular narrators in "Tereza Batista Cansada de Guerra" ("Teresa Batista Tired of War"). In his upper sixties (a guess), with the customary straw hat, he spoke of Cuíca and the "cordel," but with nothing new for me. Rodolfo was drinking some beer and was pretty "full of himself," introducing me to Camaféu as "my biographer." That did turn out to be true with the book in 1987 by Nova Fronteira, "A Presença de Rodolfo Coelho Cavalcante e a Moderna Literatura de Cordel." Rodolfo would like to visit the U.S.; it would be the height of his career. How I would love to accommodate him, but it just is not possible these days at A.S.U.

In these days I am a "regular" the Poetry Stand ("A Banca dos Poetas da Literatura de Cordel"); Rodolfo gives me copies of all the "diplomas" he is cranking out these days as a means of publicity for his own work and some donations as well. He read part of the speech that he is preparing for the Commemoration wanting some advice on the matter (I stayed clear of that!). He has just begun another of his self-promoting endeavors, the "Troubadours' Club of Bahia" and asked permission to put yours truly on the cover of the next month's edition listing me as "corresponding member from the U.S." I am familiar with his maneuvers, and begged off.

NOVEMBER 6ᵀᴴ: THE COMMEMORATION

Jorge Amado and the Commemoration

It was a memorable and beautiful day. I got a taxi to the lower city and went to the Market. Around the poetry stand there were flags, banners, tables with flowers and Rodolfo in all his glory! I spoke just a moment with him, not wanting in any way to distract or sidetrack him. I met a certain Mr. Salgueiro Antunes and his wife, he a veterinarian in Lisbon in charge of such matters at the International Airport. He invited me to stay at his home should I ever be in Lisbon. (I wondered, another example of Lusitanian-Brazilian hospitality? Or just being courteous?)

The Artist Calasans Neto at the "Mercado Modelo"

I met for the first time the artist Calasans Neto and his gracious wife Autran Rosa, recently returned from an exposition of his works in Washington, D.C. (he is also one of the narrators in "Teresa Batista") They are good friends with colleagues of mine in California – Nancy Baden and Ron Harmon from California State in Fullerton. Calasans was very open and genuine, saying he was afraid I might not like the cover of the book (quite to the contrary!)

The Researcher Edilene Matos with "Cordel" Poet Permínio
Válter Lírio and His Wife at the Commemoration

I met Permínio Válter Lírio a "cordel" poet from the years of Jorge Amado's novel "Jubiabá;" he will be honored spontaneously today by Jorge. Together from the steps of the poets' stand they will stand shoulder to shoulder, arm in arm, and in nostalgic solidarity sing "A Greve do Circular" ("The Strike of the Circular Trolley System") a protest song of the 1930s. Permínio came both before and was a contemporary to Cuíca. Edilene Matos has arranged their presence at the commemoration and is standing behind Permínio's wife, to the left.

Edilene Matos with Mario Vargas Llosa at the Commemoration

This was no small deal! The celebrated Peruvian novelist by a series of circumstances was in Brazil researching the War of Canudos (1896-1897) the war reported by the journalist Euclides da Cunha who later converted his field notes into "Os Sertões" ("Rebellion in the Backlands"), the book some say is Brazil's "best novel." Vargas Llosa was researching for a future novel "La Guerra del Fim del Mundo." Gossips say he robbed the entire plot; if you want to know the truth of it all you can find it in a future issue of "Veja" in 1984.

At any rate he was taking advantage of the time in Brazil performing the role of reporter from Peruvian television covering the Commemoration. A long time friend of Amado, his presence added much to the festivities. All this took place before he became a candidate for president of Peru, lost the election and went into "self-exile" in Spain to get over the experience. And some time later he was awarded the Nobel Prize for Literature. Like García Márquez in Colombia, he shared the glory. But unlike Carlos Fuentes in Mexico (a contemporary and also one of the "experimental novelists" of Latin America and Jorge Amado) – these did not. I always rooted for a Nobel Prize for Jorge, in fact for them both, and can only conjecture why Jorge never won. Never being the favorite of the "serious" literary critics, badmouthed for the "repetitiveness" and "commercialism" of his novels, and perhaps not "deep enough," Jorge had to content himself with several other interational awards. In a short conversation that time at his house, he said, paraphrasing, "You know they call me "just" a story-teller. It's not so easy telling these "stories." (I add: the telling of "Gabriela Clove or Cinnamon" or "Dona Flor" or "Tenda dos Milagres" or the other twenty or so other novels.)

Rodolfo Coelho Cavalcante Pronouncing His "Baroque" Speech at the Commemoration

Jorge Amado arrives and the media literally surrounds him; they seem like the famous "paparazzi" of the times. Rodolfo gave his long, involved and a bit turned upside down speech. I was occupied and preoccupied in taking photos of the moment. Rodolfo formally "called me to the table," that familiar rhetorical phrase of conferences and congresses in literary Brazil, calling me once again "my biographer" with the TV cameras rolling the whole time. I nodded hello and stepped back into the crowd. Later Jorge called me to sit in the front row, an excellent view of the festivities to come, able to hear the homages of the singer-poets to Jorge, his response to them and many improvised verses to follow.

Jorge Amado Listening to the Speeches and Improvised Verse of the Poet-Singers

Amado seemed truly moved by it all (I am sure I saw tears in his eyes). His speech could have come out of my book! He spoke of his cultural roots shared with the Bahian people and with the singer-poets. An Opinion: I believe there is still a footnote of social class in all this. There is still a large distance between the erudite and the folk-poplar. But whatever the case, Jorge Amado is still the son of a cacau plantation owner of the middle-upper class, in spite of his politics. I don't know if this is coming out right; in no way am I insinuating less than sincerity in his words. And you have to remember he ran away from the Jesuit Prep School in Bahia for such plantation owners' children, going on to live in at the time the rat trap of the old three - story building in the Pelourinho, and of course believing in and becoming an activist, at that time, in the Brazilian Communist Party. In simpler terms the major novelist of Brazil and international literary figure is not a folk-popular poet or singer of tales.

Jorge Amado Giving His Own Speech Thanking the People of Bahia

In the speech Amado thanked the "povo," the people, the poets, saying that much of what he has done (written) is a result of them and he owes to them (this author was happy because it coincides with my thesis). He recalled the "Strike of the Circular Line" of the 1930s, the song and the parodies by the poet Permínio, called him to the stage and together they sang the old protest song. It was a very emotional moment for all. It was a fitting end to the ceremony.

Jorge Amado and Zélia Gattai at the Luncheon in Camaféu de
Oxossi's Restaurant, Thanking All the Participants

LUNCH AT CAMAFÉU DE OXOSSI'S RESTAURANT IN THE "MERCADO MODELO"

Mário Vargas Llosa and Others at the Luncheon

It all took place in the restaurant on the third floor of the Mercado Modelo and was hosted by Jorge and Zélia, thanking one and all. Those I remember who were present: Camaféu de Oxossi, Calá Neto, Autran Rosa, João Jorge Amado, Zélia Amado, Jorge Amado, Mário e Patrícia Vargas Llosa, Nélida Piñón, Celestino (amigo de Jorge), singer-poets and Myriam Fraga, a well known poetess who later became a friend. She became the future diretor of the Jorge Amado Foundation in the Pelourinho and would publish my "Cuíca de Santo Amaro, Poeta-Repórter da Bahia".

The menu included: "vatapá, xinxim de galinha, arroz, molho de sir, moqueca de peixe," all in "dendê oil" and delicious. There must have been about twenty-five persons present. I ended up sitting to Jorge's left (not planned but that is the way it turned out); Zélia to his other side, Mário Vargas Llosa and wife Patrícia across the table. Llosa was enthused to hear about the "cordel." I spoke Spanish to him and his wife, and of course Portuguese to the hosts!

ANOTHER DAY: DEMEVAL CHAVES' BOOKSTORE IN THE IGUATEMI SHOPPING MALL

I took a taxi to the Iguatemi and Dmeval's bookstore now with an impressive display of my book and the table ready for autographs. I did two more interviews for TV, not feeling particularly good about either of them since the interviewers seemed to know nothing about the topic. An Aside: Cunha tells me that all the local channels covered the Commemoration and there were two minutes on the national news, mentioning my name and the book party. It is interesting to see Cunha's "modus operandi:" he arranges a good many of the events, is behind the scenes in planning but is never present. However he is at home glued to the TV to see the results. This scenario (once more, may the reader pardon me) or these scenes don't happen to a Kansas boy every day, in fact, like in 1981, never again.

Mark J. Curran

Jorge Amado Gives His "Stamp of Approval on the Author's Book

The Author and Zélia Gattai at the Autograph Party

THE AUTOGRAPH PARTY AT THE BOOKSTORE

It takes place at the newest and best shopping center in Bahia at the time, the Iguatemi Shopping Center, and at its best book store. I find myself at the author's table, pen in hand. There is time for quick but good conversation with all present: Calasans neto, and José Calasans (recalling my younger days in Salvador in 1966 when I interviewed him on his seminal book on the War of Canudos). Then Jorge came into the room, came to my side and did an interview with the TV, speaking of the book, of my projects (which he seems to have memorized), all this with the cameras rolling. At the end of the party there was a warm goodbye embrace and a request for me to call him the next morning. In sum during all these days Jorge was incredibly generous with me, demonstrating a total lack of "ego" on his part. I felt very positive toward him and this treatment; in the final analysis it was the most important of all. He certainly did not have to treat me so royally; it was out of kindness.

The scene later: the TV cameras were rolling and I was signing books for Rodolfo, for Sinésio Alves, Calasans Neto and others. Good friends Mário and Laís Barros came, and I owe Mário all the fine photos taken then which mean so much to me now and illustrate this part of "It Happened." I think they indeed enjoyed my good fortune and the moment.

Washington Luís, Director of Research of the Fundação Casa de Ruy Barbosa, was present; he spoke of a possible second autograph party, and Rodolfo was busy improvising verse. Geraldo Machado, president of the Cultural foundation, was all smiles. Thales de Azevedo, head of the Historical Institute of Salvador, Carlos Bastos, reknowned artist with some twenty of the illustrations for the original "Bahia de Todos os Santos" was there; he in fact designed that complete book for Jorge. He lives in Pedra do Sal as well, in the artist's colony, one of Jorge's neighbors. Cunha told me later that the TV coverage was great, but I never had a chance to see it. And that's the way it was.

ANOTHER DAY

I took Carlos and Edilene to a "churrascaria" on the beach as a gesture of thanks. It was there I bought the large tapestry of Kennedy as a gift for Keah showing in brilliant colors a "bahiana" amongst tropical plants, ferns and flowers, with her flowing large skirt in "folk" attire with a burning sun in the background.

I later went to Piatã Beach on the "orla" or sea coast with the Barros and later to the restaurant "O Prohibido" for the large noon meal – "shrimp in Paulistana" style. I could finally relax for the first time after the strain of the preceding days; my responsibilities had come to an end. An economic Aside: Mário informs me that he is ready to leave Brazil if the economic and social situation "explodes;" he is preoccupied by the recession and general conditions. Such complaints and stress would be repeated during the Collor de Melo regime years later (in Volume III to come) and via email as late as 2014. Mário would talk of the absolute corruption reigning in the country with no end in sight. It got much worse in 2015 with the later revelations of the huge Petrobras payoffs to politicans and others.

I did have that conversation on the phone with Jorge Amdo, he being super busy, but would like to meet again at the bookstore in Iguatemi for the autograph party for the books by Bahian authors.

I went to Rodolfo's "Banca dos Trovadores" in the Mercado Modelo to say goodbye to the poet, the main character in my book to come years later in 1987. And it also turned out to be a great "photo op" around the market and the port of Salvador, some shots I did not get years earlier mainly because of the huge changes taking place in the area, not all good from a folkloric point of view.

AUTOGRAPH PARTY OF BAHIAN AUTHORS, IGUATEMI SHOPPING

Once again this appeared to me to be perhaps a "command performance" or at least a big social moment for the Bahian intelligentsia. I chatted with Calasans Neto, Autran Rosa, Dona Zélia Gattai and Jorge (there was a warm final embrace saying goodbye). Also chatted with Guido Guerra and received some of his books.

There was one disagreeable and uncomfortable moment, recalling controversy in Bahia. I met the intellectual and writer Cid Seixas. It turns out he was/is a sworn enemy of Carlos Cunha; they had a bookstore together some years ago and it turned sour. Seixas told me, "Cunha is a viper! Look out!" The warning would be repeated in the future, and it might have been true. The only reason I even mention it here is that now I was being drawn into matters I was totally unfamiliar with and certainly uncomfortable with. What do I know? (You may recall the title of the first travel book "Peripécias" was about the "gringo ingênuo!") I can only say Carlos Cunha always treated me well and had it not been for him and Edilene, Bahia would have been much less pleasant in those many days in 1981, "winter" and "fall," and again in 1985, and twice in 1990. I owed much to them in helping with my research. Perhaps as important or more, they helped me keep my sanity in a social way in those times when I was basically alone in Bahia for the research. There were many occasions for lunch or supper with the family. It was my policy to never get into local disputes or arguments in Brazil, this during my entire career, and there were many in Salvador. The whole thing reminded me of the "poisonous" intellectual atmosphere described by Jorge Amado in "Tenda dos Milagres." But in the final analysis it would be Carlos Cunha after many efforts to publish my manuscript over Cuíca de Santo Amaro which had been "engavetado" or stuck in a drawer in the Cultural Foundation for years who would suggest I write directly to Jorge Amado about its publication. I did and it came out at the Jorge Amado Foundation in the Pelourinho with Jorge's approval and writing the "presentation" itself!

THE LAST DAY IN BAHIA

I went to Paulo Tavares' house and delivered a copy of the book, speaking of his books on Jorge Amado. Then went to Dona Hilda's house, the 1981 boarding apartment, then to the Instituto Mauá in Barra and bought some beautiful azulejo tiles of Bahianas to take home. Then to "A Portuguesa" for that last great mid day meal: soup, filé, fries, rice, beans, fruit salad, beer to drink and "cafezinho." I think it would be last time since the place disappeared later. Saudades.

Brazilian Politics of the Moment

The PDS (Partido Democrático Social) of the conservatives and the military controlled everything, but there were to be state elections in 1982. The PMDB (Partido do Movimento Democrático Brasileiro) is the "official" party of the opposition but without the "balls" to do anything in the opinion of most people. Since the political amnesty in 1980 under General Figueiredo, the radicals and the leftists are back in Brazil and are trying to regain power. The PT (Partido Trabalhista) (Lula's Workers' Party) is in the news, he being active since the famous workers' strikes of 1980 and 1981. The PTB (Partido dos Trabalhadores Brasileiros) has Ivete Vargas, a distant relative of old Getúlio. Leone Brizola is back and is governor of the State of Rio de Janeiro. Carlos Prestes is about with one of the workers' parties. Jânio Quadros is on the political scene in São Paulo. The government party controls Bahia with the governor Antônio Carlos Magalhães; his nephew, by the way, with a political plum job, is head of the Cultural Foundation of the State of Bahia. Mário Kertesz of the PDS is the mayor of Salvador and was just fired by the governor. Former governor Lomanto Júnior is apparently allying himself with Kertesz, so the "local political pot is boiling." All this is good for Brazil, still in the dictatorship, but political opinion is cynical and the people wait for the military to stay in power, and thus it was until 1984 and the great "Campaign for Direct Elections" with all the old favorites plus the millions of Brazilians in the streets bringing the eventual victory of Tancredo Neves, but more on this to come. But this moment in 1981 seems to be a "photo" of all the recent past events in Brazil.

MISCELLANEOUS MOMENTS OF THE TIMES IN THESE DAYS IN SALVADOR

The question of the "tarifa única" (single fare) on the buses. The masses are in favor; it will be cheaper for them. Renan Baleiro, the new mayor of Salvador, threw the new rule out, this because Kertesz had sponsored it.

The "land invasions" continue. One of Carlos Cunha's friends lives in an "invasion" near the lake of Piracicaba. An interesting thing: he creates abstact sculptures out of old auto parts, makes small cars of old "Fuscas" and paints them. He says the government is in the process of giving titles to the people of the "invasions."

I'm realizing the "grandeur" of what has happened, the Commemoration and my book.

New things. The news stands are full of "pornography," this because of the political "opening" and less censorship on the part of the government according to talk in the street. It all represents a sort of "backlash" to the years of repression. My take: if there is as much sex actually going on as the talk about it, it's no wonder that little work gets done in Bahia! Is this the reason for the rise in population as of late? It's a bit difficult for the "gringo" to walk in the streets, see the tight pants, the low cut blouses, and the biquinis on the beach! "País Tropical."

Under the surface there is desperation for most to earn a living or even to just get by. One can almost sense the desperation of the population. After sex, the economy is the main topic of conversation.

The ubiquitous noise; it's worse than ever! I can even hear it on the 9th floor of my hotel. "Mood Music" in the lobby of the hotel is enough to make one deaf, the TV at full volume! When I close the window in my hotel room the noise is still deafening. As I write these notes, I look out the window at the bay of Bahia and a beautiful sunset. The ships of the "Companhia Bahiana de Navegação" are crossing the green waves of the sea from the port to the Island of Itaparica. There are no longer any folk sailboats ("saveiros") in the city, but I understand some are still present on the sea coast ("a orla") near Pituba. In these past days I spent more time on the coast due to circumstances – Barra, Ondina, Rio Vermelho, Pituba and Itapuã.

Tourism. Without a car or a place to stay it would be difficult to bring the family to do tourism. Taxis are not cheap and the buses are packed and uncomfortable. Curious – with the exception of one brief time during the book party, I have yet to speak English to a North American since I arrived, a big change from 1966-1967. There is a migration of people from the old city, now for some time, to the sea coast. The valleys with their "favelas" are being leveled to build the new "interior" freeway. I only remember the 1960s when most goings on were in the old city or the Barra.

An Anecdote. During the Second World War personnel from the North American Air Force were living in Itapoã (near the international airport of today) and did their main food shopping in the Mercado Modelo in the old lower city! It was one big drive! (A historical note: these Air Force people were involved in the "air bridge" between the bulge of Brazil and the western tip of Africa, ferrying supplies, aircraft and troops to the efforts of the Allies to defeat the Italians and Germans in North Africa!)

FINAL VISIT WITH CARLOS AND EDILENE
AND DEPARTURE FROM SALVADOR

It is an atmosphere of post-celebration. Cunha is already preoccupied with preparing the scene for other events, among them a visit by the "troubadours" to senior citizens' homes for Christmas. He is highly irritated with Washington Luís of the Casa de Ruy Barbosa after an article came out in "A Tarde" with the Carioca claiming that the CRB financed my book and my studies in Brazil (nothing farther from the truth!) And there was no mention of the earlier "promise" of doing an autograph party for the book in Rio de Janeiro. Cunha says that the portion of the books designated for the Casa de Ruy in Rio will be "badly distributed." A sign of the future! The CRB kept a large portion of the copies of my book by Nova Fronteira on Rodolfo Coelho Cavalcante in 1987 stuck in the gloom of its basement, never to be marketed or distributed, gathering the dust of the ages. With this news I departed from Salavdor.

BRAZIL MAY 1 TO 31, 1985

INTRODUCTION

With a small research grant from ASU, this trip had as its purpose to bring myself up to date with the "cordel" situation and, frankly, to try to set up publications in Brazil. Looking ahead, perhaps it is better to go to the end of these notes of 1985 when I said, "The most difficult trip of all for me in Brazil." There is no need to go into all the details in virtue of some being a bit sad and pessimistic, so I'll summarize the battle for publications and talk a little about the tourism. In spite of everything, there were some good moments! We shall see that everything gets better, and in a hurry, in November of 1985 when I'll be back in Brazil under better circumstances.

SUMMARY OF RESEARCH PROJECTS, PROMISES FROM PUBLISHERS AND THE BATTLE TO PUBLISH. THE READER CAN SKIP THESE PAGES IF SO DESIRED.

Rio de Janeiro I

1. The copies of my book on Jorge Amado eventually arrived at the Casa de Rui Barbosa in Rio (the co-publisher but in name only) and are quickly out of print.
2. There was a taxi ride in the rain to the Editorial José Olympio to see if there was any news on my projects. My contact, Ivan Proença, had a falling out with JO and now has his own small publishing house.
3. Orígenes Lessa says, with subvention, perhaps Nova Fronteira may take an interest in my book on Rodolfo Coelho Cavalcante. We went there for an interview.
4. Orígenes says: take the study on Cuíca de Santo Amaro out of the Cultural Foundation of the State of Bahia; the Casa de Ruy Barbosa will publish it if I come up with a subvention of $2000 U.S. An Aside: In all this and in past and future years in Brazil I was so naïve; I really did not realize that most academic books are subsidized by the author.

Salvador I

1. Carlos Cunha says my manuscript on Cuíca de Santo Amaro would be good for the "Núcleo de Pesquisa da Literatura de Cordel" in Salvador, part of the Cultural Foundation of the State of Bahia, good for Edilene as its director and good for everyone. Edilene read the manuscript and corrected errors in my Portuguese, but the book is literally "engavetado" ("stuffed in a drawer") at the Foundation. Cunha thinks the only solution is to have a talk with Olívia Barradas, the new director of the Foundation. She is the sister in law of Governor João Durval Carneiro, thus explaining in part her post as head of the FCEB. It was an odyssey and I could give details, but

218

nothing came of it. I never flattered my way into a publication in Brazil or pleaded with someone to publish a study, and I'm not going to start now.

2. I decided to leave the Cuíca manuscript, now totally corrected and edited, at the Foundation and see what would happen. More details later.

3. I thought to myself upon leaving Salvador: write to Jorge Amado and tell him about the manuscript on Cuíca. I wrote the letter, but much later.

Rio de Janeiro II

1. I'm at the Casa de Ruy Barbosa with the director of the Research Center and Orígenes Lessa: the Casa wants the book on Rodolfo Coelho Cavalcante as long as there is a subvention; such a deal! For $500 more they will "throw in" my study on João Guimarães Rosa's "Grande Sertão: Veredas" e a Literatura de Cordel."

2. At the end of the trip I go alone to Editorial Nova Fronteira (a major publishing house in Rio), take the Rodolfo manuscript out and deliver it to the Casa de Ruy Barbosa. I spoke again to Homero Senna; the Casa will do the correction and preparation of the long manuscript, but there are no funds to publish it now. I have to find the funds.

If any reader has plowed through this, his head must be spinning (like Don Quixote after reading the Books of Chivalry). Stay tuned; it all came out all right, but took a few years time.

THE TRIP

It had been four years since I had been to Brazil. Times have changed. News of crime and violence is everywhere, especially in Rio. The people at Varig say that Rio has no more problems than any other big city in the world, but at the same time counsel me to be careful at night (they add that the robberies and muggings on the city buses are only happening in the distant suburbs). A policeman was killed yesterday at one of the subway stations. Standard advice is to not wear jewelry on the street, even a wristwatch (and buy a cheap one in case you're hit), and don't take too much cash with you on the streets. It is about this time that there are hilarilous "chronicles" by Carlos Drummond de Andrade of actually becoming friends with the local mugger because he hit him up so regularly!

AT THE CASA DE RUY BARBOSA

The Façade of the Casa de Ruy Barbosa

Antônio Marco Nedu is gone; Sérgio Pachá has bailed out and is teaching in Santa Barbara. Orígenes Lessa is the director of the "Cordel" section but has been absent for several months due to hepatitis.

An Amazing Note on "Cordel": Orígenes Lessa arranged for Rodolfo Coelho Cavalcante to come to the august Brazilian Academy of Letters and give a presentation. Rodolfo received the coveted "Machado de Assis Medal!" He calls it "My Nobel!" Rodolfo is in his groove!

ALONE IN THE HOTEL

There are reports of robbery and violence all over Rio. The former research colleagues are gone or deceased and there seems to be no possibility for my studies. I am down in the dumps! All will get better later, perhaps as Drummond says, this is just a "rock in the middle of the road" ("Uma pedra no meio do caminho" a famous poem.) More important is the philosophical part: if my "product" at ASU is Brazil itself, and if I believe less in it now, how can I possibly "sell it" to my students? I am suffering doubts as to my vocation itself and my role at ASU. The beautiful lyrics of Chico Buarque de Holanda's "Vai Passar" (referring to the military dictatorship of twenty-one years in Brazil from 1964 to 1985) are apropos. "It will pass." And it did.

ENCOUNTER WITH ORÍGENES LESSA AT HIS HOME

Still in good spirits with a great sense of humor and really clever, Orígenes received me graciously. Maria Eduarda takes good care of him and deals with his recent health problems. He spoke a lot about "cordel" and the current situation: Professor Raymund Cantel of the Sorbonne was recently in Rio and appears older and worn out. The great cordelian poet Manoel Camilo dos Santos is near death in Paraíba. Orígenes spoke of an item I heard earlier at the Casa de Ruy: of Rodolfo Coelho Cavalcante, his "Gold Medal," and how he, Orígenes, was able to set up an invitation and a trip to Rio for Rodolfo to appear at the august Brazilian Academy of Letters (Orígenes is one of the "consagrados" or members). It was a great and even crowning moment for Rodolfo's career; he now has a job in the "Núcleo de Cordel" in Salvador with a small monthly income and health benefits. Lessa is a good friend of Edilene's in Salvador and believes her when she says that there is no local funding to do my book on Cuíca de Santo Amaro, but one day, Orígenes declares, it will come out!

He tells of a competition for a short study on the "cordel" sponsored by the Casa de Ruy Barbosa and wants me to enter and send my study of João Guimarães and the "Cordel" all this by May 30th.

He says there is a great lack of interest in the "cordel" presently; there was a lecture at the Casa de Ruy by the well known Ivan Cavalcanti Proença and only seventeen persons showed up!

Bahia has no funds for publishing, not even for Edilene, the "chefa" of "cordel" there. He thinks that the name of a foreigner can mean a lot, so perhaps the "jeito" is to take by book on Rodolfo Coelho Cavalcante to Nova Fronteira Publishing House in Rio. The suggested plan is for me to leave the manuscript with Orígenes now; while I am in the Northeast he will take it to Nova Fronteira and there should be a decision by the time I return to Rio. Nova Fronteira is owned by Sérgio and Sebastião Lacerda, the sons of Carlos Lacerda, a famous Brazilian politician of the 1940s and 1950s in Brazil.

In addition he gave me some advice: take the study on Cuíca de Santo Amaro out of the Cultural Foundation of Bahia, bring it to the Casa de Ruy which will publish it with a $2000 subvention from ASU – "a good deal for everybody." The Casa has employees sitting around with nothing to do, no manucripts to edit, and no funds either!

THE FAIR OF SÃO CRISTÓVÃO, THE VISIT IN 1985

Sebastião Nunes Batista and Apolônio dos Santos at the Fair of São Cristóvão, 1985

The Author, the Poet Franklin Machado, the Woodcut Artist
Erivaldo da Silva and the Poet Expedito da Silva

I never saw fewer foreigners at the fair; I guarded my briefcase carefully. I met with Apolônio Alves dos Santos in his "cordel" stand but due to the infernal noise we set another day for an interview at the Casa de Ruy Barosa. He had good sales of the poem on Tancredo Neves, his election and subsequent death. I was also with Expedito da Silva, "Ambassador of the Order of Poets of the 'Literatura de Cordel'" in Rio and his son Everaldo who does woodcuts. Expedito believes that Raimuno Santa Helena is the "ruination of "cordel" in Rio with all his escapades and carrying on. He tells that Franklin Machado is back in the Northeast in Feira de Santana; "cordel" was not doing that well in São Paulo for Machado. And Joseph Luyten, an important researcher on the "cordel" will spend two more years in Japan. Juazeiro do Norte has some activity but it is very limited. Recife and João Pessoa have almost nothing. Rodolfo Coelho Cavalcante continues in Bahia with his job at the "Núcleo de Pesquisa da Literatura de Cordel" at the Cultural Foundation of the State of Bahia but is only writing "paid folhetos" and homages.

I ran into Gonçalo Ferreira da Silva at Apolônio's poetry stand at the Fair in São Cristóvão. He continues using the format of the northeastern "cordel", but is really a "protest" poet, super critical of the government, the politicians and the USA. I wrote in my notes, "He seems legitimate; I'll have to read his stuff." Gonçalo will only increase his visibility in the coming years becoming the "main man" of "cordel" in Rio with his "Academia Brasileira da Literatura de Cordel" in the old "Casa de São Saruê" started by Retired General Umberto Peregrino. He will actually fulfill the role of a sort of Rodolfo Cavalcante in Rio with his activities. But he later will really do a lot of work really distant from "traditional 'cordel.'"

I spent a bit of time with poor Azulão; he has only one new "follheto." His wife suffered a stroke five years ago in 1980 and has been hospitalized some five times. He does not come regularly to the São Cristovão Fair. Years later all this will change and for the better.

The Poet, Woodcut Artist and Musician Marcelo Soares

I'm with the Soares brothers. Jerônimo has the appearance of a poor northeasterner. His wife was a very pretty white girl. Marcelo was different: he wore "granny" glasses, the round ones, was younger, has studied in school and is more "representative" I think of the younger generation of Brazilians. He had a very calm demeanor and I liked him a lot; he offered me some of the last "folhetos" of his father (the famous José Soares, Poet-Reporter of Pernambuco). I had to take cash kept in my shoes to pay him. I know it's difficult to understand or imagine, but the situation of thievery and violence in public places in Rio in those days was no joke. Cariocas say nothing is safe; the "smart" thieves will even make you take off your shoes!

At this point I was feeling pretty nervous in the big fair due to the crowds of people, the cramped space between the market stalls and maybe a bit of paranoia about thieves. (The reader should note that in 43 years, knock on wood, I was never assaulted or robbed in Brasil, no small thing. Maybe a bit of precaution paid off.) But all of these warnings about the dangers were originally passed on to me by the poets in the market.

I did have a good experience at the Market, but it is evident that the atmosphere in 1985 and the general situation in Rio are different. "Cordel" was perhaps at its lowest point, and only the death of the democratic candidate opposing the military in national elections, Tancredo Neves of Minas Gerais, helped to perk up sales.

"THE PITS"

On Mother's Day I ate dinner alone in the hotel. I am paying a very high emotional price for this stage of research in Brazil. I can't allow myself to think about it too much. I did a rather "macrabre" inventory – my great friend and research colleague of years, Sebastião Nunes Batista is gone; the friend from the last research in Salvador Luís Raimundo Fernandes is in Italy; the great friend from the years at Rockhurst, Henrique Kerti, is in São Paulo; the colleague and friend of research at the Fundação Casa de Rui Barbosa Sérgio Pachá is in Santa Barbara. I was feeling a bit old, my only contacts Adriano at the Casa de Ruy and also the old and sick Orígenes Lessa. Remaining faithful to Keah – an obligation of my Catholic upbringing and of personal morality – it's my choice but with a price to pay. I asked myself: my reward? In heaven or on the return to Tempe? I change money in the hotel, even at a lesser rate, with fear of being robbed after the bank or on the streets.

APOLÔNIO ALVES DOS SANTOS AT
THE CASA DE RUY BARBOSA

An aside – thinking to myself – the trips in the future will have to have less to do with "cordel." But things would get better and a lot better – the Prize in November of 1985 and a fine trip, the book out on Rodolfo Coelho Cavalcante at Nova Fronteira in 1987, the book on Cuíca in Bahia in 1990, the book in Spain in 1991, the invitation to Brown University and meeting Sérgio Miceli in 1994, the book at the University of São Paulo in 1998 and the rest! A long lesson in perseverance.

Back to Apolônio. It was a long and good conversation. Apolônio is extremely pleasant. He said that he thinks "cordel" is reaching its end. So the reader may conclude that things were not going that well not only for the North American researcher but for Brazilians and Brazil. Returning to Apolônio's story, after years in Brasília he moved to Rio and began to sell "cordel" at the São Cristóvão Fair in Rio's North Zone. He bought a mud and wattle house in the favela of Benfica and gradually improved it, fixing it up into a pretty place, but he does not own the lot. It is all part of a "land invasion." He has no benefits from the government, no retirement savings, but does pay into the government "social security or "INPS." He was born in 1920 (he is 65 years old now but appears to be much younger). One hundred per cent of his income comes from "cordel." His wife works; there are no children. He invited me to visit him at home.

At this point in our talk colleage Candace Slater showed up and we all had lunch together. I thought at one time of doing an article or even a small book on Apolônio but Candace in effect did that in a chapter in her book, so I gave up that plan. Apolônio told me that one time when he had bought a chicken for dinner in the local corner store of the favela that he was robbed on the way home, losing the "lousy" chicken. He spoke of another poet living in Benfica, Palmeirinho, who was shot by a thief when he worked as a night watchman. Apolônio repeated that he has no retirement or real economic hope for the future. He seemed to be a simple person, clean and dignified. He was dressed in a nice looking US Top shirt, dress trousers and polished leather shoes. He seemed timid, humble but above all a good person. He touched my heart; we in the USA should get down on our knees thanking God for the peace and prosperity we enjoy in our lives!

ENCOUNTER WITH ORÍGENES LESSA, THE ODYSSY TO "NOVA FRONTEIRA" PUBLISHING COMPANY

Days later on the trip I accompanied Orígenes on the bus via Rua Maria Angélica in the Jardim Botânico to Nova Fronteira Publishing House, the most prosperous in all Brazil at this time; the owners are the wealthy family of the Lacerdas (Carlos Lacerda's sons). Orígenes proposed that they read my manuscript on Rodolfo Coelho Cavalcante, that ASU do a subvention of $2000 and that the Casa de Ruy would prepare the manuscript, creating a co-publishing agreement with Nova Fronteira. I have to phone them by the 21st of May to get their decision. Orígenes has four or five books published with them, thus the connection.

My reaction: I'm thinking to myself I'm pessimistic because Nova Fronteira does not do this kind of book. Sebastião Lacerda was very careful in the interview, a bit pessimistic in his comments, and frankly, without much enthusiasm. I understand; they feel no link or good feelings about the "cordel." I'm thinking: Cuíca in Bahia with my subvention; Rodolfo at the Casa de Ruy with ASU subvention. After these intense moments, I was tired of all this business and took advantage of the moment to do something else. The reader may be permitted a sigh of relief as well.

THE BRAZILIAN AIR PASS

I would use it several times over the years. In those days once you had arrived in Brazil via an international ticket, Varig would sell you the Air Pass which at one time allowed travel ANYWHERE on the Varig routes in Brazil for a month or two. So after the days just described in Rio it was on to Salvador.

The Arrival in Salvador

I left Rio and caught a flight to Bahia from the Galeão, not too bad, shrimp and filet mignon for the lunch on the airplane! There was that old shock of arriving at the airport in Salvador: the heat and the humidity, what a change from the "cold" in Rio's "winter." I caught a "frescão" along the sea coast road to the Hotel Bahia do Sol. There was blue-green sea, beautiful beaches, passing by Amarelinha and the Temple of Iemanjá. Jorge Amado is in Europe again, until October.

There was a re-encounter with Carlos and Edilene. The last time had been the Commemoration in 1981, so it's four years later. Carlos is the head of the "Núcleo de Cordel" and executive secretary of the Bahian Academy of Letters. Edilene is the head of the new section of Literature at the Cultural Foundation of Bahia and assistant to Olívia Barradas, the head of the Foundation. Geraldo Machado, the nephew of Antônio Carlos Magalhães is now Secretary of Culture for the State of Bahia. Antônio Magalhães is Federal Minister of Communication in President José Sarney's administration. Cunha said in passing that Geraldo Machado did so many expensive art books when he was president of the Foundation that it almost went broke! There are 200 manuscripts waiting for publication, even one by Gilberto Freyre! (Curran: do you feel better now??)

They have a new apartment. Carlos collects songbirds – "Sabiá, Cardeal, Azulão." There's a new Dalmation puppy. Bruno is now ten years old, Carole twelve.

Rodolfo Coelho Cavalcante Doing His Correspondence in Bahia

Rodolfo is now a peramanent burocrat in the "Núcleo;" he works every day, batting away letters on his old typewriter. He receives $160 per month and rights to INPS government "social security." He can publish some "folhetos" and is happy. He dresses in suit and tie every day. I chatted with him at the "Núcleo;" he seems much as he was in 1981. I copied several newpaper articles about him. Tomorrow I will bring the standard "present" ($). His newest story poem on the death of Tancredo Neves is selling well. He says tomorrow he will bring his Machado de Assis Medal from the Brazilian Academy of Letters so I can take a photo. He smiled, saying it was his "Nobel Prize." Ah, Rodolfo!

THE ACADEMY OF LETTERS OF BAHIA

It is near Piedade in an old colonial mansion with all the interior walls in Portuguese blue tile. Gorgeous! Carlos Cunha convenced then Governor Antônio Carlos Magalhães to give the building to the Academy. Carlos had been executive director there for a while. I attended a session of the writers and had a nostalgic meeting with a couple of old timers: Hildegardes Vianna from my stay in the 1960s and Hélio Simões from the 1973 Congress in Rio. Neither one remembered me, but was polite just the same.

ENCOUNTER WITH VASCONCELOS MAIA

I met the writer, intellectual, friend and contemporary of Jorge Amado and Cúica de Santo Amaro from the 1940s in Salvador. It was he and Hildegardes Vianna who were responsible for and created the tourist "space" to the side of the Elevator Lacerda in the "Cidade Alta" in the 1960s, the place where I went several nights a week to see the Capoeira Show, a wonderful moment and memory of those days in Bahia. (I wrote about it in "Adventures.") It turns out he was head of tourism in Salvador in 1959 and 1960 and responsible for creating that Capoeira Show.

The next day Vasconcelos invited me to join him at his son's restaurant in Amarelinha. We had great conversation reminiscing of old Bahia, "my Bahia" from the Jorge Amado books: the Companhia Baiana de Navegação and the passenger ships of those days, all gone now. Now there are only tourist boats over to Itaparica Island. We spoke of the scenes from Jorge's novels on Salvador, the greater part now disappeared – like the "rampa do Mercado" to the side of the Mercado Modelo. Vasconcelos still does journalism and has a regular column in the newspaper. We ate "caruru, xinxim de galinha, vatapá e moqueca de peixe." (I paid for three days with a bad stomach due to these Bahian delicacies! I've written before about the gringo's fragile stomach.) But the food tasted great and once again I was shown that Bahian hospitality. Vasconcelos was a great person. We got along well.

LEAVING BAHIA - AIR PASS TO RECIFE

It was an extremely quick visit. I spent the night in the old Hotel 4 de Outubro, spoken of earlier on as my first night in Pernambuco in 1966. The next day I took the walk to the Mercado São José and stopped at the "Livraria Cordel" along the way, all this along muddy streets, rain and what seemed immense poverty. As someone once wrote – the old part of downtown seemed like a bazaar from the Middle East. My conclusion: Brazil is a bomb waiting to go off! So, a bit down, but also seeing no real possibilities for research, the bitter taste in my mouth from the lack of action for publication from the UFEPE, I went to the airport and got on a plane for other possibilities and new adventures.

AIR PASS TO SÃO PAULO

An Aside: It is at this time that I discovered the work of Luís Fernando Veríssimo, a tip from friend Mário de Barros in Salvador (Mário is a "gaucho da gema" from Porto Alegre). Luis's "crônicas" would be an absolute necessity in my classroom at ASU until retirement in 2002. He was a "light of optimism" and happiness in Brazilian Literature and an inspiration for the title of this book!

I was in Rio, but took a taxi to the Santos Dumont, a "frescão" to the Galeão and the Shuttle Flight ("Ponte Aêrea") to São Paulo. Everything in those days was so easy with the "Air Pass," you arrive at the airport, and there are always empty seats on a flight you might want. It was at this time I took the spectacular photos out of the window of the airplane leaving Galeão and heading to São Paulo, ahead of my time before "Google Maps" with the great photos of the south zone of Rio from the air, photos used on the covers of recent books. Anyway, this flight took me to Congonhas Airport in the city.

View of Rio de Janeiro from the Air, the Flight to São Paulo

The Air Pass to São Paulo and Its Pollution

Important! After twenty years of visits to Brazil this was my first time in São Paulo. It was an astonishing moment seeing the gigantic city, the thick pollution, and then arriving at my modest hotel in the city center, all without any personal contacts or friends in the city. The hotel was the Planalto, the hotel Varig uses for the Air Pass and with the considerable discount. (Most of these good things have gone by the way as far as I know.)

The Copan Building Done by the Architect Oscar Niemeyer

The "Pátio dos Jesuítas," São Paulo

The "Pátio dos Jesuítas" represents the first construction in the city of São Paulo by the Jesuits Manuel de Nóbrega and the novice Padre José de Anchieta with the purpose of catequising the Indigenous natives of the "Planalto." It struck a chord with me since I was educated in both undergraduate (Rockhurst College, Kansas City, Missouri, 1959-1963) and Saint Louis University (1963-1968), and had learned just a bit on the role of the Jesuit Missionaries in Brazil as well as their role in writing the first Portuguese Grammar and other bits of colonial literature. In more recent days the movie "The Mission" with Robert de Nero and Jeremy Irons would romanticize their role in Brazil.

To "quebrar o galho" or "fill the bill" I took the city tour in very interesting company: three off-duty 747 airline pilots from the USA, from "Tiger Freight Lines." They were killing time, and I guess in a way so was I. So I got the blurred view of São Paulo: the Japanese "Bairro" of Liberdade, the Cathedral, the Praça da República, the Edifício Copan already mentioned, the Pátio dos Jesuítas, Pacaembu Soccer Statium, the "bairro" of Pinheiros, Cidade Universitária (the USP), and the Instituto Butantã with the snakes, Jardim América with singer Roberto Carlos' residence, Jardim Europa, and Mackenzie University. We later passed by the Parque do Ibirapuera and the monument. It was all so quick it remained a blur (I would study all this later), a cloudy image yet today. But why not? I've done the one day tour of Boston and of New York, so why not São Paulo?

Another Day. I did tourism alone in São Paulo. There were good purchases in Livraria Brasiliense. And there were gigantic portions in the restaurants – a cut of beef for lunch that could easily have been for three persons, but was the most flavorful on this trip to Brazil. It was "accompanied" by a mixed green salad with lettuce and tomatoes, rice and French fries.

A Street Scene: the return of W.C. Fields U.S. Juggler, Comedian and Movie Star. On a crowded street in the city center I saw the Brazilian version of the old "shell game" (from Fields' movies, the inveterate con-man): three small cups covering the pea and the bets from the "suckers." I saw several persons lose their money.

I later saw the Municipal Theater, the "Edifício Itália" 38 stories high, and the "Edifício Copan." An Aside: I am hearing frequent explosions (or gun fire?). The atmosphere in the city is more like New York than Brazil. I went to the Plaza of the Republic ("A Praça da República") where the "cordel" poet Franklin Maxado used to sell his story-poems; it is a sort of "hippy fair" São Paulo style. There are huge, leafy, old trees which surround the plaza and pools of water here and there. On the way home I experienced a true São Paulo traffic jam at six p.m. on Avenida Paulista returning from the tourism. What more could one want in São Paulo? And I witnessed a live bank robbery to boot a few minutes after the traffic jam.

So thus ends my first short and rather fuzzy memories of my first visit to São Paulo. Tomorrow I'll use the Air Pass to move on to "Gaúcho" country, my first time in storied Rio Grande do Sul.

AIR PASS TO PORTO ALEGRE

I have finally after more than 30 years' experience in trips to Brazil reached its far south, the fabled land of the "gaúchos" and Rio Grande do Sul. This is the state of Brazil's all time favorite president Getúlio Vargas, the state of renowned beef, chocolate, dried beef ("charque") and more recently of wines. My interest harks back to Brazilian literature to the great writer Érico Veríssimo of the "Generation of 1930" novelists in Brazil, but he of course representing the far South, and of his son Luís Fernando Veríssimo who inspired the "chronicles" in this book. Porto Alegre was the city so spoken of by some of my best friends in Brazil, the "gaúchos" Mário and Laís Barros, friends since the early 1970s. Unfortunately I did not visit the "interior" and the pampa until as a staff member on the National Geographic to Brazil in 2013 and 2014. I also had had a good taste of it in Uruguay in 2013 and 2014 with visits to "estancias."

The city of Porto Alegre is surrounded by the Rio Guaíba, and there are huge ocean going cargo ships docked alongside at the river. The downtown seemed empty to me. I was lodging at the old Hotel Royal, supposedly now owned by soccer star of the national selection, "Falcão." After checking in at the hotel, I walked up to the "Praça da Sé" or Cathedral Plaza and whiled away an hour or two just trying to absorb a bit of atmosphere of Rio Grande do Sul. The plaza was calm, there were many families with children about, matronly leadies doing their crochet, people sitting on the park benches with their "cuias" drinking "chá mate" tea. I probably spent an hour chatting with one of the families. There was no sign of vagrants, no danger about, all very calm and content with their "mate." Afterwards I went to mass in the Cathedral to the side of the plaza.

That night. Recall I am alone in all this, not a single contact. I found out about the "Parque da Harmonia" and its "galpão crioulo," a Gaúcho "churrascaria," the real thing! This night would stand out in my memory as another of the most unforgettable of times in Brazil, and all this in spite of being alone. The garçons were dressed in the "gaucho bombachas" those wide pantaloons, and were wearing heavy leather boots. They all had the large, long knives prepared to cut the portions of meat. But what made my day and night was the music. There was a "gaucho" band – accordion, guitar, drums, all beautiful music to my ears, the "milongas" especially pleasing, and wonderful local "folk" dancing by men and women in regional, folkloric dress. The men were in "bombacha" trousers and polished leather boots with spurs, dancing with beautiful young ladies in full dresses I associated with what I had seen in Mexico. There was a lot of "stamping of feet," and indeed it did make me think of the mariachi music of Mexico.

A funny thing – all the waiters seemed tall, big and in very good health and appearance, contrasting with memories of the same in let's say Pernambuco, Bahia or even Rio. "It just might be the German or Italian heritage of the Gaúchos," I thought. The girls were beautiful with more of a Latin appearance, almost Spanish. There was no "Girl from Ipanema" look at the galpão!

The food was spectacular for my tastes: a huge cut of "churrasco" beef and a lettuce and tomato salad that filled a platter large enough for an entire family. And there was icy cold "choppe para regar." What can I say? I was aware of being quite alone at my table, but that food and music and dancing made a lasting impression.

The next morning I'm downtown at a very good book store. So ended my ever so brief introduction to southern Brazil. I would eventually return and in style, on staff on the National Geographic Explorer.

AIR PASS AND THE RETURN TO RIO.

I'm lodged again at the Hotel Novo Mundo to the side of the Parque do Catete, and at one end the old national palace of fame of President Getúlio Vargas and his suicide in 1954.

An aside: I saw much more Brazilian "futebol" on television on this trip. They are in the process of chosing the national "selection" for the World Cup of 1986 in Mexico and in the process have just fired the coach and are bringing back Telé Saldanha of the Cup of 1982 when the selection lost to Italy in the finals. The return of Zico, Sócrates and Falcão from Italy is raising the level of enthusiasm. A small aside: it seems Zico owes hundred of thousands of dollars in taxes to the Italian government.

Another aside: This was the trip that at the end, killing time before the taxi to the airport, I saw the movie "The Terminator" with Arnold Swartzsnegger and it came close to giving me nightmares on the airplane. I thought to myself, "Perhaps apropos of the whole trip." Everything is really going to take a turn for the best, and dear reader, you can be relieved as well because the last chapter of 1985 takes on a new and much more positive turn!

Not really in a good space, I was ready to leave Rio and return home. And it was a battle until the last moment: the mad taxi ride to the Galeão with a huge traffic jam on the bridge on the "Ilha do Governador" leading to the airport. I believe I was suffering a bit from nerves, but in the end it all turned out well. There was an uneventful flight to Miami and then to Phoenix and Keah and Katie waiting for me in the airport. As I already said at the beginning, it might have been the most difficult stay ever in Brazil (in spite of some good times) but with a nice turn of events to come. 1985 brings happiness and hope for the future.

BRAZIL, NOVEMBER OF 1985, THE ORÍGENES LESSA PRIZE, THE TRIP WITH KEAH AND GREAT HAPPINESS IN BRAZIL

INTRODUCTION

A note to the reader: this part of "It Happened" is mainly tourism and diversion. As the Spaniards say, "En Buena hora!" ("It's About Time.") Enough about research and the efforts to publish in Brazil! I received news in October of 1985 that I had won the Orígenes Lessa – Lençóis Paulista Prize in a competition sponsored by the Casa de Ruy Barbosa for my monographic study "Grande Sertão: Veredas e a Literatura de Cordel." It was Orígenes himself who had encouraged me to enter into the competition in May of 1985. I later learned that there were forty entries, national and international, so I felt flattered and proud of the deed.

The genesis of the study may be of interest: this was the study I wrote in a rustic, fishing cabin on Grand Mesa in Colorado during the month of June of 1972! I recall writing when there were still about four feet of snow on the level outside the cabin window, and Keah and I kept warm with constant apple wood fires in the hearth. In spare time to clear out the cobwebs (and it indeed did) I climbed down the hill covered with snow to fish for trout in a just thawing lake. The people in Brazil wanted me to come to receive the prize in person. It seemed the proper thing to do, and was an honor, so I wangled part of the travel expenses from ASU (the Deans always had an eye out of publicity, particularly international publicity) and the Casa de Ruy provided some local living expense. The best is that Keah would come along, her first time in Brazil since the "honeymoon" of 1970.

THE TRIP

Gallery of Photos from Rio de Janeiro

Keah and the Varig DC -10, Brazil 1985

View of Flamengo Beach and the Sugar Loaf

Sunset, Flamengo and the Sugar Loaf

Flamengo Beach and Keah from Urca Hill

The Cable Car Climbing to Sugar Loaf

The View of Copacabana Beach from Sugar Loaf

Botafogo Bay and "Corcovado" from the Sugar Loaf

The plane reservations were fouled up a bit so there was a monkey wrench in the plans which we had to straighten out in Miami. I remember that even in November there was "Musak" Christmas Music in the airport. We were packed like sardines into the seats of the air liner, but arrived well to Rio where we caught the "frescão" (I had figured out a "system" for Rio transportation – avoid the expensive taxi ride in from the Galeão and getting the first taxi at Santos Dumont), in this case to the Hotel Novo Mundo in Flamengo. The room was comfortable if modest, but with a beautiful view of Guanabara Bay and the Sugar Loaf.

We were traveling on the now well known "Air Pass," so we went immediately to Varig's office in Copacabana to set up all the internal air travel and reservations in Brazil. We decided to go to both old and new places if possible (new at least to Keah). So we would both "matar saudades" "cure homesickness" for old spots and make the whole thing a second honeymoon.

In passing, after the Varig agency, there was a walk along the beach in Copacabana and both Keah and I got to see the "piranhas," boobs and buns on display, the skin tight pants and all in brilliant colors! Unhappily, there would be national elections the next day, so all bars closed, so we had to put off our introductory "caipirinhas."

Later we made a courtesy visit to the home of Orígenes and Maria Eduarda Lessa; they were happy to see us and treated us well in a very happy encounter.

On the return "home" to the hotel in Flamengo, the taxi driver scared the hell out of us with stories of robbery, assaults and muggings in the city. He said a stolen passport would go for $500 USD! We ended changing dollars at the front desk of the hotel, maybe making a shade less in the trade, but avoiding problems in the streets with the "Parallel" market in sway.

NOVEMBER 15: TO SÃO PAULO AND THEN LENÇÓIS PAULISTA

We took a taxi to Santos Dumont, the downtown Rio commuter airport, a "frescão" to the Galeão and the flight, always on Varig, to Guarulhos, the city airport of São Paulo. These were other times: the flight was practically empty, the 737 with perhaps ten passengers, so I was able to take some incredible slides out the windows as we passed the entire South Zone.

Upon arriving at the airport in São Paulo we "hitched" a ride to the city, confiding in a new friendshop with a nice young fellow on the flight, "Seu Antônio" on "holiday" in São Paulo and Santos. He spoke of his "paixão," making movies, and his latest on "the psychology of the woman." He did not know São Paulo, so there were lots of wrong turns, wrong streets, he frankly being lost (but never admitting it! Are all male drivers the same?) There was no GPS system yet in those times.Finally we arrived in the center of huge city, to the Santa Efigênia District with our hotel set up and paid for by the prize people.

It was all set up that we would drive to Lençóis Paulsta where I would receive the indeed modest prize, traveling with Zélia Cardoso. She was second prize winner and asked to come along by the prize people. Her husband teaches English and American Literature in a local "colégio;" she teaches Classics (Latin and Greek languages) at the renowned USP. She said in an aside that she had very little time to prepare for the competition, thus writing her study in a real hurry as a "reflexão posterior." (Does this mean as an after thought?) Her sister Lilian is to be our guide and driver for the entire trip. Thus began a bit of a true odyssey, "Brazilian style." An adventure it was and not a bit calm at that.

We left huge and smoggy São Paulo by the "Autovia Castelo Branco," the main highway heading out of the city to the west with 4-6 lanes on each side of the freeway. The surrounding terrain was quite green, hilly and with many cattle ranches. We passed by Sorocaba seeing the huge termite mounds (a first for Keah and me); I recalled the anteater is a well known "character" in Brazil's comic books. There were also many "Zebu" or Brahma cattle in view. Lilian drove her little "Fordzinho" as she called it at maximum speed, and she seemed to be a bit distracted in her driving. At least this was the "take" on it from the two passengers in the back seat. It took four hours to arrive in Lençóis. To the side of the road we saw coffee trees, bamboo, and huge plantations of Eucalyptus trees (I would see these years later in far southern Brazil on field trips of Lindblad-National Geographic Society Expeditions). As we drew closer to Lençóis, we entered the vast lands of sugar cane plantations, from horizon to horizon. Sugar was indeed the main product of the region. I was a bit of a veteran of sugar cane plantations but in the old Northeast. I had never seen the huge cultivation of the same in São Paulo, in reality larger than in the Northeast. We would soon get to know it well.

Lençóis, the Outings

The city itself is the birthplace of Orígenes Lessa or at least where he grew up, the son of Protestant missionaries. It is a prosperous sugar cane region. The mayor's name is Ideval Paccola and it was his brother who showed us around the old family sugar cane plantation and mill. There is a significant Italian immigrant population in the region dating from the end of rthe 19th century.

We met our hostess, Marly Montoro, widow of Franco Montoro, nephew of the governor of the State of São Paulo. Marly's husband died in a motorcycle accident. She works three or four days a week in the library (which will be known from now on as the "Biblioteca Orígenes Lessa") and another two days in the main business of the family, buying scrap metal ("sucata") which is then sent to the forges to be made into steel, a very prosperous business!

Green Corn Pizza in Lençóis Paulista

Our lodging was quite modest due to the small size of the town, the "Pousada dos Arcos," rustic but comfortable, and the open varanda with a nice cool breeze in the evening was a great place to have a beer or soft drink. Marly took us that first night to a local pizzeria (Italian naturally) where I tried something new: green corn pizza, tuna pizza and Brazilian vegetable "palmito". Interesting! And of course icy draft beer! The conversation that evening was on the veranda of the Pousada – Marly, Keah, Zélia, Lilian and I. Marly is from the city of São Paulo and is still trying to get used to life in this small town. The library however is far from that of a small town thanks to the efforts of Orígenes Lessa. All the books are from his vast collection plus those donated by Austregésilo de Atayde, President of the Brazilian Academy of Letters in Rio, and the collection of the local library itself. It was no small affair.

Visit to the Paccola Sugar Cane Plantation Mill

A Field of Sugar Cane, the Paccola Sugar Cane Plantation and Mill, Lençóis Paulista

Fermination of the "White Stuff" ("A Branquinha") Keah and the Paccola Sugar Mill

They plant the sugar cane; it grows and produces for five years. The harvest time is from April to November. This is the old mill but still mechanized, at least in comparison to those from the Lins do Rego family I visited in Paraíba in 1966. The reader perhaps may be familiar with one of Brazil's major novelists, one of the "Novelists of the 30s" or "Novelists of the Northeast," José Lins do Rego who wrote several novels in his "sugar cane cycle" and is compared by Brazilians to our own William Faulkner.

Large trucks bring in the stalks of sugar cane, already burned in the field, this to make the hand cutting easier (the sky over the entire region was filled with smoke from the burned fields). From the truck a forklift takes it out of the truck and puts it on a long conveyor belt which moves it into the mill to be ground. The products from this old mill are: "cachaça, caldo de cana, álcohol, melaço, vinhaça" and sugar itself. Once the stalks of sugar cane are washed, they are "trituradas" (split open) and crushed by several successive grinders. The resulting liquid, the "caldo," flows into one canal, the "bagaço" or waste into another. The waste will be dried and used as a combustible to power the grinders. And part of it is returned to the fields to be used as fertilizer; this is the part known as "vinhaça."

We saw the fermentation process in large vats, perhaps three meters wide and just as deep, in which the "caldo" is boiled to separate impurities and comes out clear and ending as "cana" or "cachaça" sugar cane rum, the final product.

An aside: Mr. Paccola after the tour took us to an old cellar, locked with a very rusty old padlock, difficult to open with the key. But it turned out to be a storehouse for the "fine wine," in this case for the oldest "cachaça," - "da prima." End of the story: he insisted that we take some ten large bottles (liter size) as souvenirs (I think we actually got three or four of them home as baggage on the plane to the U.S.) But one in particular, the oldest of the "branquinha" in an antique bottle ended as the main component in "caipirinhas" in our house for some time in Arizona. The others, "finer" rum of darker color, are still "aging" today.

The Ceremony – The Prize at the Library of Lençóis Paulista

The Author and the Orígenes Lessa Municipal Library in Lençóis Paulista

Our Hostess Marly and Mark

I must say it like it is: this was a modest award from a small town. On the other hand it was exactly this that provided the charm of it all: an important event for such a place and far, far away from the normal madness of the huge cities of Brazil. It was a little humorous in some ways. Dona Vera, the "Presidenta da Biblioteca," took great pains to show us around the collection, and Marly showed us the "rare books." One document catching my curiosity was a photocopy of the infamous northeastern bandit Lampião's birth certificate! Any fan of "cordel" would drool over this! The mayor of the town is there, Mr. Ideval Paccola, and a little bored by it all. There is a small ceremony with speeches and local protocol, and then some words of thanks by the North American praising Orígenes Lessa (a friendship since 1966), Sebastião Nunes Batista (friend and research colleague since 1966-1967), Marly and Lençóis. I should add the official prize had the moniker of "The Sebastião Nunes Batista Prize of the Orígenes Lessa Municipal Library of Lençóis Paulista." Or it was something like that; I don't think I have the document to prove it.

Then came a funny "reponse" by the mayor; he seemed a bit like the prize winner, a country boy at heart, nervous and fidgeting a bit, but following the accostumed protocol in the region. Later Marly took her turn with a speech dedicating the library to Orígenes Lessa. A local photographer snapped some shots; it was all very quick and pleasant.

Visit to the "Barra Grande" Sugar Cane Refinery

Visit to the "Barra Grande" Sugar Cane Refinery

The "Romeo and Juliet" Trucks at "Barra Grande"

This added much to the trip, the place and the time. Such refineries are still the basis of one of the major aspects of the Brazilian national economy, and I daresay, we will probably not see one like it again. This is a phenomenon of Brazil in the 1980s. There are 6000 field hands and 1,200 more at the refinery itself. It is the epitome of the modern sugar cane refinery. There are one thousand truck loads of sugar cane per day, 16,000 sacks of sugar produced each day, plus the alcohol and other side products. The trucks, for Brazil, are huge, and are called "Romeo and Juliet" (truck cab and cargo trailer). We all donned yellow hard hat construction helmets, obligatory for the refinery and began "the grand tour."

We saw the trucks unloading; before each truck is unloaded, a sample sugar cane stalk is tested (we saw a demonstration of this). The "caroço" or sugar fiber is taken to a laboratory where tests are done to test the acidity, the sugar content, and then place a price on that particular truckload of raw sugar cane. The testing laboratory is totally air conditioned (there was incredible heat outside in the rest of the refinery). Mr. Maurício led the tour. To the side of the refinery there were huge mounds of "bagaço" or sugar cane trash which is used as a combustible to power the entire refinery when the trash is burned and converted to steam power. The excess sugar cane trash is sold to other smaller refineries in the area. This refinery owns 48 other smaller refineries in the region and many sugar cane plantations. (A far cry from the Lins do Rego plantations in Brazilian literature!) There are even more plantations that provide and sell their sugar crops to "Barra Grande." Maurício allowed that some try to cheat on the price by selling sugar cane of low quality, this finagled through the test of the "caroço."

The biggest grinder is under repair ("estava em obras"), but I climbed the refinery scaffolding anyway, just to get an idea of the immensity of the operation – there are six different grinders. Later we saw a smaller grinder (ladies and young girls are not permitted to climb up into the scaffold – the workers below, all men, can look up and see everyone on the scaffold, thus with a good view under the ladies' skirts). The heat was overpowering and the smell almost nauseating. Then we went to an even hotter place, gigantic, with the huge tanks where the crude sugar cane liquid is heated and cooked. The result is a sort of molasses ("melaço") which is then dried, whitened, and converted into crystal sugar. The molasses which is not graded and chosen for sugar is converted into alcohol. The rest of the product is the "vinhaça" which is dried and spread in the fields as fertilizer (friend Mário Barros in Salvador told me once that in the old days the "vinhaça" was dumped into the local rivers and polluted the waters and killed the fish.)

By this time all of us were overheated, and we decided to not do the rest of the tour. Guide Maurício was visibly upset about this. I had hoped for a small packet of the "Barra Grande" refined sugar as a souvenir, but none was offered. We left the refinery feeling pretty miserable - hot, dirty, thirsty, and even nauseated, but the experience for us was a once in a lifetime thing. (It gives me an idea, on a huge scale, of what our friend Richard Arms' father did as a head manager of sugar mills and refineries in Cuba before Castro and then in Colombia and Paraguay.)

The reward for our suffering the heat: after taking cold showers, we went to a "churrascaria" on the local highway entering into Lençóis, it seemed like in the middle of nowhere. The menu was: tomato salad, peas, potato salad, all in the "rodízio" style; cuts of chicken, sausage, beef sirloin and filet mignon, all served with huge portions of French fried potatoes (a product of the region coming in frozen from Piracicaba). Keah's personal waiter wants to be "an international waiter" and is learning English via cassete tape. Another Maurício, whose passion in life is sugar cane, gave us a ride to the hotel; he is Marly's boy friend and is the CFO of a sugar cane operation in the region. He spoke beautiful, clear Portuguese, something always appreciated by the ole' "gringo" Portuguese professor while in Brazil.

The Return Trip – "God Help Us"

"Deus nos Acuda!" It was a test of all our patience. Unbelievable. Dona Lilian is crazy! She insisted on going by a city in the region, "Barra Bonita," to see its handicrafts, but she never figured out where it was! She refused to ask for directions from anyone. We, the passengers in the car, saw road signs which indicated the right road and she ignored them. So the return trip was a meandering through lands and lands of sugar cane, rolling hills and fertile soil. Keah and I were frustrated by this time and "crazy" for all that to end. We followed the Rio Tietê, saw excursion boats (and thank God were one half hour too late to get on one or we would have never arrived "home" on time). We did see another huge refinery with long lines of trucks waiting to unload their sugar cane. Ignoring our suggestions and also those of her sister Lúcia Lilian took the wrong turn and road and was actually heading back to Lençóis. She was hunting for folk art of the region. Finally, when we did arrive to the correct highway she wanted to turn in the wrong direction, returning the way we had come, opposite to the correct direction. At that point all the passengers were exasperated and yelled our protests. Lilian at that point ceded to our pleas, turned right and at maximum speed took us back to São Paulo, her car literally "vibrating" due to the maxium speed. It was frightening. We finally arrived in the outskirts of São Paulo city, took a wrong turn, passed by the bus station, a subway station and finally arrived at the Hotel do Planalto. There we all said good bye, wishing each other well! What a relief! ("Que alívio!")

The hotel was in a state of confusion – at that very moment two huge tour buses full of tourists from Buenos Aires arrived. It reminded me of the little hotel in Medellín, Colombia in 1975 when the place was inundated with short Indian-tourists from Bolivia, all jamming the tiny lobby and elevators with their huge suitcases, and all rushing to get to their rooms (evidently) before anyone else.

The next day we went to mass at Santa Efigênia with armed guards at the entrance to the church. Then we went to the Praça da República and its Sunday morning "hippy fair." There were a few "folhetos de feira" by Benedita of Bauru and some by Franklin Maxado (who now is in Feira de Santana, Bahia, his home town), another person in charge of his former small shop in greater São Paulo. Benedita began writing poetry in the "concretista" style, but is doing "cordel" now, and is involved in the "Centro Zumbi da Cultura Black." We later bought some nice ceramic pieces from a grandfatherly type from O Porto, Portugal. He asked me, "O senhor é português?")

On the return to the hotel we witnessed a bank robbery in progress! There were some men with their pants down to their ankles and all kinds of policemen in VW Police Cars ("Fuscas"). We were walking nearby, perhaps fifteen meters away. It turns out to be a common happening in the city, the thieves with their hands on the building walls, their pants on the floor, being searched by cops. And there were lady cops present as well.

Trying to check out of our hotel, the young fellow behind the counter who was supposed to do this was on his cell phone obviously talking to a girl friend or the like (we could get a lot of the conversation), instead of checking out customers. But we got through that, took a "ônibus executivo" (like a "frescão") to Guarulhos airport which took forty minutes, and with nothing pretty to look at, a lot of pollution, and the Rio Tietê incredibly polluted to the side.

At the airport we attempted the check-in with those ten liter bottles of "cachaça," the "gift" from Lençóis, and actually got it done. We put them all in a luggage locker at the Galeão before the flight to Bahia. An introduction to that flight was a glass of Campari for Keah and a glass of Scotch whiskey served with ice for Mark. Both were served in Brazilian airline style, sufficient to make two or three normal drinks.

An Aside: In the newspaper of São Paulo there was an article about Ex-President Jânio Quadros going shopping at a corner store, buying toothpaste and Cepacol; the paper even gave its price. Then Jânio shouted, "Get the hell out of here you dogs! Let me go shopping in peace." The papers are talking of a possible political alliance betwwen Quadros of the PTB and Leonel Brizola. Anything is possible!

KEAH AND MARK IN BAHIA

The Author and Friend Mário Barros at Itapuã Beach

Friends Mário and Laís Barros met us at the airport, accompanied by Mário's father João, his mother and Carla his daughter. Son Eduardo cold not be present as he was doing fancy horse riding ("hipismo"). We then went to their house in Itapuã and had a good conversation bringing everybody up to the present, and gave Mário and Laís our gifts from Arizona. There was a walk along the beach at Itapuã, and then they took us to the Hotel da Bahia (used by Varig for the Air Pass people) where we would be stayng. We had dinner that evening at the side of the pool with a very pleasant breeze in that hot Bahia climate. It was all quite pleasant.

News of the Barros: Mário is going to represent Ford Inc. in Brazil in its division of agricultural equipment. There is a possible outing planned for Florida where they will rent an RV motor home. The company where Mário has worked for some time, Formac, is doing better. Laís is studying English, the kids are in the "Escola Americana" and Mário is on the school board. There is talk of a possible major move to Florianópolis in southern Brazil where Formac has an affiliate. The schools are better than those in Bahia. Formac has been robbed three times in recent months; Mário thinks it may be traced to the night watchman working with neighborhood thieves. Laís is learning how to use a pistol (protection in the house when Mário is gone.)

November 18th. The "café da manhã" in the hotel is to be noted: the waitresses are all in the "bahiana" dresses and outfits; there are scrambled eggs, bacon, all kinds of breads and juices and an excellent "café com leite." The reader may recall that this is Keah's first trip to Brazil since 1970 and she loved the breakfasts. Afterwards we caught a taxi to the Lower City and to the "Mercado Modelo." There was a huge traffic jam along the way, so life is "normal" in Bahia.

The Author and "Cordel" Poet Rodolfo Coelho Cavalcante at the "Mercado Modelo"

We surprised Rodolfo Coelho Cavalcante with a visit to his poetry stand outside of the Market; he had many "folhetos" from the Editorial Luzeiro from São Paulo, but little from the Northeast. Happy to see me, he reported that he had been invited to go to Paris and the Sorbonne by some "French poets." He was of good appearance, suit, tie, but a little disheveled. He is going to "lançar" or put out a new story-poem at 3:00 p.m. today in the Cultural Foundation of the State of Bahia on the historian Pedro Calmon (the "Cadillac" of my1973 notes from Rio, the author important for me because of his "O Brasil na Poesia do Povo").

Keah and I did a bit of shopping in the Market, dolls for our daughter Kathleen and souvenir t-shirts, etc. An Aside: The character in the market wanting to sell us the dolls went "over the top" in demonstrating the same: to show they were well made he batted their heads on the concrete floor of the market, and then took out his cigarette lighter and tried to light them afire! We did not buy the dolls.

Political Demonstration and the "Trio Elétrico" Truck for Mayor Mário Kertesz

This is truly politics Bahan style! It all happened when we were in Camafeu de Oxossi's restaurant on the third floor of the Market. While having a drink, we heard this huge commotion outside on the streets: it was a huge political demonstration in favor of Mário Kertesz of the MDB. He is now the new mayor and by virtue of a staggering majority vote. There was a huge truck in the style of the "trio elétrico" of Carnvial in Bahia blaring rock music, many people dancing in the streets, fireworks going off, and an atmosphere of Carnival. Kertesz had "paid a promise" (in this case political not religious) for being elected: he walked the entire way from the old church of Conceição da Praia to the Church of Jesus do Bonfim on the peninsula, some 6-10 kilometers distant! This was a memorable thing to do, only to be seen in Bahia!

Mark J. Curran

View of Bahia from the Lacerda Elevator in the Upper City

Keah in the Restaurant "Solar da Unhão"

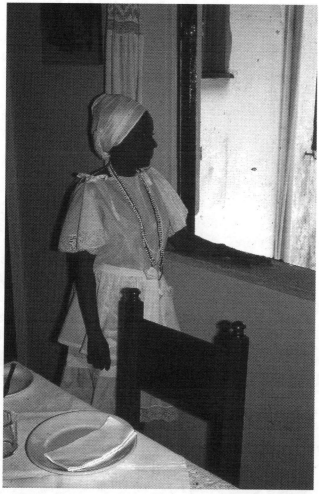

The Beautiful Bahian Waitress in the "Solar da Unhão"

After the political manifestation we got on the Lacerda Elevator to the Upper City (a very folkloric ride yet today; you are "with" the Bahian people!) to see that unforgettable view of the Bay of Bahia, then a taxi to our hotel, and then a big Brazilian lunch in the "Solar da Unhão" Hotel in the restaurant "Casa da Gamba," a five-star restaurant with a view of the bay and waitresses in full "Bahian dress." Ours was fifty years old but looked much less. We had the "full treatment" – "batida de coco, de limão, casquinha de siri e camarão à Gamboa, e camarão à Grego;" the first was a little like Keah's shrimp creole, a Southern dish from back home. And there was icy "Brahma choppe" beer to drink. The owner after discovering who we were and my past intellectual efforts in Salvador insisted that after our already complete meal that we try the "real Bahian specialities of the house." I protested; she won the day and we were offered "a oferta da casa," – "vatapá, caruru, xinxim de galinha e camarão, tudo em azeite de dendê." The result some time later was that both Keah and Mark had digestive problems, the price paid for the Bahian incredible hospitality.

In the afternoon we went to the Cultural Foundation of Bahia to see Rodolfo's big "festa." The historian José Calasans gave a long speech about Pedro Calmon; Thales de Azevedo of the Historical Institute and other Bahian intellectual dignitaries were present. And there were poet-singers from "cordel" and Rodolfo reciting the new "folheto." Presidenta Olívia Barradas gave a speech, and it all was very dramtic. Rodolfo in full figure and form acted as master of ceremonies for it all; it was a big Bahian "show." There was improvised verse by the singer-poets; it must have lasted two hours. Keep in mind Keah did not understand much and me not a lot more.

Afterward we returned exhausted to the hotel. We took advantage of a beautiful sunset on the bay from our room and wrote these notes. Then we went to the travel desk of Varig in the hotel and tried to arrange the Air Pass to Iguaçú Falls, but unfortunately it did not work out. Second choice did: a return to Manaus for me (first time for Keah) but lodged at the beautiful "Hotel Tropical."

We then took a taxi to Carlos and Edilene's house. We had brought presents from home and it was all greatly appreciated. Daughter Carol is a real beauty by now, and son Bruno is playing soccer. Edilene seemed tired (and with good reason); she is studying and preparing her Master's Thesis at the Federal University of Bahia for December. The thesis will perhaps be published by Editora Vozes in Rio. Edilene is "secretary" to Olívia Barradas still at the Foundation (Olívia has one and one half year's left on her sabbatical from the Universidade Federal do Rio de Janeiro). Carlos Cunha has returned to the "Núcleo de Cordel." He is also the executive director of the Bahia Academy of Letters, trying to establish his reputation as manager there, but at present with no salary.

Keah Overlooking the Port of the Barra, Salvador

Another day. There was a big breakfast at the Hotel da Bahia: cocoanut yogurt,etc. then to Barra Beach and to the Church of Santo Antônio, then to Santo Antônio Fort with its incredible view of the bay, then the rather intense shopping and buying the artistic tiles of the Bahianas that still decorate our kitchen in Mesa. A Brazilian Aside: We saw a billboard showing a beautiful young Bahian girl in a very small swimming suit bottom. It said, "An old style suit spoils your summer!"

There were many more huge cargo ships in the Bay, perhaps the beginning of the oil boom in Brazil's Atlantic, all seen from a beautiful view of the bay from our hotel room. The hotel had a beautiful swimming pool and is near the old fort. The room was the best of Bahian tourism at the time: calm, all outside noise blocked! It had good, quiet air conditioning, excellent television, good, clear phone service, floor and walls of marble, the ubiquitous "frigobar" and with a telephone even n the bathroom. Big fluffy bath towels changed twice a day. The lobby of the Hotel has a Stern's Jewelry Store, beautiful modern paintings, huge views of scenes of Bahia, and a fine restaurant. Our bill: 888000 or $44 USD per day with meals and laundry, all pretty amazing with the Varig Air Pass Discount. The reader may wonder why I dwell on this; the reason is that this is the only time in all my years in Brazil when I or we went "first class."

And I do recall the student and research days of decades past when a $5 room near the bus station or a hammock in a pilgrim's stall in Juazeiro were this traveler's fare.

An Update on "Cordel:" Notes from a Conversation with Carlos Cunha

Carlos says now in 1985 there is no interest in "cordel" or support for the same in Salvador, not by the masses and not by the other social classes. The books in the library of the Núcleo have disappeared, probably stolen; less than ten serious researchers appeared this last year at the "Núcleo." Rodolfo has a poetry stand in front of the Mercado Modelo, but there is little interest by the public. (All this will change in a few years with the personal computer and printer at its side used by a new generation of "Cordel" poets.) Cunha says that he even has less interest today; he is focused on the political moment in Brazil – the sudden death of the "Hero of Democracy" "The New Tiradentes" Tancredo Neves and the anxious moments for his successor former Vice-President José Sarney. All this is indeed another story relating the trajectory of Brazilian politics since the Military regime and the euphoria of the "new democracy." An Aside: I shall tell it all in a future volume in Brazil, "A História do Brasil em Cordel" in 1998 by the editorial press of the University of São Paulo.

Carlos says that the Commemoration for Jorge Amado in 1981 was the high point of cultural festivals in Bahia; my small book the only one to result. There has been nothing like it since that moment! The "silver tongue" wagging again, he says that Alfredo Machado (Jorge Amado's publisher in Brazil) would like to publish my monograph in São Paulo, and I should write to him from Tempe. Cunha says that I was a "pioneer of studies of 'cordel' in Brazil; Edilene says the the Volume of Studies from the Casa de Rui Barbosa in 1973 is still the best thing in the field. I, "at the right place at the right time" in the company of Manuel Cavalcanti Proença, Manuel Diégues Júnior, Théo Brandão, Ariano Suassuna, Raquel de Queirós, Bráulio do Nascimento and others. Carlos and Edilene were both extremely surprised to hear I had won the "Orígenes Lessa Prize" (the reason for this trip); they had not heard of this news.

Cunha spoke of a local journalist Paulo Marconi who had seen my Cuíca manuscript (Cunha showed it to him; I scolded him for doing so). He says that Marconi was astonished that a foreigner could come up with such a study capturing the spirit of Cuíca. Marconi's thesis is to "unmask" the image of Cuíca de Santo Amaro ("Defender of the poor masses of Bahia") and show him as the scoundrel he was ("Cuíca o Cafajeste" as a possible title.) He has documents of Cuíca in jail, etc. and of his "bad character." Cunha thinks there will be little duplication in the two studies, both with very different approaches.

And it turns out Edilene has done a biography of Cuíca (another "surprise" not hinted at earlier in the days with them in Salvador) a small book; I appear in the bibliography. The book was paid for by the UFEBA; the Cultural Foundation had no money. An Aside: Cuíca chose the pen name "Cuíca" due to his penchant for trying to play the guitar and make it sound like a "cuíca." So this resolves all the searching by folks to determine the origin of the name.

Conclusion from Bahia

The city and the streets have more people and in fact were totally jammed with people. There is huge growth along the "orla" (one can see my photos from 2013 and 2014 coming in by sea and witness all this). There is a freeway through the interior of the city now with new buildings, houses and shopping centers. The days of the 1960s "are all gone." I was impressed as ever by the people, but I still like Bahia after all these years. "Cordel" as well just "used to be" (" já era").

THE TRIP TO MANAUS

The Flight to Manaus

Using the Air Pass we caught the international flight of the brand new DC – 10 of Varig's (the flight that continues after Manaus to Caracas, Mexico City and the U.S.) It offered the fine international service, the time of the flight being three hours an a half from Salvador to Manaus (I am fairly confident this is the same flight as that in Jack Pizzey's documentary film "The Amazon" in those days).

The "Hotel Tropical"

The Blue Macaw and the "Hotel Tropical," Manaus

Keah and the Blue Macaw, the "Hotel Tropical"

We were lodged at the famous "Hotel Tropical" on the outskirts of the city of Manaus on the banks of the Rio Negro. It was and still is a magical place; after checking in we walked through its many gardens, seeing the small zoo with macaws, and several large cats including one Jaguar ("onça" in Portuguese), monkeys and the like.

Mark and the Swimming Pool at the "Hotel Tropical"

Keah in the Swimming Pool of the "Hotel Tropical"

Keah at Sunset on the Patio of the Pool of the "Hotel Tropical"

Then we went to the round swimming pool with its own "falls," ("catarata") and heard live music (calm, much like the old "Bossa") while sitting under the hotel arches from which one could spy views of the great Rio Negro in the distance. The music was the best music yet on this trip, quiet guitar, very soft percussion and soft voices. We had drinks at the side of the pool, swam, and then rested, sitting on the terrace and watching a beautiful sunset over the river and the forest. I recall drinking a Malt-90, a Brahma Choppe and Keah had her favorite a wonderful "batida de coco." There was a light dinner and we "repaired" to our room (recall this was our "second honeymoon").

Describing the inside of the hotel: there was a very high ceiling with a central atrium, this with palm trees, pools of water and white egrets. The corredors are wide and elegant, all in colonial style, the floor of Brazilian tropical hardwoods, the doors all carved wood, antique "steel" lamps, and ornamentation of polished drift wood from the Solimões and Rio Negro throughout.

The room has a high ceiling, a huge "armoire" or closet of tropical wood, wooden floor, color TV and the "frigo bar." The view outside the window was a distant view of the Rio Negro and one heard all kinds of birds. On that first night there was a heavy tropical rainstorm all night long. There was a radio, telephone in the bathroom, and Portuguese tiles of tropical plants.

That afternoon we did a walk along the beach in front of the hotel, its name "Ponta Negra" or "Black Point," then walking through the dense and wet gardens to the small dock and tour boat of the hotel.

Second Day in Manaus, November 21st
The Floating Dock and the Market

We started the day with the big breakfast at the Tropical Hotel: freshly squeezed, icy orange juice, slices of fresh pineapple, banana, scrambled eggs, bacon, a sort of Brazilian pound cake and "café com leite." We were seated to the side of the atrium, waiters in formal dress all around us, a maitre'd in black tuedo, all very upscale.

We took the hotel bus to the city, a matter of twenty to thirty minutes, passing by military bases to the side of the river. The city of Manaus, its downtown that is, was full of life, many more tall buildings than in 1967, my last visit, but the scene seemed very familiar down by the docks. You could see the old Hotel Amazonas, aged by the climate (rain and humidity). Near the docks was a large commercial area but with "small commerce," many poor people selling tourist gadgets, clothing, and even plastic watches. I did find a "cordel" stand but with only two local story-poems, a few from the "Lira Nordestina" of Juazeiro do Norte and the rest from the Editorial Luzeiro of São Paulo and its colored "comic book style covers."

The Docks at Manaus at Low Water Stage on the "Rio Negro"

The main entryway to the floating dock is closed to the public; only those having to do with the big ships, cargo ships and tourist ocean liners may enter. (What a change from 1967 when I wandered freely all through the docks seeing everything from ocean going cargo ships loading "cashews" from Brazil, small passenger boats and a sleek United States research ship (full of the requisite antennae) thought by the locals to be a "spy" boat. It may be worth while for the reader to see my "Adventures of a 'Gringo' Researcher in Brazil in the 1960s" to see the contrast.)

The Fish Market Modeled on Steel Structures in Lisbon and Paris

We went to the Central Market, made of steel, similar to the construction of the Elevador Santa Justa in Lisbon) constructed in the 19th century during the "rubber boom" days of Manaus. We whiled away some time, not in any hurry, standing outside the market leaning against the railing and looking down to the docks, the small boat traffic and commerce along the banks of the River, just watching "a banda passar." The side of the river was full of small passenger boats and cargo boats, all from the interior up and down river, boats that go up and down the Rio Negro, the Solimões and out to the encounter of the waters where the true Amazon begins, this plus the myriad tributaries of the Amazon region. We watched the loading and unloading of the small cargo boats – fish, wooden cases of Guaraná, beer, all carried on the shoulders and heads of the porters. There were stacks of PCV, sacks of manioc flour, all transported via the the river. I noted "businessmen" with the ubiquitous leather briefcases under their arms, but mainly "povão."

The air was full of the scent of frying fish, all kinds and with Indian names. There was a lot of filth and bad odor, all explained by the fact that the river is at its lowest level of the year, perhaps twenty feet below the high water marker on the stone wall to the side of the scene. In the distance one could see a long line of wooden market stalls on stilts. (In 1967 I was there in high water season in April and all this was floating.) But at present it was surrounded below by a mountain of rubbish.

We saw men unloading cocoanuts, one by one, tossing them in the air from one man on the boat, another on shore and in succession up the banks to the market. And there were mounds of green bananas. All this was amidst an incredible coming and going of people. The locals tell me that the "milk boat" I took from Manaus out to the tributaries of the region is still in operation and traverses many large and small streams picking up milk cans full of milk, fish, and passengers to and from Manaus.

To the right of this scene is the main dock, floating on the huge pontoons in service now for years; the large tourist boats and cargo ships can be seen in the distance.

Returning to the inside market we saw an amazing variety of fish (I'm sorry I cannot tell you the names, unlike a later trip to the market in Belém do Pará where they were all labeled for the buyers and tourists) but with the expected smell associated with the same. Then we walked to the "Mercado de Miudezas," the "stuff" market with its t-shirts and local artisan items which I did not particularly care for thinking the markets in the Northeast of Brazil were much better – hand made arrows and bows, dolls made from gourds with feathers in headdresses. I remember one such market, perhaps in Belém do Pará, where there were key chains made of "piranha" heads, or so they claimed.

We returned to the old Hotel Amazonas, had a light lunch, and then walked toward the principal destination: the "Teatro Amazonas" or Manaus Opera House. The busy business district was replete on both sides of the street with dozens of shoe shops (recall Manaus is a free port or tariff free commercial zone in Brazil free for export and import), watches, electrical applicances (we were not yet in the computer, cell phone, smart phone and "app" age but rather of household applicances, color TVs, refrigerators, stoves). And all manner of clothing. I can report that when one arrived at the "International" airport of Manaus, all the Brazilians came with huge empty suitcases, ready to fill them in the "free zone" and take the "stuff" to the far corners of Brazil. It may be added that later Manaus became one of the principal places for computer manufacturing in Brazil. You don't exactly expect this of a city carved from the jungle a century before!

The climate. It was not as extreme as I recalled from the 1960s. If you are in the shade and there is a bit of a breeze from the river, it seemed tolerable, but if one or the other was lacking, look out! You perspire doing nothing!

The Opera House ("O Teatro Amazonas")

The Opera House ("O Teatro Amazonas"), Manaus

The Opera House is located on a small hill; in 1985 the paint was peeling and the color was perhaps not as brilliant as it might have been (it was rose colored when I visited in 1967). The Theater was closed and redone in 1975. We saw it all by virtue of the entrance price of twenty cents U.S. Its history is impressive: it was inaugurated in 1896 and remains as the most important monument of the riches of the "Rubber Barons," yet another of the economic "cycles" reflecting Brazil's history. One might recall sugar cane, tobacco and coffee in the Northeast, the gold and precious stones of Minas Gerais, the coffee boom of the late 19th century in São Paulo, and the industrialization of the twentieth century, all this followed by the huge force of mechanized agriculture and cash crops for export which brought the opening of the savannah of central Brazil and the later devastation of the Amazon for ranching. These are just the main economic booms; there were others like placer mining in the rivers of the North.

In part the Opera House owes its existence to an effort to match the "Teatro de Belém do Pará," far to the east on the Amazon's way to the Atlantic, this with its own opera company. The "Teatro Amazonas" has the main floor plus three more floors with private boxes or "camarotes" (see the photo). The decoration of its interior supporting columns is to be noted: busts and masks dedicated to the greats of the world of theater, opera and classical music: Moliére, Rossini, Mozart, Verdi, and others. One should not forget the panygryic to Carlos Gomes, the best known of creators of opera in Brazil. The stage curtain is the theme of the encounter of the waters of the Rio Negro and the Solimões but in mythological terms.

The visitor first notes, before entering the building itself, the tremendous cupula: it is comprised of 36,000 pieces of shell in "cerámica esmaltada" and "telhas vitrificadas" coming from Alsácia, in the colors of the Brazilian flag: blue, green and yellow.

What may be of most interest is the "folklore" of the place (notions garnered from I don't know where in my travels and studies but ending in my mind): that the great "stars" of European Opera came for one-night stands! That the Rubber Barons sent their dirty clothes to be laundered in Europe! That the great Enrico Carusso sang there! I do not know if any of these wild notions is true, but it would be nice if they were!

What is true based on scenes I have seen from documentary films over the years is that the labor used to build the huge edifice came largely from the indigenous natives of the region. It is a fact that the indigenous population of the Amazon was decimated over the years, to the point that the Barons by the end of the nineteenth century and beginnings of the twentieth were forced to bring hired labor transported from the far Northeast of Brazil. All this is documented in the story-poems of the "literatura de cordel." Horrendous accounts of the long journey by ship from the coast of Ceará and Maranhão, the inhuman working conditions, and the dangers to the rubber workers from hordes of biting insects, poisonous snakes, crocodiles and even big jungle cats abound. And this was just for openers! Bad food or too little food and servitude brought on by that so familiar institution of the "company store" brought misery and little hope to the "seringueiros" or rubber workers.

I saw the Opera House for the first time in 1967 (the story told in "Adventures ..."). It was no less impressive the second time around. I recall that the first time when I arrived it was "under renovation" ("em obras") and I had to bribe a door man to let me look inside. Image a traveler and a trip of literally thousands of miles ending with "Sorry for the inconvenience; we are closed for remodeling." It's a little like my friend from Guatemala who traveled all the way to Arizona's Grand Canyon and arrived on one of those rare days when a weather inversion brought clouds and fog which literally covered the canyon, nothing to be seen below

The Author and the "Speech from the Opera Box" in the "Teatro Amazonas"

The Famous Tapestry of the "Teatro Amazonas" Depicting the Legend of the Amazons

Describing the scene a little more: as I said there are three floors with private boxes, the stage with the great curtain so described, painted as it were, the curtain itself coming from Europe – the scene of the meeting of the waters of the Solimões and Rio Negro forming the Amazon River, this not too far from Manaus. The curtain was of deep red velvet, the same color as the chairs in the "plateia" and in the "camarotes," these with their own "privacy" curtains. One imagines what might have gone on behind those curtains over the years! Many chairs were caned, probably according to the necessities of the climate. I always wondered: how did the gentlemen in their formal dress of tuxedos and the ladies in their fine ball room gowns deal with that heat? I do not recall seeing the normal, ubiquitous ceiling fans of the tropics. One surmises that today all is air conditioned, but for sure it was not then!

The "Salão Nobre" was inaugurated in 1896, a salon for formal balls, the floor of parquet, of Brazilian Rosewood ("Jacarandá") and other precious tropical woods; crystal mirrors from floor to ceiling are on at least one wall, all imported from Italy, and there is a large entry door of marble. The windows of the "Salão Nobre" sport paintings of "O Guarani" a famous indigenous legend made romantic novel by José de Alencar the greatest of such novelists in Brazil, and other Amazon scenes. As in the main theater, on the interior columns are busts of famous Brazilian and Portuguese figures of the arts at that time, many from the world of literature and classical music, already mentioned. And the tapestries come from Europe.

There are many such scenes in the fine buildings of Europe, and many probably surpass what I have described. What makes the impression is to find this is the sweltering heat of a tropical boom town literally one thousand miles from the Atlantic Ocean via the great Amazon River!

A lighter note: before and after visiting the Theater we enjoyed the best cocoanut ice cream I have ever tasted; nothing comes close! I cannot imagine finding better ice cream, chock full of cocoanut! And freezing cold! I would repeat the trip for the ice cream (well, maybe not, but then again … .)

After walking through the downtown once more, we caught the bus to the "Hotel Tropical." We went immediately to the swimming pool, swam and drank caipirinhas and then to the room, second honeymoon, right? We returned to the terrace by the pool to watch the sunset and then enjoy a wonder dinner of "churrasco – maminha de alcatre," all kinds of salads, dessert of "doce de coco," fruit and cafezinho.

Outing by Boat on the "Rio Negro" and "Rio Solimões"

Let's put it all together in a "gallery of photos."

Mark and the "Liana" to the Side of the Rio Negro, Playing "Tarzan"

The Excursion Boat of the "Hotel Tropical" and the Trip
to the "Rio Negro" and the "Rio Solimões"

Mark and Keah in the Dugout Canoe ("Piroga") in the Amazon Forest

Cashew Nuts and Icy "Antártica" Beer on Board the Tourist Boat

Mark and the "Encounter of the Waters" ("Encontro das Águas")

Goodbye to the "Rio Negro," the "Hotel Tropical" and to Manaus

November 21ˢᵗ. We got up at 6:15 a.m. to heavy rain. There was an excellent Brazilian breakfast ("café da manhã") and then our walk from the hotel to the small private hotel dock on the Rio Negro. With the heavy rain we used improvised umbrellas - the towels of the hotel. The dock has a problem, so we were taken out to the boat in a small canoe of the Hotel. The boat was very similar to one of the dozens of small passenger boats one sees at the main dock in the port of Manaus – pretty, freshly painted, two levels, Amazon style, and diesel powered. We sat up front in the bow in front of the small pilot's cabin, this in order to feel the fresh breeze coming off the water. The day was cloudy and with rain until we arrived at the far side of the Rio Negro (an hour's trip with little traffic in this part of the river). They told us the Rio Negro varies from three to twenty-two quilometers in width, with a depth of 90 meters, and with few fish due to the acidity of the water (the acidity comes from the leaves washed into the water from a long distance north of Manaus, the same leaves giving the river its "Coca Cola" color. (I have pictures from 1967 with this same colored water in the zoo of Manaus, incidentally where a non-paying passenger came onto our largely wooden bus- a sloth on a stick relegated to the back of the bus by the driver.) The Rio Negro begins far to the north in the State of Amazonas.

Then it was time for the "walk in the forest," about an hour in length. We disembarked the excursion boat, walked parallel along the wide beach of the river, and then scrambled perhaps twenty to thirty feet up the sand to the trail in the forest (remember this was low water season;

in April the water is at the level of the trail.) Our short trek was parallel to the river, always visible to our right. At this point there was light rain, the heavy rain of the past night and early morning had passed, but everything in the forest was soaking wet. We used clear plastic bags and fashioned them into a type of poncho, walking through a forest dense with vines, trees, many of them extremely tall, but with little useful knowledge provided by the guide. Yet, the feeling one had was yes, to be in the middle of the Amazon rain forest.

We arrived to a large lagoon in the middle of what seemed to me to be pristine Amazon forest, so dense that it was not possible to penetrate into it from the trail. At that point we were granted a thirty minute canoe trip ("piroga", an Indian name) through the stream channels ("Igarapés") and a large lagoon with water lizards and the famous blue butterflies ("Morphos"). An Aside: we were mightily entertained by a young couple from Florida (they could have been newlyweds on honeymoon) totally decked out in African Safari dress, and he with a huge butterfly net. At one point in a walk through the nearby forest he tripped and fell into the side of the dense forest, no harm done but nor did he catch a Morpho. An Aside: every tourist to the Amazon basin, whether at its beginnings in Belém do Pará, upstream at Santarém or Manaus, or to the far reaches on the border of Colombia or Ecuador, has seen the tourist souvenirs at the markets: a plastic case with a blue Morpho inside. I confess now that we purchased two such items, not thinking of the ecological ramifications. The color has not faded yet today, years later.

After the canoe trip and walk, guests are offered the option of spending the night at a lodge the Hotel maintains on the lake, including restaurant and bar; the big attraction is to hunt (or at least spot) alligators at night. No one on our trip took them up on the offer. I regret this now, not catching alligators, but being able to experience a night in the dense forest with what I am sure are dozens of terrific night sounds.

The "jungle lodge" was a nice, pretty cabana, with a thatch roof, round, large and relatively comfortable, even with its little bar. I'm sure the Brazilians blasted their "mood music" even there. It is in the middle of said lake; the guests were given an opportunity to swim but no one accepted the offer. There were many birds, bird songs, but the most impressive to me was sight of the dense forest ("mata"), the calm, and a total lack of human noise in the place. A great experience! This was many years prior to Keah and my interest in birding, a pity.

So after the "walk in the forest" we returned to the side of the Rio Negro to yet another cabana where they served a "typical lunch" of the region: "batida de maracujá, caldeirada de peixe, batata inglesa, cebola, e arroz." The fish was "Tucuri" if I caught the name correctly. There was fruit salad for dessert and a good "cafezinho." The view of the river was beautiful, and fortunately there was a cool breeze along with the immensely high humidity. Perfect. I realize this was just a "hotel trip," but it was fine and fulfilled its purpose: just an introduction and "taste" of the Amazon.

The Return to Manaus

It should have been a trip of about one hour (we passed the time drinking coffee, then an icy Antártica Beer with cashew nuts). We passed the "Encounter of the Waters" with its black and "café com leite" colored waters mingling, the result of the joining of the Rio Negro and the Rio Solimões which then forms the Amazon. At the point of encounter of the Solimões and the Rio Negro ("The Encounter of the Waters") and later when the two form the Amazon, the river is at a depth of 270 feet and 55 kilometers wide. Here, yes, there is a richness of aquatic life and fish, therefore the waters are full of all sized fishing boats. I don't recall well, but I think we got a quick glance at the famous rose colored dolphins.

On up stream to the side of the river there were a lot of factories including a petroleum refinery and a jute factory. In the middle of the river there were floating gasoline stations. We saw huge ocean going oil tankers and now there was a lot of traffic on the river (from the Rio Solimões and its tributaries). I remember there was almost no traffic from Manaus up river on the Rio Negro. And we saw a huge ferry boat that was crossing the river from the Port of Manaus connecting with the Humaitá "Highway," the latter city some 600 kilometers from Rio with the original asfault highway long ago destroyed by the rains. This was one of many of the roads imagined by the military in the 1960s, 1970s and early 1980s to "open up the Amazon" and continue the "March to the West" to the borders of Ecuador and Peru.

At some point after the "Encounter of the Waters" they took us to the opposite bank of the river to a tiny native village where we saw cacau trees and the famous "seringa" or rubber trees on a rubber plantation. We were told that five percent of the tires manufactured in Brazil are made of natural rubber. We witnessed the way they cut the bark of the tree in "arrow shaped" cuts; place a small cup below the cut and the raw white liquid rubber drips into the cup. One can only imagine the number of trees necessary during the rubber boom to explain the huge production and the decimation of Indians doing the harvesting! (We already spoke of them being replaced in the 20th century by massive numbers of Northeastern migrants and their tales of woe.)

On the return we saw very muddy water, great visible poverty to the side of the river, and much river traffic. Upon actually reaching the Port of Manaus (and later to the hotel dock) there were many houses on stilts, many small home made wooden docks in front of them, and many boats being made. It was a busy, informative and interesting hour on the river.

Returning to the hotel there was swimming, a "caipirinha," and dinner on the varanda by the pool.

November 23. The Final Morning in the "Hotel Tropical"

We walked through the gardens, took photos of the hotel (including the "quartos de luxo" on the second floor with small varandas and woven hammocks), and photos of the macaws. There was a final "caipirinha" with "bossa" music by the pool before check out and departing. We were a bit sad to leave this "tropical paradise," but were jolted back to reality by the hot bus ride to the airport, the long line at customs (recall Manaus is a free port so there are customs entering and leaving as though leaving the country). I killed time at the airport making small talk with the pretty girls in the Stern's Jewelry shop.

THE RETURN TO RIO DE JANEIRO

The flight was familiar – the Varig D C – 10 to Rio via Brasília. The huge plane was jammed until Brasília, a flight of two and one half hours from Manaus with the international service once again. Cocktails and two meals! It was 26 degrees centigrade in Brasília; the air was fresh and clean after a rain shower. We could see the buildings of the North Zone in the distance but nothing from the government sector. I have to recall the famous quip about President Reagan's trip to South America: he arrived at the Brasília airport much as we did, had a "formal" appearance outside the plane on the stairway, and said, "I am so happy to be here in Bolivia." Or so goes the story.

From Brasília it was an hour and a half to Rio, a bus to Copacabana and our three star hotel the "Excelsior Copa," one of Varig's Air Pass Hotels. As one might imagine, we were a bit depressed by it all after the "Hotel Tropical." The air conditioner in the room did not work and it was incredibly noisy with street noise and traffic outside. One saw only a minimal slice of view of the beach from the room, and below in the street and entrance to the old hotel the chaos of tour buses from Argentina. Plus we were exhausted.

November 24th, Rio de Janeiro

Breakfast in the hotel dining room was without electricity and we had to use candles to see our way in the interior stairways from the room to the restaurant and back. It all was a shock after the beautiful experience at the "Hotel Tropical" in the so-called "underdeveloped Amazon."

Because I had missed it so far on the trip that Sunday morning we caught a taxi on the new "freeway" under the Túnel Rebouças to São Cristóvão, $2.50 USD with a great driver. The fair was large as usual, "Forró" Music, hammocks, "caldo de cana, milho cozido, cachaça" and all the flavors of "batidas," and meat cooked on a spit. The noise from the "Forró"stands was deafening. There were endless stands with all kinds of northeastern food, clothing, raw meat and live blue crabs.

I saw all the "old" follheteiros – Elias de Carvalho, some poet-singers, Expedito F. Silva, Gonçalo Ferreira da Silva, and Apolônio Alves dos Santos. There were a lot of duplicates from the story-poems purchased earlier in the year, including several on current events.

From the Fair we took a taxi back to Copacabana and went to mass at a church only three blocks from the hotel – Nossa Senhora de Copacabana – a modern church, progressive, with a very communicative priest, and the church totally packed. It is a huge parish with nine Sunday masses.

Lunch was at the "Merage" on Copacabana beach – "caipirinha, choppe, couvert (ovos de codorniz, azeitonas, paté e queijo) e "chateau" com batatas portuguesas." It was too much! Back to the hotel for a nap.

Sunday afternoon we took a small bus called the "jardineiro" to Ipanema to Praça General Osório and the hippy fair. It was fun and we found some souvenirs: small stained glass scenes of Rio de Janeiro. The smell of marijuana ("maconha") filled the air. There were articles made of leather, paintings and I took many photos.

We walked along Ipanema beach, taking photos, and then caught the "Jardineiro" back to Copacabana where we hung out on Copa Beach in front of the Copacabana Palace Hotel just taking in that great "carioca" beach scene. There were many games of soccer on the beach, a submarine spotted out in the sea beyond the beach, the great Copacabana kites (called "papagaios" or parrots) and all manner of folks getting their exercise and strolling on the "calçada" (some still call the walking "fazendo Cooper" a term garnered from the British in Brazil). All kinds of people were walking all kinds of dogs, and there were the maids "babás" in their white uniforms with sometimes ornate and huge baby carriages. Copacabana seemed like Brazilian middle class; Ipanema seemed to have a different atmosphere, more prosperous and newer. What do I know? There was time for ice cream on the beach and a return to the hotel to make plans for the final days.

An Aside: as I write this so many years later I realize how different this trip really was from all my stays in Brazil. This was not quite the "folklorist doing fieldwork in the outback"!

November 25th, Rio de Janeiro

We enjoyed a good breakfast at the Excelsior than a taxi to the Othon Hotel to see one of their rooms and reserve a room for our last night there to celebrate Keah's birthday, with a discount of 30 per cent from the Varig Air Pass. The hotel has 30 stories, faces the beach and is on Posto 5. We chose the so called "quarto de luxo" facing the beach and from the balcony window could see the entire crescent of Copacabana Beach, that is, the full curve.

We then went for a final, short visit to the Casa de Ruy Barbosa and a brief reunion with Adriano, Orígenes and Homero Senna. They were all very nice to us; I handed out the presents we had brought from Arizona amidst good talk and lots of jokes. They said the study for the Orígenes Lessa Prize would come out at José Olympio in 1986; I would get one copy by air mail and the rest by surface mail (a standard practical solution to international postal fares at that time). Ha ha. It never happened.

There is a new edition of "Literatura Popular em Verso: Estudos I," the original book of 1973, by Itatiaia in Belo Horizonte, my name with all the others on the cover. The copy I received has disappeared over the years.

Then we took the subway (still perfectly clean and shiny in those days) to downtown and had a tasty lunch of "galeto" in the huge Avenida Central Building. Then "book stops" to Livraria AGIR, the store at FUNARTE, to the café at the Municipal Theater, to the Convent of Santo Antônio, and the subway back to Botafogo and Copa.

All this flurry of activity was followed by settling in the room at the Othon, a visit to the top floor restaurant and bar, the Skylab, for the view, a long walk on the beach, etc. We ate dinner at an old familiar place on the beach, "Restaurante Lucas." I bought roses for Keah, and returned to our room. You could see below on the beach lit candles from the "Umbanda." Exhausted after this busy day, we looked forward to the great day tomorrow.

November 26th, Celebrating Keah's Birthday

Keah and the View of Copacabana Beach from the Othon

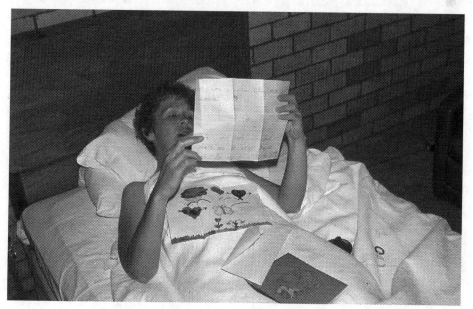

Opening Birthday Cards from Daughter Katie

Breakfast in the Room, Keah's Birthday, and the View of Copacabana Beach

We awoke at 8:00. Keah read all her birthday cards from me and Katie. A special breakfast was served elegantly in the room with roses and a view of the sea. After that we dressed and went down to the beach in front of the hotel where we body surfed in those nice waves and watched the parade of "mini-tangas", volleyball games, the gulls flying in the wind and diving for small fish in the ocean and just watching the beach scene.

Later we went to a tourist agency, Viagens do Norte, to trade our last dollars on the parallel market and then to shops to buy presents for Katie. There was the usual array of tourist stuff: toucans painted on leather, blue Morphos in plastic, and other gadgets for tourists. We later bargained with the beach vendors and bought no less than sixteen tourist t-shirts!

Tired, we walked back to the Othon and took the elevator to the 30th floor for a beautiful sunset. Later there was time for another walk on the beach in early evening, dinner at Lucas, noting Umbanda candles on the beach and the Carioca "ladies of the night" peddling their wares. In the end it was a great Copacabana beach scene all in all.

November 27th, Last Day in Rio and in Brazil

Breakfast was in the "Tropical Garden" of the Othon on the 3rd floor, all very calm with a 180 degree view of the beach, a leisurely hour to "ver a banda passar." Then to the room to pack the bags. There was the last lunch at the Othon, caipirinhas and then filet, and from four to eight p.m. we sat in the lounge on the third floor, enjoying that tourist life in Rio, had one or two caipirinhas and looked at Copa. There was once again futebol on the beach, volley ball, gulls flying over head, fender-benders along Avenida Atlântica, incredible p.m. traffic along the beach, many tour buses arriving. We watched the waves, the time passing pleasantly and not too slowly at all. It was a time for laughter, memories of the trip, and a fine end to the adventure.

That evening we took the safe Taxi Transcopas to the airport, the driver with 26 years experience as a taxi driver in Rio, from Sobral, Ceará. The ride was quick and no problems (unlike many other times heading to the Galeão).

We spent the last of the Brazilian money in shops at the airport: a beautiful coffee table book on Brazil, more t-shirts, an Elba Ramalho tape, and a few books on Brazilian Literature. We are on Pan Am and it's on time, but there was time to remember and do these final notes.

Miscellaneous Moments, Commentary, Brazilian Politics of the Moment and My Apologies to the Reader

There were very good relations with the now Fundação Casa de Ruy Barbosa. The Varig Air Pass was superb, including the thirty per cent discount to the Varig-connected good hotels. This was the first (and perhaps last) time that I and Keah were to go "first class" in Brazil. No remorse. After those cheap hotels near the bus stations in the Northeast, the bus rides, the student apartments and boarding houses, it was a nice change. But I did not feel much like a folklorist. We enjoyed the country, the small city of Lençóis Paulista and the sugar cane area of São Paulo State, and especially the "Hotel Tropical" outside of Manaus. Rio seemed more turbulent than ever and much noisier (it was a relief to be one night on the 30th floor of the Othon when the roar of the traffic was more distant). But the country seemed as "alive" ("vivo") as ever, an exciting place with all its ups and downs.

I was impressed now in 1985 by the growth and richness of this "third world" country. Brazil is truly the "sleeping giant perhaps awakened" with incredible resources. One recalls the autos, buses, transports, new roads and freeways, and newly asphalted roads in the interior of São Paulo State, all not much different then the U.S. "Huge and crowded".

We were impressed once again by the racial mixture and mingling of social classes in Rio, everyone together on the beaches, an example of what the Brazilians like to call the "Brazilian democracy." But we saw more poverty on the streets and beaches of Copacbana; the impression garnered is that the poor seen in the South Zone are not only from the North Zone but down from the hills in the favelas which surround a good part of South Zone Rio. The wealthy zones are still Ipanema, Leblon, São Conrado and the Barra (remember I speak of 1985). The buildings in Copacabana seem old, suffering from the passage of time. I do not pretend to comment on the rest of greater Rio from this short experience.

The people we were with treated us extremely well and seemed more open to us, perhaps in part due to my improved Portuguese over the years – Orígenes Lessa, Maria Eduarda, Marly in Lençóis, Homero, Adriano at the Casa de Ruy, the Barros and Carlos and Edilene in Salvador.

An Interesting Presidential and Literary Aside: Orígenes says that Brazilian President Sarney will go to Lençóis soon to help inaugurate the "Biblioteca Municipal Orígenes Lessa." I'm sure this is related to their being both buddies and members of the Brazilian Academy of Letters.

TV is everywhere, the principal channels ruling (TV Globo for one), leveling the regional differences in spoken languages throughout the country I think. Carlos Cunha believes TV has pretty much "done in" the greater part of "local culture" in Brazil – it features soccer, national news and soap operas. A Cultural Aside: We saw "Grande Sertão: Veredas" on TV. Diadorim was well done, Riobaldo less so, but dialogue was extremely difficult for me to understand. However, even Brazilian friends admitted to having difficulties dealing with the "fala regional," even Dona Wilma, Adriano's wife from Rio Grande do Norte.

"Cordel." It was almost the same as the earlier visit in May. There are few of the old poets and it is extremely expensive for them to publish. Editoral Luzeiro continues to be seen throughout the country and dominates the remaining market. To its credit it is still publishing the 32 page narrative poems ("romances") and sometimes "classic" story-poems. There does not seem in 1985 to be a new or significant production of "cordel." (Writing now in 2009 I saw all this change with a renaissance of "cordel" being written on the computer and printed on the printer to its side as well as the Internet and its effect on all social classes in Brazil). I wrote in 1985: "It's time to do the "definitive" book, well written and done with patience." (Definitive for me that is.) I did and it would be years before it would come out in 2011 at the Editorial Ateliê in São Paulo, "Retrato do Brasil em Cordel." A foot note to all this, and to be seen in another volume of "It Happened" will be the flurry of books I would do in retirement after 2002.

Politics

There is great euphoria with the return to democracy, but also the situation is chaotic. November 15th, 1985, was the day for elections for mayors of cities. The greatest competition was in São Paulo where the PTB and old Jânio Quadros won! Gossip has it that there may be a coalition between Leonel Brizola and Jânio Quadros for congress in 1986. And after that the time will be here for the new Constitutional Assembly; this will be the Constitutional Congress, new in Brazil since the end of the military dictatorship. The debate now is: who and which shall be the representatives in congress to do the new constitution?

In Brazil it is personality and the personalities that win in politics; not the ideas. Tancredo Neves is now a saint in Brazil! The "cordel"edition of his death by Editorial Luzeiro can be found all over Brazil. There seems to be a lot of confusion as to the future: one hears little so far from Sarney, the "interim" president. His party is the PFL (Partido do Frente Liberal) and is still basically Catholic and conservative. The PT is headed by Lula, the PTB by Brizola or perhaps Jânio Quadros. Orestes Quércia of the old PMDB lost to Jânio in the election for mayor of São Paulo. The PCB ("Partido Comunista Brasileiro") has less than five per cent of the vote in November of 1985. I wrote a note to myself: try to keep up to date on all this via "Veja" magazine.

Summary of November, 1985

The entire trip was really a second honeymoon; the travel together with the prize will not be repeated. And the trip renewed my enthusiasm for Brazil and gave me some ideas for the future – projects like "História do Brasil em Cordel" and the English version "Portrait of Brazil – the Universe of the 'Literatura de Cordel.'" I was not even thinking then of all that would happen in retirement.

The Pan Am flight landed at 5:00 a.m. in Miami, Keah with a very bad sore throat and sickness coming on. We took the "monorail" to customs and had a very long wait for the bags (including all that "cachaça" given to us in Lençóis.) From there the trip continued to Marathon, Florida, for a reunion with Keah's brother and girl friend, but that's another story.

So, again, this trip and event will not be repeated. We must however cherish the trip, the closeness it brought to Keah and me and the enthusiasm for trips in the future. There was a huge contrast between this trip with Keah and my first in 1985 (I apologize to the reader for the heavy moments in the latter). And as I said at the beginning of the 1985 account, "The worst trip of all in Brazil," but just the same, important in the Brazilian "Odyssey" through the years. The improvement now on the second trip is explained by the circumstances: the prize, the Air Pass, and most of all, Keah's company. It will be a sign of the future; all will get better, even with ups and downs in coming years.

And, after all, it is only one year of all that took place in "It Happened in Brazil – Chronicle of a North American Researcher in Brazil II."

So we reach the end of "It Happened." A third or perhaps even a forth volume will be forthcoming in future years and eventually bring us to the present in the Brazilian odyssey of the naïve North American researcher in Brazil. Future volumes will tell of research trips to Brazil in 1988, 1989, 2000, 2002 and 2005. Some will be a return to the Northeast and wonderful reunions with people like Ariano Suassuna and others. Others will take me to the megalopolis of São Paulo for some important moments. Those long years of research, writing, and waiting for pubished results would all come to fruition with books in 1987, 1990, 1991, and especially in 1998 while still active faculty at ASU. Among highlights will be the "100 Years of 'Cordel'" in São Paulo in 2001 and new travel to Iguaçú in Southern Brazil. Retirement will bring a flurry of writing and publishing activity and a totally new adventure: Staff on Lindblad's National Geographic Explorer from Brazil to Buenos Aires in 2013 and 2014.

Like Cuíca de Santo Amaro used to say on the back cover of one of his poetic "bombshells" in Salvador,

STAY TUNED!
("AGUARDEM!")

ABOUT THE AUTHOR

Mark Curran is a retired professor from Arizona State University where he worked from 1968 to 2011. He taught Spanish and Portuguese and their respective cultures. His research specialty was Brazil and its "popular poetry in verse" or the "literatura de cordel," and he has published many articles in research reviews and now some sixteen books related to the "cordel" in Brazil, the United States and Spain. Other books done during retirement are of either an autobiographic nature – "The Farm" or "Coming of Age with the Jesuits" - and /or reflect classes taught at ASU in Luso-Brazilian Civilization, Latin American Civilization or Spanish taught at ASU. The latter are all found in the series "Stories I Told My Students:" books on Brazil, Colombia, Guatemala, Mexico, Portugal and Spain.

Published Books

A Literatura de Cordel. Brasil. 1973

Jorge Amado e a Literatura de Cordel. Brasil. 1981

A Presença de Rodolfo Coelho Cavalcante na Moderna Literatura de Cordel. Brasil. 1987

La Literatura de Cordel – Antología Bilingüe – Español y Portugués. España. 1990

Cuíca de Santo Amaro Poeta-Repórter da Bahia. Brasil. 1991

História do Brasil em Cordel. Brasil. 1998

Cuíca de Santo Amaro – Controvérsia no Cordel. Brasil. 2000

Brazil's Folk-Popular Poetry – "a Literatura de Cordel" – a Bilingual Anthology in English and Portuguese. USA. 2010

The Farm – Growing Up in Abilene, Kansas, in the 1940s and the 1950s. USA. 2010

Retrato do Brasil em Cordel. Brasil. 2011

Coming of Age with the Jesuits. USA. 2012

Peripécias de um Pesquisador "Gringo" no Brasil nos Anos 1960 ou 'A Cata de Cordel" USA. 2012

Adventures of a 'Gringo' Researcher in Brazil in the 1960s. USA. 2012

A Trip to Colombia – Highlights of Its Spanish Colonial Heritage. USA. 2013

Travel, Research and Teaching in Guatemala and Mexico – In Quest of the Pre-Columbian Heritage

Volume I – Guatemala. 2013

Volume II – Mexico. USA. 2013

A Portrait of Brazil in the Twentieth Century – The Universe of the "Literatura de Cordel." USA. 2013

Fifty Years of Research on Brazil – A Photographic Journey. USA. 2013

Relembrando - A Velha Literatura de Cordel e a Voz dos Poetas. USA. 2014

Aconteceu no Brasil – Crônicas de um Pesquisador Norte Americano no Brasil II, USA. 2015

It Happened in Brazil – Chronicle of a North American Researcher in Brazil II, USA, 2015

Professor Curran lives in Mesa, Arizona, and spends part of of the year in Colorado. He is married to Keah Runshang Curran and they have one daughter Kathleen who lives in Albuquerque, New Mexico. Her documentary film "Greening the Revolution" was presented most recently in the Sonoma Film Festival in California. Katie was named best female director in the Oaxaca Film Festival in Mexico.

The author's e-mail address is: profmark@asu.edu

His website address is: www.currancordelconnection.com